ETHNOGRAPHY IN SOCIAL SCIENCE PRACTICE

Ethnography in Social Science Practice explores ethnography's increasing use across the social sciences, beyond its traditional bases in social anthropology and sociology. It explores the disciplinary roots of ethnographic research within social anthropology, and contextualizes it within both field and disciplinary settings.

The book is in two parts: Part I places ethnography as a methodology in its historical, ethical and disciplinary context, and also discusses the increasing popularity of ethnography across the social sciences. Part II explores the stages of ethnographic research via a selection of multidisciplinary case studies. A number of key questions are explored:

- What exactly is ethnographic research and what makes it different from other qualitative approaches?
- Why did ethnography emerge within one social science discipline and not others?
- Why did its adoption across the social sciences prove problematic?
- What are the methodological advantages and disadvantages of doing ethnographic research?
- Why are ethnographers so concerned by issues of ethics, politics, representation and power?
- What does ethnography look like within different social science disciplines?

The book is aimed at social science students at both undergraduate and postgraduate level and each chapter has pedagogic features, including reflective activities and suggested further readings for students.

Julie Scott Jones is a senior lecturer in sociology at the Manchester Metropolitan University. Her research interests focus on identity, worldview construction and meaning systems. Recent publications include 'Fundamentalism and Global Security' in *Encyclopaedia on Globalisation and Human Security* (Praeger Security Press, 2009) and *Being the Chosen: Exploring a Fundamentalist Worldview* (Ashgate, 2010).

Sal Watt is a lecturer in psychology at Liverpool Hope University. Her interests include organizational behaviour, identity and commitment. She is active in teaching and encouraging wider application of qualitative research techniques and, in particular, ethnography in psychology.

ETHNOGRAPHY IN SOCIAL SCIENCE PRACTICE

Edited by
Julie Scott Jones and
Sal Watt

Routledge
Taylor & Francis Group

LONDON AND NEW YORK

First published 2010
by Routledge
2 Park Square, Milton Park, Abingdon, Oxon, OX14 4RN

Simultaneously published in the USA and Canada
by Routledge
270 Madison Avenue, New York, NY 10016

Routledge is an imprint of the Taylor & Francis Group, an informa business

© 2010 Julie Scott Jones and Sal Watt; individual chapters, the contributors

Typeset in Times New Roman PS by
Florence Production Ltd, Stoodleigh, Devon
Printed and bound in Great Britain by
TJ International Ltd, Padstow, Cornwall

British Library Cataloguing in Publication Data
A catalogue record for this book is available from the British Library

Library of Congress Cataloging in Publication Data
Ethnography in social science practice/edited by Julie Scott Jones
and Sal Watt.
    p. cm.
    Includes bibliographical references.
    1. Ethnology – Research.   2. Ethnology – Methodology.
    I. Jones, Julie Scott, 1966–.   II. Watt, Sal.
    GN345.E7825 2010
    305.8001 – dc22   2009039719

ISBN 10: 0–415–54347–9 (hbk)
ISBN 10: 0–415–54349–5 (pbk)
ISBN 10: 0–203–87630–X (ebk)

ISBN 13: 978–0–415–54347–7 (hbk)
ISBN 13: 978–0–415–54349–1 (pbk)
ISBN 13: 978–0–203–87630–5 (ebk)

FOR MILLIE AND ANNA

FOR DINK, FREDA AND MY BOYS

CONTENTS

CONTENTS

CONTRIBUTORS

John E. Goldring is a lecturer in sociology at the Manchester Metropolitan University. He is an ethnographer and has spent much of his research career exploring gay men's relationships – with each other, their families and friends – and their health and well-being. His experience of being a gay married man has encouraged him to consider alternative gay identities and to attempt to give 'voice' to those who could be considered on the margins of the 'gay community'. His research has taken a late-modern perspective to explore the changing social and legal climate that gay men have faced since the decriminalization of 'homosexuality' in 1967.

Anna Graham is currently a lecturer in education at Liverpool Hope University. She trained as a primary school teacher at Homerton College, Cambridge and has been a practitioner and researcher since 1995. She completed her MPhil degree at Queens' College, Cambridge and is currently completing her PhD. Her research examines the implications of poverty and social exclusion for children's primary schooling.

Helen Jones is a principal lecturer in criminology at the Manchester Metropolitan University. She is a feminist, teacher, researcher, writer and activist. She teaches on a range of criminology and criminal justice topics. At a national level, Helen has been a consultant on the Home Office Sex Offences Review; the Victims of Violence and Abuse Prevention Programme (VVAPP); and the Inter-Ministerial Advisory Panel on Sexual Violence. Over the years, she has provided consultancy and training to the Rape and Sexual Abuse Centre in Merseyside and often speaks about the rape crisis movement at conferences and in the media. She continues to provide consultancy to the national Rape Crisis organization and in 2008 co-authored *Rape Crisis: Responding to Sexual Violence*.

Rosemary Kilpatrick prior to retirement was professor of childhood and youth studies at Liverpool Hope University and previously held the position of Director of the Institute of Child Care Research at Queen's University, Belfast. She has extensive professional experience as a forensic psychologist working with children and young people in the education, care and justice systems. Her academic career has mirrored this professional experience with a focus on marginalized young people and an increasing interest in, and use of, participatory and visual techniques.

Wendy Laverick is a lecturer in criminology at the Manchester Metropolitan University. Her research interests span all aspects of violence, harm and social justice. She has an interdisciplinary interest in issues of gender and globalization and is currently applying these substantive areas to the study of transnational crime.

Duncan Light is associate professor in the Department of Geography at Liverpool Hope University. He is a cultural geographer with particular interests in post-socialist Central and Eastern Europe. Most of his recent research has been undertaken in Romania, a country he has visited regularly for 15 years. He is currently exploring the relationship between tourism and national identity in the context of 'Dracula tourism' in Romania. He is also interested in the significance of the 'place myth' of Transylvania in the Western imagination. He is a member of the editorial board for the *Journal of Tourist Consumption and Practice.*

Clive Palmer is a senior lecturer in the School of Sport, Tourism and the Outdoors at the University of Central Lancashire. His doctoral research was an ethnographic study entitled *The Aesthetic Evaluation of Men's Artistic Gymnastics*. He is the editor of the *Journal of Qualitative Research in Sports Studies* and is active in promoting student research to communicate their experiences and discoveries in sport. His academic interests include aesthetics in gymnastics, applied ethnography, philosophy of sport and physical education, coaching theory and outdoor education.

Dave Randall is a principal lecturer in the Department of Sociology at the Manchester Metropolitan University. With Mark Rouncefield, he has written books and published many journal articles on the relationship between ethnography and the design of computer systems. He has been involved in a number of studies of organizational and other contexts where new technology has been introduced. Domains that he has studied include air traffic control, the banking system, museums, schools, mobile telephone use, a 'smart' house, 'ontologies' and wearable cameras.

Mark Rouncefield is a senior research fellow in the Department of Computing at Lancaster University. He is widely published in the areas of Computer Supported Cooperative Work (CSCW) and Human Computer Interaction (HCI). He has conducted fieldwork in a number of areas, including studies of medical work, banks, a steel works, legal work, mobile telephone use and 'mundane' computing. He has recently been working as a Microsoft European Research Fellow.

Julie Scott Jones is a senior lecturer in sociology at the Manchester Metropolitan University. Her doctoral research was an ethnography of a Protestant fundamentalist community in the USA. She has published in the areas of American Protestant fundamentalism and identity; secularization theory; and social research methods. Her research interests focus on identity, worldview construction and meaning systems.

Sal Watt is a lecturer in psychology at Liverpool Hope University. Her doctoral research was an ethnography which investigated the effects of Human Resource Management as a strategy for change in the Civil Service. Within this context her research has focused on how Civil Servants negotiate change and associated risk. Her interests include organizational behaviour, identity and commitment. She is active in teaching and encouraging wider application of qualitative research techniques and in particular, ethnography, in psychology.

PREFACE

This book is very much the result of a personal journey through our experiences of doing ethnography as fieldworkers and as teachers of research methods, particularly qualitative ones, to social science students. This book is the product of our shared joy and frustration as ethnographers; joy that ethnography has become more widely adopted within mainstream social science disciplines, beyond its traditional base in social anthropology. This is demonstrated by its appearance on research methods courses for undergraduates and its use as a research methodology in diverse subjects such as criminology, education studies and business studies. Even psychologists seem to be getting in on the act. But frustrations remain around the representation of ethnography to students, as illustrated in most mainstream research methods textbooks, which can be as simplistic as 'nodding sympathetically with a smile on my face' or 'going undercover and spying on people' as two of our undergraduate students put it. Too often ethnography is viewed as a generic qualitative method: any form of unstructured interview or any form of observation that entails some degree of researcher participation. Our backgrounds as a social anthropologist now teaching as a sociologist, the other as a sociologist now teaching psychology, gave us as ethnographers an interesting standpoint from which to reflect.

As usually happens with academics, this book started life as a whinge about students' understandings and (mis)perceptions of ethnography. The whinge soon turned into discussions about students, textbooks, curricula, colleagues, and disciplinary boundaries and peculiarities. Eventually the talk turned into this text. The book does not seek to be a definitive guide to doing ethnography; such books already exist. Nor does it seek to make some grand theoretical statement concerning the state of the art with respect to ethnography. What we want this book to do is to explore the questions that we first encountered in its conception: just what is ethnography? Are there core ethnographic values across the social sciences that breach disciplinary boundaries? Does it matter that different disciplines have different 'takes' on ethnography? In addition, just what does an ethnography look like in actual practice within different social science disciplines? This book is for our students, the very ones who started us on this journey in the first place. We hope it gives them a sense of ethnography as a challenging yet ultimately satisfying methodological approach, which takes us to the very heart of what social science should be all about; getting up close and personal with life as it is lived.

Julie Scott Jones
Sal Watt
August 2009

ACKNOWLEDGEMENTS

We would like to take this opportunity to acknowledge and thank those who have been instrumental in helping us to get this project off the ground and through to fruition. At the outset we would like to thank Patrick Brindle and acknowledge his valuable advice and support of our original idea and book pitch. We owe immense thanks to those people at Routledge who ran with our idea and who have been immensely helpful and supportive throughout our journey; special thanks to Gerhard Boomgaarden, Miranda Thirkettle and Jennifer Dodd.

We would like to thank our respective institutions and colleagues for their continued support, namely the Social Science Faculties at the Manchester Metropolitan University and Liverpool Hope University. A big thank you goes to Martin Guest for his patient and continued IT help and support. Importantly, we would like to thank our respected colleagues who generously agreed to give of their time and contribute chapters to this text; thank you – we hope you are as proud of the book as we are. Finally, it goes without saying, we owe immense gratitude to our respective families for their support, patience and understanding; we now owe you time.

Part I

THINKING THROUGH ETHNOGRAPHY

1

INTRODUCTIONS

Julie Scott Jones

Looking back

My introduction to ethnography came as a first-year social anthropology undergraduate. My first week of lectures was on Bronislaw Malinowski's fieldwork in the Trobriand Islands (see Young 1979), given by a deeply charismatic lecturer who had spent years doing ethnographic field research in the Amazon. By the end of that week, I had learnt two basic 'truths': first, that ethnographic field research was what social anthropologists 'did' and, second, that Malinowski was the 'founding father' of all things ethnographic. Furthermore, ethnography entailed long-term participant observation in far-flung, 'exotic' places, where the researcher might even 'go native' (that is over-identify with the research participants and thus lose all sense of object-ivity), and that was not necessarily a bad thing. To my class of first-year social anthropologists it all seemed exciting, glamorous and far superior to anything the sociology or psychology students were doing with their questionnaire-based surveys or lab experiments. At that stage, we did not see that these established 'truths' were more akin to 'myths' and highly problematic in relation to representation, power, ethics, and many other related methodological (and political) issues. We had not yet read Malinowski's diary (1967) or engaged with the debates that ensued within the discipline (see for example Okely 1975 and Geertz 1984). Also, we had not yet come across ethnography in other social science disciplines: we thought ethnography was purely the domain of the social anthropologist.

By the end of my undergraduate studies ethnography was a far more problematized methodological approach and far less romanticized. This book seeks to explore many of these problematics around power, representation, politics, ethics and so forth; the issues that ethnographers today see as essential aspects of 'doing' an ethnography, which were absent from the classical ethnographies to which my first-year class was introduced. Chapter 2 of this book explores social anthropology's relationship with ethnography, and how and why these issues became important, so there is no need to review them here. It also explores the 'myth' of Malinowski that my undergraduate class was taught and believed.

3

Nevertheless, ethnography remained something that social anthropologists 'did'; indeed it often seemed like social anthropology's *raison d'être*. During my doctoral studies, I began to appreciate that social anthropologists were not the only ones to use ethnographic field research. I conducted my field research in the USA and found anthropology 'at home' problematic in relation to social anthropology's traditional focus on non-western cultures. It was then that I began to explore ethnography in sociology and found that some sociologists had pursued ethnographic research, often influenced by the classical ethnographers that I had studied as an undergraduate. The Chicago School remains the best and most influential example of this work, but they were not mainstream within sociology until the latter half of the twentieth century. It is interesting to reflect on how disciplinary boundaries can blind us to alternative and often innovative uses of the same methodology – something that is discussed in Chapter 4 in particular reference to psychology.

Today, as a lecturer in sociology, I teach qualitative research methods, including ethnography, but remain frustrated by how ethnography, typically, is presented to students in the mainstream research methods textbooks. That representation presents ethnography as a form of participant observation (which it is) that entails a bit of reflexivity. Obviously, texts that are more specialized provide greater detail than generic methods books can, but there is a danger that students believe themselves to be doing ethnographic research when they are not. Students often have a stereotype of ethnography that it is any form of participant observation, or any form of qualitative research, that involves being a 'bit touchy feely', as one of my students put it. My co-editor, Sal Watt, as an ethnographer herself and a lecturer in research methods to psychology students, felt similar frustrations. Additionally, as we both migrated across disciplinary boundaries, from social anthropology to sociology and sociology to psychology respectively, we became aware that ethnography was often represented and viewed in different ways, depending on the disciplinary context.

This book emerged from our desire as ethnographers (and teachers) to explore a number of related issues:

• What exactly is ethnographic research and what makes it different from other qualitative approaches?
• Why did ethnography emerge within one social science discipline and not others?
• Why did its adoption across the social sciences prove problematic?
• What are the methodological advantages and disadvantages of doing ethnographic research?
• Why are ethnographers so concerned by issues of ethics, politics, representation and power?
• What does ethnography look like within different social science disciplines?

These issues are explored throughout this book, which seeks to place ethnography within broad historical and disciplinary contexts. As ethnography is becoming increasingly popular across the social sciences, we wanted to explore what ethnography means to researchers outside its traditional havens of social anthropology and sociology. Indeed, does ethnography look the same to a psychologist or sports scientist as it might to a social anthropologist? Does it matter if it does not?

The importance of context

We did not want to write a 'how to do' ethnography textbook; there are already some very good books that do this, for example, Hammersley and Atkinson (2007) and Brewer (2000). What we wanted was to write a book that allowed students to see ethnography in action in a variety of field settings and within different social science disciplines. 'Social science' is a label that has become increasingly unfashionable in the past thirty years due to the many 'turns' (for example, feminism, post-structuralism, postmodernism, postcolonialism, etc.) in theory that have influenced, shaped and altered how so-called 'social scientists' see their disciplines. As objectivity, validity and empiricism make way for subjectivity, politics and deconstruction, social scientists find the word 'scientist' highly problematic. In addition, 'social scientists' increasingly 'deconstruct' and dissect their own subject areas, motives, preconceptions and so forth; unifying ideals that may operate across disciplinary boundaries can seem opaque. Increasingly we have retreated into our disciplinary boxes to a greater degree. However, the editors and contributors of this book would make a case for utilizing the label 'social science' as the more we peer over disciplinary boundaries and attempt interdisciplinary work the more we appreciate common goals and motives. At a basic level, we could identify a desire to engage with and understand the social world and individuals' lives within it. An appreciation and awareness of historical and cultural contextualization, as well as social constructionism, are also shared across the 'social sciences'. Social scientists might also acknowledge shared usage of key concepts and terminology, a point Sal Watt makes in Chapter 13 of this book. Therefore, we use the term 'social science' deliberately and consider there to be sufficient commonalities across the social science disciplines for the material in this book – even though each chapter is written within a particular disciplinary perspective – to be of use and 'speak' to students in a range of social science subjects. It will become clear as the chapters progress that what unites us is not our categorization as 'social scientists' but as 'ethnographers'.

Each chapter of this book will place the reader in a different field setting and within a different social science discipline, including social anthropology, sociology, criminology, psychology, geography, education, sport and health. This list is not exclusive; as the bibliography demonstrates, ethnography has also been used in, among others, economics, business studies, nursing, hospitality studies and within IT development. I hope that the reader will also grasp that ethnography is no longer 'just' colourful description but can be applied in academic, policy and commercial settings (as Chapters 3, 5, 6 and 7 vividly demonstrate). In other words, ethnographic work can have an influence beyond academia and, more importantly, can change lives; Helen Jones, in Chapter 3, sees the ability of ethnography to change research subjects' lives as the central goal of any piece of ethnographic research. This point is echoed by many of the other contributors.

The overall intention of the book is to demonstrate the potential range of field settings available to would-be ethnographers, as well as to illustrate how ethnography may be conducted within different disciplinary boundaries. It is worth noting, as Sal Watt does in Chapter 4, that ethnography has such a low profile in some disciplines that researchers may not even categorize their work as ethnographic or may not wish to due to disciplinary norms. One of our contributors, Duncan Light (see Chapter 12), 'came out' so to speak as an ethnographer while writing his chapter as he realized the commonalities his work shared with that of the other contributors. Within his discipline of geography, ethnography is still an emerging methodology. This book demonstrates that although ethnography may look 'different' when conducted within specific disciplinary contexts; this 'difference' is superficial and beneath the surface lie shared values: what we might call 'core values' common to all ethnographers, irrespective of social science discipline. We might also categorize ethnographers as having a shared worldview, or what Dave Randall and Mark Rouncefield, in Chapter 5, call a 'sensibility'.

An ethnographic sensibility?

The conventional academic style would be for an introductory chapter to offer a discussion of definitions of 'ethnography', before presenting the editors' particular shared definition. This introduction (and book) deliberately omits such a discussion. Debates on definitions are always interesting (and often entertaining) but can also be nothing more than semantic diversions. Numerous texts explore the issue of definitions (see for example Brewer 2000; Hammersley and Atkinson 2007). In bringing together a range of ethnographic examples from across the social sciences, we have found diversity in approaches to field settings and how fieldwork was conducted. I am the only one of all the contributors who actually lived long term with their field subjects; to my undergraduate social anthropologist sensibilities this would make my work the only 'proper' ethnography. However, as many of the chapters demonstrate, one can move in and out of the field setting and yet still immerse oneself in a particular social world. The relationships created and maintained with field subjects can be just as meaningful (and close) as powerfully demonstrated in Chapters 3, 6 and 9. As noted in Chapters 5 and 12; some research might only last a week or two and yet, as these chapters show, a wealth of 'thick' data that is certainly ethnographic can be obtained. Many of the field settings could not be lived in by the researcher for practical reasons; most obviously in Wendy Laverick's prison work discussed in Chapter 6. Some settings, by their nature, require the ethnographer to live apart from the field. Yet all the chapters show a high level of participation within the field setting and a strong commitment to field subjects that overwhelmingly identify the work as 'ethnographic' in style and orientation. We could argue, then, for a shared sensibility common to all ethnographers, built on a set of common, core values, that shapes the way they see and orientate themselves towards their discipline, their field setting and ultimately their research: a sensibility that identifies them as ethnographers rather than 'just' qualitative researchers or indeed 'social scientists'. What exactly might these core values be?

Our core values?

The chapters in this book demonstrate that, no matter where ethnographic research is conducted or within whatever social science discipline, there remains a set of shared, what we might call, core values. These values include the following:

- *Participation*: conventionally ethnography is represented as utilizing participant observation as its central method. However, not every field setting can allow the researcher to participate fully, for example, Wendy Laverick, in Chapter 6, could not live the life of a prisoner. She had to rely on focus groups and interviews to collect her data. Yet her work is ethnographic because she participates in their lives, not in a literal physical sense but, as she clearly discusses, in an emotional and mental sense. Her participation is a commitment to enter the prisoners' social worlds emotionally and mentally. Participation need not be the model of the fully immersed participant observer; field settings mean that levels of participation vary and may alter over time. Ethnographers make a commitment and demonstrate a willingness to participate in the social worlds of their research subjects on different levels: physical, social, mental and emotional. This commitment means that ethnography is highly subjective and physically and emotionally draining; a point fully explored in Chapter 13 on 'Leaving the field'. Using ethnography and participant observation as synonymous terms ignores the fact that the latter may be a very superficial level of physical or social participation, without the emotional or mental participation ethnographers usually engage in.
- *Immersion*: ethnographers strive to immerse themselves within a cultural setting; they want to 'learn the language' literally and metaphorically. This is not the same as 'going native', but rather a commitment to doing as much as you can to become akin to what we might term a 'knowledgeable tourist' or a 'trusted outsider'. Immersion means that ethnographers (to

paraphrase the Chicago School sociologist, Robert E. Park) get the seat of our 'pants dirty' literally and metaphorically. Or to use another analogy, we seek to get 'up close and personal'.

- *Reflection, reflexivity and representation*: we might call these the 'Three Rs' of ethnography. Ethnographers reflect constantly on their work, their writing, their motives, etc. This reflective practice works to inform their research at every stage. Thus, ethnography is not a mechanical methodology where one 'goes out' and collects data, analyses it and then writes it up. Ethnography is highly reflective. Ethnographers are also committed to reflexivity, as Sal Watt discusses in Chapter 13. Reflexivity is more than mere reflection but rather a theoretical, ethical and political stance whereby ethnographers consider their position within their research, their relationship to their field subjects and their wider cultural context. Reflexivity involves thinking through issues of gender, race, sexuality, class, power, ethics and so forth. It is more than just pondering how your participants might act differently towards you and more to do with a commitment to being aware of and willing to challenge issues of power, control and so forth. Chapters 2, 3 and 13 discuss the rise of reflexivity in more detail. Finally, reflection and reflexivity have at their heart a concern with representation of the field setting, the field subjects and their social actions. As discussed in Chapters 2 and 3, the past thirty years have seen the issue of representation shift to the heart of social science practice. This involves a concern for how we accurately depict our research subjects in a way that facilitates 'understanding', but, more importantly, it relates to an awareness of the political power of representation. In other words, how we represent a social group or culture has political ramifications, something classical ethnographers failed to consider. John E. Goldring's research (in Chapter 9) vividly demonstrates the importance and potential consequences of representation. Representation particularly relates to the writing process and consideration of how we construct texts that represent field subjects in a realistic, critical and empowering way; the concern for giving 'voice' in text is part of this concern. As Duncan Light discusses, in Chapter 12, ethnographers are as reflective about their writing as they are about their actual research and, for that reason, 'writing up' ethnographies is, perhaps, more time consuming and challenging than other forms of research writing. Ethnographers acknowledge that ethnographic writing is not objective and neutral but inherently political.
- *'Thick' description*: ethnographers record their data in a specific way; they do not just record everything they note in a descriptive manner; rather, they strive to describe the field setting and actions that occur within it in as much detail as possible and with as much contextualization as possible. This is called 'thick description' (Geertz 1975) and, if done well, it not only recreates the field setting as accurately as possible but also affords sufficient context to allow 'understanding', in a phenomenological sense,

to occur. Ethnographers, therefore, are scrupulous in their recording of data and their collecting of all forms of data, whether field notes, photographs, recipes, artefacts and so forth, that might help create a 'thick description' of the field setting. 'Thick description' is discussed at greater length in Chapter 12.

- *An active, participative ethics*: all social science researchers take ethics seriously. However, ethnographers view ethics as an active part of their research, rather than something to be sorted out prior to fieldwork. Ethics becomes a political issue for most ethnographers, with a concern to empower rather than disempower participants. Ethnographers seek informed consent throughout their fieldwork and strive to create field relationships whereby there is a continual dialogue about ethics. Issues of privacy, sensitivity, representation, power and consent become central concerns in most modern ethnographic work. Ethnographers view ethics as participative, which can involve allowing field subjects to view field notes or letting them feed back into finished ethnographies. Obviously covert work would seem to go against these principles, as discussed in Chapter 8; but even covert researchers strive to be as ethical as they can be within their research setting, for example, using pseudonyms and committing to giving 'voice' to participants in the finished text. Although there are many examples of covert ethnography, the majority of ethnographers do overt research and place the rights and well-being of their field participants at the centre of their work and above all other research concerns.

- *Empowerment*: linked to the previous values is that of a commitment to empower field subjects. Empowerment can be direct, as in John E. Goldring's research (Chapter 9) on gay married men and Wendy Laverick's research (Chapter 6) on violent offenders, where the participants became empowered by telling 'their stories'. However, empowerment can also be gained by ethnographic research being used to influence wider social policy or legislation. In Chapter 3, Helen Jones, cites numerous examples of criminological ethnographies that have influenced government policy, for example on rape, and in turn helped to empower people. Ethnographers are sensitive to issues of power and abuse; they are reflective of the history of social science research and the many examples of unethical work (see Chapter 3 for a further discussion). Many ethnographers view the positivistic, natural science model of research that dominated the social sciences until the 1980s as inherently disempowering and open to abuse. It should be noted that ethnographers are very aware that they may be unable to empower their research participants, but at least they are committed to not disempowering them.

- *Understanding*: finally, we might argue that at the heart of all ethnography's 'core values' is 'understanding'. As Chapter 2 notes, the German phenom-enological tradition greatly influenced the development of ethnography as a methodology. Weber's concept of '*Verstehen*', with its aim of creating interpretative bridges or frameworks for 'understanding' are at the very centre of everything that ethnographers seek to do. All researchers want to understand the social world they are researching, but often they do this by imposing an objective, distanced theoretical framework. Ethnographers allow data, and thus explanations, to emerge from the field experience and obtain an insight into lives as they are actually lived; rather than how the researcher thinks they are lived. Malinowski (1922: 25) saw the ethnographer's goal as 'to grasp the native's point of view'. As Geertz (1984: 135), drawing on phenomenological theory, notes, this 'communion' is not possible but rather ethnographers are trying to create relationships within the field whereby 'understanding' is more like 'grasping a proverb, catching an illusion . . . reading a poem'. Geertz's description of 'understanding' is valuable as it makes clear that ethnographers can never see the world as the 'natives' might, but at the same time insights, however fleeting, are possible and can be profound.

Describing ethnography as a form of participant observation, a mere method, confuses method and methodology. Ethnographers use a range of methods to gather data, although participant observation remains a central one. Ethnography is a methodological approach that sits within the broader context of qualitative research. By identifying core values that all ethnographers hold, we can get away from definitions that are exclusive to only a handful of disciplines and instead acknowledge the diversity of approaches within the broad heading of 'ethnography'. It also allows us, as ethnographers and social scientists, to open up interdisciplinary dialogues that can further understanding of social worlds and actions.

Thinking through ethnography

This book is in two parts. The first part, 'Thinking through ethnography' seeks to offer a historical and theoretical background to ethnography as a methodology. In Chapter 2, the origins of ethnography within social anthropology are outlined and the reasons for the dominance of ethnography within that discipline are discussed. The chapter also reviews ethnography's development within other social sciences. In Chapter 3, Helen Jones discusses the importance of ethics within ethnography and how ethics (and politics) became increasingly central to ethnographic research. She draws on a variety of examples from criminology. Finally, in Chapter 4, Sal Watt discusses ethnography's position within psychology; reviewing that discipline's adoption of the natural science model, as well as more recent attempts to popularize ethnography within psychology. Part II of the book, 'Ethnography in context', seeks to take the reader through the different stages of ethnographic research, as well as discuss some key methodological issues. Each chapter draws on a specific example of ethnographic research, within a specific social science discipline. By the end of the book, the reader should have a sense of the process of doing an ethnography, as well as an appreciation of how ethnographies might differ across disciplines. The contributors have deliberately written their chapters in a reflexive and personal style. Every chapter offers an insight into how contributors negotiated key areas of the research process, including how they chose their research areas; formulated working research questions; negotiated access; made their work ethical; recorded their data; worked with field subjects; and 'wrote up' their results.

In Chapter 5 Dave Randall and Mark Rouncefield discuss the pros and cons of doing applied ethnographic research across subject disciplines, drawing on their extensive work in commercial settings. They make the point that applied ethnographic work can lead to difficult compromises, based on commercial demands. In Chapter 6, Wendy Laverick draws on her work with violent offenders to discuss issues of access and particularly the demands of doing research in a 'closed' institutional setting (specifically a prison). Her chapter demonstrates that close field relationships can be fostered despite the obvious restrictions present in a prison. In Chapter 7, Anna Graham and Rosemary Kilpatrick, review the issue of researching 'vulnerable subjects', specifically children. All research subjects are less powerful than the researcher is; but children are perhaps the most powerless and therefore specific techniques must be used when doing research involving children. The chapter powerfully demonstrates that children's views of the world can challenge adult inter-pretations and open up new ways into long-standing social problems, in this instance educational underachievement and poverty. Sal Watt and Julie Scott Jones, in Chapter 8, discuss participant observation in two contrasting case studies; one overt and one covert. The chapter illustrates that all participant observation is fraught with problems and that covert research might be justified in some research contexts. Chapter 9 focuses on the issue of empowerment in relation to field participants. John E. Goldring draws on his research with gay married men to explore issues such as field relationships, giving 'voice' and over-identification with field subjects. An ethnographic example from sports studies is discussed in Chapter 10; Clive Palmer draws on his work on male gymnastics to discuss strategies for data recording and organizing field data. In Chapter 11, Julie Scott Jones and Sal Watt discuss different strategies for analysing field data; drawing on two contrastive case studies. Duncan Light, in Chapter 12, reviews the final stage of ethnographic research: 'writing up'. He uses examples from his research into 'Dracula tourism' in Romania to explore issues around writing and representation. Finally, Sal Watt, in Chapter 13, draws many of the book's themes together in a discussion of reflexivity and 'leaving the field'. She utilizes a series of vignettes, written by some of the book's contributors, to explore ethnographers' emotional, physical and social ties to their field settings, and the challenges they face when returning to 'normal' life.

Looking ahead

Reflecting on my own ethnographic 'education' in social anthropology makes me realize how much ethnography, and indeed the social sciences, have changed in the past twenty years. It seems as if we have finally processed the social and theoretical transformations of the past forty years; the social sciences have emerged changed, typically for the better, particularly around issues of methodology, representation, ethics and diversity of subject areas. Ethnography mirrors this in its normalization of representation, active-participative ethics, concern with text and embracing of diversity. The rather tired classical ethnographies that I read as an undergraduate seem more like archaeological artefacts than anything of theoretical relevance in the twentieth century. That is quite harsh but reflects how quickly subjects and teaching curricula change. This text demonstrates the process of doing ethnography today, in a variety of disciplines; the potential of interdisciplinary work is certainly something that needs to be explored further. It also shows the insights that can be gained, as well as the impact research can have on individual lives: social and personal change is possible, which is a powerful message that social scientists and ethnographers, in particular, should never tire of repeating.

Suggested further reading

Brewer, J. D. (2000) *Ethnography*, Milton Keynes: Open University Press.

Chambers, E. (2000) 'Applied Ethnography', in N. K. Denzin and Y. S. Lincoln (eds) *Handbook of Qualitative Research*, 2nd edn, Thousand Oaks, CA: Sage.

Coffey, A. (1999) *The Ethnographic Self: Fieldwork and the Representation of Identity*, London: Sage.

Crang, M. and Cook, I. (2007) *Doing Ethnographies*, London: Sage.

Fetterman, D. M. (1998) *Ethnography*, 2nd edn, London: Sage.

Hammersley, M. and Atkinson, P. (2007) *Ethnography: Principles in Practice*, 3rd edn, London: Routledge.

Reflective activities

1   Thinking about 'ethnography' generally; use a social science dictionary and look up its definition for 'ethnography'. Is the definition clear? Review the way some of the suggested readings listed above define 'ethnography': how do they differ and how are they similar? What makes 'ethnography' different from other qualitative methodologies?

2   Review the difference between 'method' and 'methodology'; what is the difference between the two?

3   Thinking about your academic discipline: What is the position of ethnography within your specific academic discipline? Is it popular and widely used, or rarely mentioned and underused? How might you account for ethnography's position in your academic discipline?

4   Select a specific research topic and then consider how ethnographers in different social science disciplines might research that topic.

2

ORIGINS AND ANCESTORS

A brief history of ethnography

Julie Scott Jones

This chapter will outline the history of ethnography as a methodological approach. Specifically, it will focus on ethnography's origins within the traditions of social anthropology and will discuss the reasons why it came to dominate this discipline's methodological orientation and indeed continues to do so today. This chapter will also review ethnography's problematic and piecemeal adoption by, and expansion into, other social science disciplines.

A long history?

The word 'ethnography' has its provenance in Greek; a combination of the words '*ethnos*' ('people' or 'tribe') and '*graphia*' ('writing'). Literally translated it means 'writing about a people' and therein lies a clue as to a central tenet of ethnography, which is to describe in as rich a detail as possible a culture or group of people. The word was first used in English in the 1830s usually synonymously with 'ethnology'[1] and 'anthropography';[2] it is believed to have originated in Germany. But it was not until the latter half of the nineteenth century that the term became adopted in a truly methodological sense; a point to which we will return.

It could be argued that ethnography is a very old research method and in one sense this is true. Highly descriptive accounts of other cultures can be found throughout most literate societies from the classical era onwards (Scott 2002). However, although some of these accounts presented genuine attempts to describe other societies, more often than not they were ideological; serving as tools to justify colonization, imperial ambitions and to reinforce long-standing worldviews. For example, the Romans often portrayed the northern European tribes that they encountered as cannibalistic barbarians (Arens 1979); such accounts are strikingly similar to those written by French, Spanish and British writers during the era of European empire building over a thousand years later. The Greek origins of the word again provide a clue as to its ideological power; '*ethnos*' does not just literally mean 'people' but implies a particular category of 'people', namely 'non-Greeks'; thus the 'other' or those that are not 'us'.

Europeans would use the derivation 'ethnic' to refer to 'heathens', 'savages' and all those neither Christian nor Jewish. The ethnographic focus on 'the other' would later prove to be a central preoccupation of anthropological and other social science ethnographies (Comaroff and Comaroff 1992; Kuper 1988). So 'ethnography' has never been a neutral term, nor used as a neutral tool for collecting data – something that we should be mindful of in our practice today.

These so-called early ethnographies are little more than cultural descriptions rather than serious attempts to analyse a social group within a broader theoretical framework. Many of these early descriptions were embellished to entertain the audiences 'back home' in Europe, while others were fictitious accounts constructed in the imaginations of imperial historians or philosophers (Kuper 1988). We should be mindful that rarely were such accounts produced in a neutral, unbiased or even systematic way; most had an ideological point to make. That said, these early 'ethnographies' do serve a purpose in that they can give us an insight into colonizing powers and the way that such powers construct 'the other' (Stocking 1991). A good example of this would be the work of Arens (1979) on accusations of cannibalism. Such accounts tell us much more about the beliefs and values of those doing the accusing than it does of the so-called 'cannibals'. So social scientists today might use earlier accounts to explore themes of 'otherness', ethnicity, racism and so forth. But we cannot call these works ethnographies in a truly methodological sense.

Armchair ethnographers and colonial collectors

Ethnography as a methodological approach emerged in the late nineteenth century. Originally, ethnography was a research method rather than a methodology in its own right. A research method is a tool to collect data whereas a methodology is the theoretical, ethical, political and philosophical orientations of the researcher to the research. In other words, one's methodology informs one's choice of research method.

There are three key reasons why ethnography became a popular research method at this time: positivism, imperialism and evolutionism. Positivism was the dominant theoretical position of the newly emerging social sciences in the early nineteenth century. The social sciences were so named as they were to apply scientific principles to the study of society, specifically modern societies. The shift into modernity had precipitated the impetus to study social change and the very nature of the 'social'; hence the emergence of the 'social sciences'. These new academic disciplines adopted a scientific focus with an emphasis on empiricism in order to construct 'laws' or theories of society, just as a physicist might use evidence to construct laws of motion. Thus data became important to these new social scientists, marking the shift away from philosopher-theorists who constructed theories with little attempt to prove them using evidence or data. In theorizing modern society, social scientists worked within a dominant theoretical position, namely evolutionism. Again, we can see the influence of the physical sciences, specifically Charles Darwin's theory of evolution. Early social scientists theorized that just as animals evolved over time and adapted to their environments, so too did cultures; and just as the study of a more 'primitive' organism might lead us to understand more complex organisms and their evolution, so too might the study of more 'primitive' cultures inform us about modern (read here) European society. Thus, the data upon which to build theories of social evolution for these positivist social scientists was to come from the non-European world. One final factor was also at play, namely imperialism. The nineteenth century was the highpoint of European imperialism and, as European powers expanded and colonized large areas of Africa and Asia, they encountered new cultural practices and beliefs. There was both a 'scientific' curiosity about such cultures but also an ideological agenda. In order to reinforce the imperial mindset one must construct stereotypes of the colonized that serve to justify their colonization. As we noted earlier, throughout history colonizing powers have constructed colonial 'others' who were depicted typically as 'primitive', 'barbaric', 'uncivilized' and so forth, and therefore in need of the civilizing forces of an imperial power, whether it be the Romans in Europe, the Spanish conquistadors in South America or the British in Africa. These three factors fed into one another to create a demand for accounts of 'primitive' beliefs and practices.

Most of the accounts (early 'field' data if you will) that were sent back were collected by myriad individuals, few of whom were trained social researchers, for example, civil servants, colonial police officers, doctors, missionaries, travellers, and so forth. Some data may have been collected in a systematic way, for example, as part of a census, but rarely for a specifically social science purpose. Thus, there was a distinction between professional social scientists (so-called 'armchair ethnographers') who would do the theorizing and interpreting of data, and the amateur data collectors 'in the field' who collected data. This meant that cultural beliefs and practices were typically taken out of context, and often manipulated to fit existing theoretical models rather than to create new understandings. For example, the social evolutionist theories of James Frazer (1890) are built on a collage of contrastive cultural practices that lack contextualization. This was common practice. Emile Durkheim's classic piece of social theory *The Elementary Forms of the Religious Life* (1915) drew on data on Australian aboriginal culture that he pieced together from different field accounts. However, his reliance on second-hand data meant that he misinterpreted aboriginal religion: a key criticism of his theory (Hamilton 2001). The era of the 'armchair ethnographer' went into decline as the nineteenth century ended because of a new generation of social theorists who wanted to go into the field and also because of the rise of a new methodological framework in the social sciences that challenged positivism.

Exploring 'out there'

As the nineteenth century neared an end, a new generation of social scientists sought to 'get out' into the field. Charles Booth's extensive field research amongst London's poor remains a classic of early sociological field research (1902). However, typically the 'field' was much further away: there was a trend for anthropologists and psychologists to join scientific survey voyages to specific regions of the world to chart local cultures and customs, as well as do medical, geographic and zoological surveying. For example, W. H. R. Rivers and Alfred Haddon conducted extensive ethnographic research on the 1898 Torres Straits expedition (Kuper 1996). Indeed, Rivers first highlighted the importance of systematic field research via immersion in a culture:

> A typical piece of intensive work is one in which the worker lives for a year or more among a community of perhaps four or five hundred people and studies every detail of their life and culture; in which he comes to know every member of the community personally; in which he is not content with generalized information, but studies every feature of life and custom in concrete detail and by means of the vernacular language. It is only by such work that one can realize the immense extent of the knowledge which is now awaiting the inquirer.
>
> (Rivers 1913 cited in Kuper 1996: 7)

Rivers was critical of earlier survey work, which he saw as piecemeal and often misleading in its portrayal of a culture. This changing view of ethnographic research was partly prompted by serendipity; that is Rivers's participation in the expedition to the Torres Straits changed how he viewed data collection. If he had followed his initial instinct not to go, then perhaps his views would have remained unchanged (Kuper 1996). However, at this time there was also a growing methodological challenge to positivism within the social sciences that would influence the growth of ethnography, particularly in the USA.

Positivism had dominated French and British social science research and theory for most of the nineteenth century. However in Germany a different approach had developed. Whereas the majority of Enlightenment philosophers had privileged rationality, objectivity and logic; the German philosopher Immanuel Kant critiqued these concepts and placed an emphasis on subjectivity and perception (1881 [1771]). Kant's work, which was developed further by the likes of Hegel (1967 [1821]), Dilthey (1988) and Weber (1949), influenced the development of German social science to be anti-positivistic in orientation, with a stress on hermeneutics, subjectivity and interpretation. Dilthey's (1988) concept of '*Verstehen*'; a form of 'empathetic understanding' that researchers should adopt as a methodological stance towards creating an environment where interpretation or explanation may be possible was developed further by Max Weber (1949) and became a characteristic of what became labelled 'interpretivist' sociology. The key aspect of this approach was its focus on how field subjects viewed or interpreted their social world. This was in contrast to positivism's emphasis on detachment, objectivity and validity. Interpretivism by its nature demands that the researcher embrace subjectivity, build relationships with field subjects and become immersed in the field environment. However, neither Dilthey nor Weber were fieldworkers and their methodological ideas remained theoretical at this stage. However, they represented the beginning of a new approach to thinking through cultures and methodology that would come of age in the twentieth century.

A founding myth, a founding father

By 1906 'ethnography' had been adopted as the term used to refer to 'descriptive accounts of non-literate peoples' (Kuper 1996: 2). The focus was on description and recreating social worlds but it was not at this stage attached to a formalized methodological approach. One key figure changed this: the Polish-born social anthropologist Bronislaw Malinowski (1884–1942). It has already been noted that professional fieldwork had already become common by the early 1900s within social anthropology. Social anthropology had adopted ethnography as its central methodological approach in contrast to sociology and psychology's focus on positivism and empiricism. Malinowski is a key figure because his fieldwork became the template for later ethnographic practice. In 1914 Malinowski travelled to New Guinea to conduct initial fieldwork; during this stint he learnt the local language, which he stressed was a key advantage for any would-be ethnographer. Previous fieldworkers had relied on interpreters. In 1915, Malinowski settled in the Trobriand Islands to conduct long-term fieldwork over two years between 1915–16 and 1917–18. Malinowski's 'founding myth', that was later built up around him as he became a prominent figure in social anthropology, portrayed him as stuck in the Trobriand Islands due to his being a 'foreign alien' (his citizenship was Austrian, although he was actually Polish) in Australian territory during the First World War. However, he could have returned to London if he had wished: but it all added to the myth that would be later built around the man (Kuper 1996). During his two years in the Trobriand Islands Malinowski established proper, systematic, modern ethnography (Kuper 1996: 12). Malinowski stressed that the ethnographer's ultimate goal (1922: 25) is 'to grasp the native's point of view, his relation to life, to realize his vision of his world'. Malinowski's ethnography involved several key aspects (Young 1979):

- Live in the field; immersing yourself in this social world.
- Learn and use the language of your field subjects.
- Isolate yourself from 'outside' influences (he was referring to European influences).

- Collect as much data as you can on everything in the field setting, from folklore stories, to social rules and customs, descriptions and observations.
- Take copious field notes.
- Participate in field activities where possible; thus, participant observation is a key element of ethnographic research.
- Keep a detailed field diary to use as a safety valve to release emotional pressures.

The Trobriand fieldwork produced three volumes: *Argonauts of the Western Pacific* (1922); *The Sexual Life of Savages in North-Western Melanesia* (1929); and *Coral Gardens and their Magic* (1935). These highly detailed accounts of Trobriand life have three key themes:

1 Cultures or cultural practices cannot be studied in isolation: the fieldworker must contextualize a culture through immersion within it.
2 One cannot rely on an informant's description of the social reality; rules are not always followed as people say they are, therefore only through participant observation can social reality actually emerge.
3 Through contextualization the ethnographer will come to realize all things cultural are relative and therefore one should not make judgements on the rationality or irrationality of others' cultural practices.

Malinowski's work also stressed the importance of cross-cultural comparisons to challenge Eurocentric conceptions of the universality of certain customs or beliefs; for example, his work on sexuality challenged Freud's theory of the Oedipus complex. He also stressed a relativistic approach that placed customs in their cultural context; in other words beliefs and practices, which may seem 'irrational' outside of their context, become 'rational' within their cultural milieu. Malinowski was not just a methodological innovator, he also stressed the importance of linking data to social theory; description was not enough and needed to be framed by a theoretical paradigm. Malinowski's was Functionalism, a theoretical approach that had been popular prior to Malinowski's fieldwork and that stressed that all social phenomena have a function within a society. Durkheim's work (1915) is a good example of a functionalist approach. However, Malinowski could be considered the first Functionalist (and fieldworker) to collect original, primary data to support his theories. Malinowski returned to the University of London after the First World War; a deeply charismatic figure he influenced the next generation of social anthropologists and ethnographers. His influence as a social theorist waned after his death as Functionalism came to be heavily critiqued. Nevertheless, he remains a key figure as the person who established not only what an ethnography could and should look like, but also how one should go about 'doing' an ethnography.

Social anthropology's rite of passage

Ethnography had already been adopted by social anthropology as its central methodological approach as early as 1909 (Radcliffe-Brown 1952: 276), but it was the so-called 'Malinowskian Revolution' (Kuper 1996: 32) that established ethnography as the methodological and theoretical heart of social anthropology. Malinowski's approach and orientation to his field setting and subjects became a template for how social anthropologists 'did' ethnography. The act of 'going off' into the field and immersing oneself in a culture became effectively a rite of passage (Kuper 1996; Okely 1996; Okely and Callaway 1992) for professional social anthropologists; the successful survival of the experience and the 'writing up' of an ethnography allowed entry to the anthropological 'club'. This remains essentially a rite of passage today; the majority of doctoral programmes in social anthropology still insist on long-term fieldwork as a key criterion and many undergraduate programmes encourage dissertation students to conduct fieldwork. This raises a criticism of social anthropology as elitist, dominated by academics and students from high socio-economic class backgrounds with the time and access to financial support to participate in such fieldwork. The subject does still recruit students, and therefore by implication academics, predominantly from the higher socio-economic classes (Mills 2003).

Malinowski's work also encouraged the over-identification of the ethnographer/anthropologist with their field setting, implying a sense of ownership; for example, these were Malinowski's Trobrianders, Firth's Tikopia (1936) and Evans-Pritchard's Nuer (1940). This became a style of ethnographic authorship/ownership that would later become problematized and critiqued; a point to which we will return. The 'field' was taken as meaning non-western cultures; in other word's anthropology's gaze was on the 'other', typically the colonial 'other'. This allowed social anthropology to position itself apart from sociology, whose focus has always been on western, typically urban societies. Jackson (1987) makes the point that anthropology 'at home', i.e. in urban or western contexts, had a relatively low status until the 1980s, and even then it often remained focused on what we might class as the fringes of western cultures, for example peasant or rural cultures. However, at the same time that British social anthropology was being revolutionized by Malinowski's work, his ethnographic principles were being adopted by a group of sociologists who wanted to explore the subcultures of the western urban setting.

The urban 'other'

Sociology has always been closely linked to social anthropology but a classic way to distinguish between the two is that the former typically focuses on western, urban settings and utilizes quantitative, empirical methodologies, while the latter focuses on non-western cultures, using ethnographic

19

methodologies. The point was made earlier that British and French sociology adopted positivism as its central methodological orientation. However, German sociology, particularly the work of Dilthey and Weber, had offered up an alternative methodological orientation, which could be broadly labelled 'interpretivism'. The German tradition also drew on the work of phenomenologists such as Husserl (1931) and Schutz (1970) to explore theoretical frameworks for understanding social action; this was far more theoretically sophisticated than the 'simpler' functionalist theories dominating British social anthropology in the inter-war years. It should also be noted that American social and cultural anthropologists, such as Franz Boas, Alfred Kroeber, Ruth Benedict and Margaret Mead, also drew on these German theoretical perspectives while promoting long-term fieldwork in a style akin to that of Malinowski (Stocking 1983).

A synthesis between the ethnographic practice of Malinowski and the philosophical and theoretical perspectives of the German tradition occurred at the Department of Sociology of the University of Chicago: the so-called 'Chicago School'. Becker (1999) points out that the 'Chicago School' became more a myth of origin (similar to that of Malinowski) and a catch-all label for a disparate group of sociologists. That said, the 'Chicago School' remains significant in the history of both sociology and ethnography (Plummer 1997). The University of Chicago was the first to establish a department of sociology in the USA (in 1892); it produced the first main sociology journal (the *American Journal of Sociology* in 1895) and the first major sociology student textbook (Park and Burgess's *Introduction to the Science of Sociology* in 1921). Finally, it had a core focus on empirical urban fieldwork, heavily influenced by German phenomenological theory, which would give rise to the key sociological theories of Symbolic Interactionism and Ethnomethodology. Two of its founding members, W. I. Thomas and Robert E. Park, had studied in Germany and drew on German phenomenological theory in developing their own work, in turn influencing the development of the 'Chicago approach'. Perhaps more significantly, both Thomas and Park promoted the importance of fieldwork and thus the use of empirical data to build theoretical models. Chicago was a city in flux in the post-First World War era: its population was being transformed by immigrants drawn to the industrialization going on in the city and consequently there were extremes of wealth and poverty. The city itself was to be a living 'social laboratory'. Park exhorted his students in 1927 to:

> Go and sit in the lounges of luxury hotels and on the doorsteps of the flophouses; sit on the Gold Coast settees and on the slum shakedowns; sit in the Orchestra Hall and in the Star and Garter Burlesk. In short go and get the seat of your pants dirty in real research.
>
> (Becker 1999: 4)

The concern was to explore social change as it happened, and to access and understand social worlds in the phenomenological or interpretivist style. A series of now classic studies emerged, including, Anderson's *The Hobo* (1923), Thrasher's *The Gang* (1927), Wirth's *The Ghetto* (1928), and Shaw's *The Jack-Roller* (1930). Initially the focus was on direct observation, but later participant observation, based on long-term immersion in that context (albeit without actually living with the field subjects), was used. As Becker notes (1999: 10) the Chicago style of fieldwork was heavily influenced by the social anthropological tradition established by Malinowski, affording 'all the romance of anthropology but [you] could sleep in your own bed and eat decent food'. Field data allowed the construction of theoretical models to understand social worlds within the city. Perhaps the most famous example of a 'Chicago School' ethnography is Whyte's *Street Corner Society* (1943), which, Becker notes, became a 'model for all of us of what a Chicago style field study ought to look like' (1999: 7). Whyte lived for just over three years (including eighteen months living with one family) in a slum district in Boston populated by first- and second-generation Italian immigrants. His study describes the different activities, groups and events within this social world. It is perhaps the closest that sociology has ever got to the Malinowskian model of ethnographic fieldwork. Whyte's work is also significant as it had been influenced by the now relatively forgotten W. Lloyd Warner, who encouraged his students to draw on the British social anthropological approach to fieldwork; Erving Goffman was another Warner-influenced researcher.

The 'Chicago School' remains the best example of the use of ethnography within the sociological tradition and, despite the clear theoretical differences, within the Chicago style there was a commitment to the use of extensive participant observation based fieldwork to explore and understand urban social worlds. It should also be noted that the 'Chicago School' also mimicked the anthropological tradition in its exoticization of urban 'others': while anthropologists focused on colonial non-European 'others', the Chicago sociologists typically focused on those in the lower reaches of western urban society, such as immigrants, the working class, vagrants and so forth. Again, we have relatively affluent, male, upper middle-class (and white) fieldworkers researching 'others' without reference to issues of power or ethics (let alone gender, race or class); a key criticism that would be raised against this style of classical ethnography during the social and cultural transformations within the social sciences in the latter half of the twentieth century.

Ethnography elsewhere

While social anthropology adopted ethnography as its core methodological doctrine to the point of dogma, sociology's relationship with ethnography focused on the 'Chicago School'. British and French sociology remained in the positivist tradition, privileging quantitative research methods. In psychology the research approach also remained resolutely quantitative, experimental and deductive (see Chapter 4 for a more detailed discussion of this issue) until the emergence of cultural psychology in the 1980s, as exemplified by the work of Shweder and Levine (1984). Although the 'founding fathers' of psychological method, particularly those in the psychoanalytical tradition such as Freud and Jung, saw the importance of investigating (and by implication understanding) patients' lives, we cannot classify their subsequent detailed case histories as ethnographies in the sense of those of Whyte, Malinowski or Radcliffe-Brown. In terms of other social sciences, such as geography, economics, business studies, sports studies and education studies, quantitative, deductive approaches dominated the research focus. The social sciences until the 1960s (and in some cases beyond) remained very much in the 'science of society' mould first established in the early nineteenth century. However, the social sciences, particularly sociology and social anthropology, would come to be transformed, theoretically and methodologically, by the social revolutions of the 1960s.

'Others', 'invisibles' and the issue of power

The 1960s brought a series of socio-political movements that would transform western society and in turn have a profound impact on the social sciences. The civil rights and gay rights movements, along with the second wave of feminism, campaigned on issues of equality, justice, political rights and against discrimination, whether on the grounds of gender, race or sexuality. One key element of these different campaigns was a concern with representation and visibility: for example, women and homosexuals were either not highly visible in the media or crudely stereotyped. Representation became a key political issue: how, why and who can represent an individual or social group? The concerns of these movements, particularly feminism, challenged the social sciences to think seriously about issues of representation, power and ethics. In simplistic terms, it meant opening up new research areas, for example, the social worlds of women and how they differ from those of men. If most researchers were men (and usually white at that), then inevitably their focus would be on the lives of men; practically, they might not be able to access women's lives. However, this inevitably led to misrepresentations of a culture: for example, social anthropology's tendency to focus on male activities like hunting, rather than female activities like gathering which actually provide most sustenance to hunter-gatherer communities. A good example of this is the work of Weiner (1976), whose fieldwork in the Trobriand Islands offers an interesting contrast with Malinowski's, particularly with regard to gender and the significance of women's activities. By the 1970s, the effect of feminism on the social sciences saw women's lives becoming a legitimate area for research and meant that gender (and sexuality and race) could not be overlooked within research; in other words, women were no longer treated as invisible. In addition, feminist ethnographers (see for example Okely 1975) began to challenge the macho culture of surviving (and suffering) fieldwork as a rite of passage, particularly within social anthropology.

Against the backdrop of these social movements was a transformation in social theory that fed off wider social changes as well as theories within other disciplines: this transformation goes under many labels: 'the cultural turn', 'the literary turn', 'the post-structuralist turn' or the 'postmodern turn'. This chapter will use the phrase 'post-structuralist turn', but all the labels signify a shift in how we look at, think about and understand the social world around us. From the 1950s onwards, particularly in literary studies and philosophy, there was an increase in theorists interested in the construction of knowledge, issues of representation and power, and the importance of contextualization. The work of theorists like Lyotard (1984), Lévi-Strauss (1968) and Foucault (1972) fed off and into wider social transformations. By the 1980s, this 'turn' became very influential in social anthropology and sociology, and consequently changed how ethnographers think about their work. We might view 1967 as the year ethnography started its transformation from the classical Malinowskian model to what we now understand ethnography to be today. That was the year that Malinowski's personal diaries from his time in the Trobriand Islands were published as *A Diary in the Strict Sense of the Term*. It should be noted that the diaries were never meant for publication; however, they reveal underlying misogyny and racism towards the Trobrianders, as well as sexual fantasies about the women (Okely 1996). They effectively destroyed the Malinowski myth, as well as the myth of the impartial, relativist, neutral ethnographer innocently and earnestly trying to understand 'the natives' (Geertz 1984). These diaries began the process of reflecting on ethnography, which would culminate in the landmark publication in 1986 of *Writing Culture* by James Clifford and George Marcus.

Let us illustrate the impact of post-structuralism on ethnography. When the likes of Malinowski or Whyte conducted their fieldwork or wrote up their ethnographies they excluded themselves from their work, i.e. they did not see themselves (white, male, middle class) as having an impact on how field subjects might view or act towards them. They also did not reflect on how their view of the world was shaped by their gender, class, race and so forth, and how that might affect their interpretation of the social world around them and ultimately how they represented it. The imbalance of power between them as professional, academic ethnographers (and eventually authors) and their field subjects, who were usually 'other', was not acknowledged or explored. For example, within social anthropology, most ethnographers had been upper middle-class, white, men (bar a few exceptions, such as Margaret Mead) looking at black, colonial 'others', ignoring issues of race, gender and class and, by implication, power. Today the work of Evans-Pritchard, Firth or Radcliffe-Brown seems paternalistic at best and patronizing, sexist and racist at worst.

In terms of ethics, ethnographers did not seek informed consent or complete ethics forms, yet what impact might their work have had on their participants? Not to mention issues of privacy and confidentiality. However, classic ethnographies were also presented as timeless through the use of the 'ethnographic present', yet what of the wider socio-cultural context within which ethnography was produced? Such ethnographies were also presented as the definitive vision of that social world, ignoring the fact that different researchers at different times might produce alternative views. A good example of this might be the work of Derek Freeman (1984) on Margaret Mead, offering differing views of Samoan culture. The 'writing-up' of ethnographies had been presented as a mechanical thing rather than a political issue in itself. The post-structuralist 'turn' meant that ethnographers (and social scientists generally) could no longer remove themselves from their ethnographies or work; they could not continue to ignore issues of power, ethics or representation and had to take seriously issues of text construction and subjectivity. The work of Clifford and Marcus brought these issues together in their influential text *Writing Culture* (1986), which had a profound effect on ethnography, especially within social anthropology.

The long-term impact of this shift means that reflexivity, ethics and text construction have become central to the work of the ethnographer; some might say to the detriment of actual data collection. Reflexivity means that ethnographers must think through their prejudices, biases and how their very subjectivity affects their work at all stages, whether planning, in the field or 'writing up'. This can place tremendous pressure on ethnographers to face up to what might be uncomfortable truths about themselves and their work (Okely 1996). Nevertheless, through the act of reflexivity the aim is to add depth to understanding (see Chapter 13 for a more detailed discussion of reflexivity). Ethics too becomes important at all stages; gaining ethical approval, seeking informed consent, giving participants 'voices', considering issues of power and so forth. Finally, ethnographers today focus greatly on how they 'write up' their ethnographies: questions arise such as, 'how will participants be represented?'; 'how might they be given "voice"?'; 'how might the text be genuinely collaborative with field subjects?'; 'how are subjectivity and reflexivity incorporated?', alongside more traditional issues such as 'how do I bring this social world to life?' Ethnographers today present their work as contextualized, subjective interpretations of social worlds or cultures; they do not suggest that their works are timeless, grand narratives (see Chapter 12 for a further discussion of the writing process).

Ethnography's discontents

The post-structuralist 'turn' in the social sciences has had two key consequences in relation to social research. First, the dominance of post-structuralism has led to criticisms outside of and within the social sciences that there is too much navel gazing, abstract theorizing and textual deconstruction going on, rather than practical, applied research with a wider social impact and relevance. This is crude stereotyping of what contemporary theorists are trying to do, but there is an imbalance towards abstract theory within some social sciences, particularly in sociology. Social anthropology, with its traditional focus on non-western, often colonial or postcolonial cultures was particularly affected by the rise of post-structuralism, postcolonial studies and feminism. The very foundations of the discipline were critiqued and deconstructed through the 1980s and 1990s. To illustrate this point I recall attending a postgraduate seminar in the early 1990s where the doctoral students concluded that in order to be 'good' ethnographers they should actually not attempt to 'do' an ethnography such was the mania for dissecting and challenging every aspect of practice, almost rendering it impossible to actually conduct research. This is and was an extreme position and everyone present actually did go on to do interesting and useful ethnographic work. This soul-searching has ultimately been a good thing for a discipline so long characterized and dominated by upper middle-class, white, male academics complacent regarding issues of race, power and gender. The discipline has modernized and consequently new insights and subjects areas have emerged.

But we might argue that ethnographers today, in reflecting and deconstructing what they do, are actually better placed to reveal important 'truths' about people's lives and cultures. The use of ethnography within criminology is a good example of that, such as the work of Barton (2007), Lees (1996) and Westmarland (2001). Similarly, in social anthropology the use of ethnographic techniques in applied settings has had an impact on famine relief and the work of non-governmental organizations (NGOs) (see for example De Waal 2005). More recently, the increasing use of ethnography within psychology (see for example Shweder 1991) allows greater exploration of core concepts such as 'mind', 'self' and 'identity' within wider cultural contexts, and therefore new ways of thinking about mental illness.

The rise of the ethnographic?

The second consequence of post-structuralism has been the decline in quantitative methods within the social sciences and the rise in qualitative techniques, particularly ethnography. This has had a great impact in sociology in particular, where there has been a steady decline in the teaching and use of quantitative approaches. Ethnography would seem to have come of age in the past twenty years as a methodology that fits in a social and academic context that places great importance on ethics, relativism, representation, inclusion and subjectivity. Ethnography, so long the domain of the social anthropologist, can now be found on undergraduate curricula and in student research methods textbooks across the social sciences, from psychology and business studies to education and health studies. However, has the growth of ethnography led to it losing its identity? Is every discipline's version of ethnography the same? Does it matter that many research methods textbooks present ethnography as synonymous with participant observation? This issue is something to be explored through the chapters of this book and for the reader to consider.

It takes us back to the issue discussed in the introduction concerning the confusion between method and methodology and the importance that students understand the difference.

Ethnographers do use participant observation as a method but ethnography as a methodology involves a commitment to a series of principles:

- A relativist stance.
- A desire to accurately provide a 'thick description' of a social world.
- An intention to seek ways to 'understand' a social world through immersion (long or short term) in that environment.
- The importance of historical and cultural contextualization.
- The intention to present the 'native's point of view'.
- The stress on ethics, representation, 'voice', power and inclusion.
- The importance of reflexivity.
- An awareness of subjectivity.

We can trace most of these principles back to Malinowski's basic view of what an ethnographer should do, but strengthened by the insights we now have from feminism and post-structuralism. Ethnography has come through the past forty years of social, theoretical, academic and cultural transformation a better and more useful methodology.

Can ethnography make a difference?

Ethnographies, whether classical or contemporary, endeavour to represent in detail specific cultural contexts or activities. If done well, an ethnography should take readers into that social world and allow them to gain insights and understandings. However, a key criticism of ethnography that has remained since the early twentieth century is 'What is the point of it?' After all, ethnographies present snapshots of cultures that are context-specific and subject to social change; indeed, by the time an ethnography is 'written up' the social world it seeks to represent inevitably will have changed. Ethnographies are highly subjective and low on validity and reliability. Can they actually make a difference beyond that of satisfying curiosity? As was noted above, the use of ethnography within some disciplines or sub-disciplines has been particularly effective in revealing social insights that can have an impact on policy, for example, in criminology and education, both of which are discussed in later chapters of this book. Ethnography can be applied, but it is often unattractive to those funding applied social research and policy work as it takes time and therefore can cost more to do in comparison to survey-based research. In addition, politicians and policy advisers find statistics easier to digest and present than the more detailed (and often challenging) data that emerges from ethnographic work. Nevertheless, there is an increasing use of ethnography within applied, funded contexts, particularly within education, health and criminology. One final point that we can make regarding the motivation for doing an ethnography is that ethnographers have always sought, through their work, to make a difference to people's lives by 'getting out there' and uncovering often 'hidden' social worlds: that is a worthwhile and important act in itself.

Suggested further reading

Clifford, J. and Marcus, G. E. (eds) (1986) *Writing Culture: The Poetics and Politics of Ethnography*, London: University of California Press.

Geertz, C. (1975) *The Interpretation of Cultures*, London: Hutchinson.

James, A., Hockey, J. L., Dawson, A. H. (eds) (1997) *After Writing Culture: Epistemology and Praxis in Contemporary Anthropology*, London: Routledge.

Kuper, A. (1996) *Anthropology and Anthropologists: The Modern British School*, London: Routledge.

Moore, H. (1988) *Feminism and Anthropology*, Cambridge: Polity.

Okely, J. (1996) *Own or Other Culture*, London: Routledge.

Okely, J. and Callaway, H. (eds) (1992) *Anthropology and Autobiography*, London: Routledge.

Reflective activities

1   Read a short extract from one of the classic studies mentioned in this chapter and then read an extract from a more contemporary ethnography. Compare and contrast the differences between the two texts: are they so different or are there core similarities? How might you account for the differences?

2   In a small group, attempt a group participant observation in a social setting. All members of the group should try to record everything going on around them (including how people interacted with you) in as much detail as possible. Afterwards you should compare your field notes and try to account for the differences recorded in the light of issues discussed in this chapter, such as reflexivity, subjectivity and so forth.

3   Using your field notes from the above task attempt to 'write up' your notes into an ethnography, considering issues of 'voice', representation, power and so forth that have been discussed in this chapter.

4   Imagine you are conducting long-term ethnographic fieldwork: what problems and pressures do you think you would face?

5   Take one of the classic studies listed above and imagine the characteristics of the ethnographer were changed, such as, gender, race, class; how would that have affected the data collected?

Notes

1   The comparative study of different cultures, i.e. comparing and contrasting different cultures.

2   Literally meaning 'writing about man'.

3

BEING REALLY THERE AND REALLY AWARE

Ethics, politics and representation

Helen Jones

This chapter will explore the ethics and politics of ethnographic research; how such issues emerged within the social sciences and why they shifted from marginal concerns to central methodological issues, particularly in relation to ethnographic fieldwork. It will draw on a range of examples from within sociology and criminology. Within this, it is important to consider how researchers confront ethical issues and what strategies they use to incorporate consent, representation and empowerment within their research on the social world. This chapter will ask what the ethical and political implications are of doing ethnographic research and why we should choose to conduct such research; it will also consider examples of unethical work to illustrate the possible consequences and impact this can have. These questions underpin all research which takes the daily life of human participants as its key focus. A critical ethnography which is aware of social dimensions and relations of research, does not come simply or easily.

A brief history of the ethics and politics of ethnographic research

I like to think of research as theory in action: you have an idea and you seek to find out about it by doing 'something'. If we consider ethnography to be a way of 'finding out', we might begin by wondering how this approach differs from other methods of research.

From the nineteenth century, social science research was largely guided by a conceptual paradigm informed by the natural sciences, with researchers seen as value-free technicians, applying methods to problems to establish 'truths' in a supposedly objective and ethically neutral manner in the disinterested pursuit of knowledge. Sociologists are deeply interested in the values held by different people and societies, but sociologists are also part of society and are influenced by the values which exist around them. Within criminology, value neutrality might be held to support the notion of equality before the law and the presumption of innocence, but as the sociology of deviance began to take a more qualitative approach to the study of crime in the mid-twentieth century, so the issue of value neutrality came to be challenged (Garland 2002). Critics have argued that there are political and ethical dimensions to supposed 'neutral' research, and that 'researchers who represent themselves as detached only camouflage their deepest, most privileged interests' (Fine 1994: 15). The question is not 'whether we should take sides, since we inevitably will, but rather whose side are we on' (Becker 1971: 123).

Often supposedly ethically neutral research entails the harm, or potential harm, of human participants (for example the work of Humphreys 1970, Milgram 1974 and Zimbardo 2007 discussed later in this chapter). Supposedly ethically neutral scientists might be concerned with the ethics of science (i.e. the protection of the 'purity' of the data), but ethically aware social scientists have the additional burden of concern for the ethics of the research participants, that is, the protection of their legal and human rights.

What many early researchers – particularly within mainstream twentieth-century sociology and criminology – did not realize was that their commitment to 'objectivity' and value-neutral research was highly subjective in the value-laden worldview of their predominantly, white, middle-class, masculine perspectives (Garland 2002; Harding 1987). This has been described as 'the view from above' (Haraway 1991: 197), and a challenge to this came initially from the Chicago School of ethnography, which emerged in the 1920s in the Department of Social Science and Anthropology at the University of Chicago. American cities were experiencing increased population growth following the First World War and sociology was undergoing a paradigm shift away from positivistic quantitative methods towards a more social policy orientated, problem-identification and problem-solving direction, utilizing 'naturalistic' observational qualitative methods. Notable ethnographers working at the University of Chicago included William Thomas (1937), Herbert Blumer (1969), Robert E. Park and Ernest Burgess (1969). They were interested in almost every aspect of city life, from crime, ethnicity, class, poverty and the family, to urban geography and even the role of the press. Their influence on sociological debates on theory and methodology in the twentieth century endured for many decades, and even into the 1950s and 1960s the second wave 'Chicago School' boasted members such as Erving Goffman (1956), Howard Becker (1966) and Gary Fine (1995). However, as discussed in the previous chapter, the 'Chicago School', despite privileging fieldwork and engagement with field participants, still represented the 'gaze' of white, middle-class men looking at predominantly lower-class, marginalized or ethnic minority men. The Chicago School overlooked the lives of women and could be said to have fetishized the 'deviant' over the everyday – particularly the first wave of the Chicago School. The Chicago School ethnographers rarely engaged with the issues of ethics and power in their fieldwork practice.

Nevertheless, the point should be made that the 'Chicago School' did represent a move away from the laboratory towards ethnography: 'the study of the cultural processes that occur in efforts to respond to particular human problems' (Chambers, 2000: 856), but this shift was not total and ethically dubious research was evident during this period.

Don't try this at home: unethical research

Is it possible to be aware of our intentions, our interpretations and our relations of power and still act in a way that might be harmful and unethical? Most research is conducted with integrity and care for the participants. Most researchers will explain the purpose of the research, its general aims and, if promises of confidentiality are made, they are generally upheld, except in circumstances where it cannot be maintained (Israel 2004). Participants have the right to privacy and the right not to be exploited. However, research has deceived, participants have been exploited and questions are still raised about the balance between the rights of research participants and the merits of deception.

In the mid-twentieth century, the Second World War had left many people questioning whether those accused of war crimes were justified in their claim that they were simply 'obeying orders' (Arendt 1973). Stanley Milgram, a professor at Yale University, conducted experiments that have since been widely described and documented (1974; see also Blass 2004; Zimbardo 2007) to examine whether human beings are inherently evil or if good people would be obedient to authority and do things they knew to be wrong. In his experiments, a participant was required to give 'electric shocks' to another person as part of what had been described to them as a 'learning experiment'. An overwhelmingly large number administered 'shocks' when urged to do so by the researcher, even when it was obvious that this was dangerous and even life threatening. The participants were deceived because the electric shocks were not real and the true aim of Milgram's experiment was to test obedience to authority.

The same questions about the nature of human behaviour, morality and obedience were also of interest to Philip Zimbardo, a professor at Stanford University. Zimbardo's 'prison experiment' aimed to study the process of de-individualization – a process which 'makes the perpetrator anonymous, thereby reducing personal accountability, responsibility, and self-monitoring' (2007: 295). Zimbardo constructed a 'prison' in the basement of one of the university buildings and recruited a number of students to take on the roles of 'prisoners' and 'guards'. Over a period of six days and nights, the students gradually took on the roles while Zimbardo and his researchers watched the distress of the 'prisoners' and the brutality of the 'guards':

> The obedient participants in Milgram's many replications typically experienced distress for their 'shocking' behavior, their participation

lasted for only about one half hour, after which they learned that no one was really harmed. By contrast, participants in the SPE [Stanford Prison Experiment] endured 6 days and nights of intense, often hostile, interactions that escalated daily in the level of interpersonal aggression of guards against prisoners.

(Zimbardo et al. 2000: 1)

Ethical standards insist that participants must not be deceived. Deception was certainly evident in both Milgram's and Zimbardo's research. Both researchers assert that there were no long-term negative consequences of the deceptions endured by their participants, but this does not negate the necessity for ethical standards, regulations and guidelines. It is questionable whether either study would make it through an ethics review today. Another ethically questionable study, conducted at around the same time, aimed to challenge the stereotypical beliefs held about men who committed sexual acts in public lavatories (Humphreys 1970). This ethnographic approach used participant observation where Humphreys took the role of 'watchqueen' (to cough if a stranger or the police were approaching the public lavatory). He also secretly followed some men and recorded their car licence plate numbers. After persuading a police officer friend to trace the details of the licence numbers, Humphreys used the addresses to call at the men's homes to ask questions about their marital status, employment and other personal details. The ethnographic, subcultural tradition of Chicago School sociologists, who did not give priority to ethical considerations, is evident in Humphreys's research and these three research projects highlight the point that what might be seen as ethically acceptable by some, at some points in time, is never static and always open to revision.

Projects such as Milgram's, Zimbardo's and Humphreys's have been criticized across the years by ethical reflections on the methodology employed. Zimbardo himself experienced anguish over the way in which he allowed himself to be ethically blinded by his fascination with the project and apologized to the participants again over thirty years later in a recent book: 'I apologize to them again for any suffering they endured during and following the research' (Zimbardo 2007: xv). This illustrates the argument that research ethics extends from choosing a topic through to beyond the completion and the reporting of the findings.

A 'cultural turn': seeing personal experiences as political issues and acting ethically

To think ethically is to think beyond one's own interests, but from where did a concern for ethics come? It emerged most fully in the 1960s during the counter-cultural shift that encompassed the civil rights movement, the women's rights movement, the gay and lesbian rights movement, and the 'cultural turn' towards a more nuanced understanding of the crimes of the powerful. This shift brought into focus the importance of 'voice' and visibility; that the personal is also political; and the need for the social and political appreciation of previously 'hidden lives'. Certainly, Greenhouse (2003: 270) has suggested that the reason to undertake an ethnographic study is 'not just to perfect our knowledge of crime and punishment, but also to maintain the vital connection between the practice of social science and the question of its fundamental social value'. The concern to fully represent the 'voice' of the research participant led to a sense of responsibility to identify communities, codes and customs to better understand the world and to uncover injustice.

This move away from a focus on men of a certain class, of a certain colour and of a certain sexuality saw the emergence of representations of other lives within ethnography. As the 1960s gave way to the 1970s, ethnography brought these lives into sharper focus within mainstream research, but this was not without risk. Stacey argues that ethnography, with its focus on participant observation, has the potential to betray feminist principles of trust and collaboration: 'ethnographic methods also subject research subjects to greater risk of exploitation, betrayal, and abandonment by the researcher than does much positivist research' (1988: 21). For others (such as Visweswaran 1997), ethnography has allowed for processes of research which value non-exploitative relationships and there is now a large body of feminist research within sociology and criminology. Indeed, Heidensohn (in Gelsthorpe 1997: 791) suggests that, 'there has been a significant shift in the study of crime because of feminist perspectives on it', and this may be because feminists 'have attempted to focus on the relationship between the researcher and those studied' (Belknap 2001: 21).

The emergence of a greater awareness of the potential to harm within qualitative research heralded the development of ethical codes. Although ethics are relevant to many other academic disciplines, key themes are common to the British Sociological Association and British Society of Criminology ethical codes:

- Respect for the individual person.
- Promotion of the participant's rights.
- Promotion of social justice.
- Work that is for the benefit of others.

These values do not deny the opportunity for covert research or for observation of public events; for example, at a criminal trial it would be nonsense to assume that the consent of the judges, court officials, witnesses and accused need to be obtained. The Social Research Association (SRA) states: 'there can be no reasonable guarantee of privacy in "public" settings since anyone from journalists to ordinary members of the public may constitute "observers" of such human behaviour' (2003: 33). The values within ethical codes, however, do form the basis for principles such as informed consent, non-deception, the absence of psychological or physical harm, privacy, confidentiality, and a commitment to collecting and presenting reliable and valid empirical data. However, guidelines that are valid for some purposes are not always applicable in others and the Economic and Social Research Council (ESRC) acknowledges that:

> Other ethical frameworks for research on human subjects, such as that which addresses biomedical research, may not be appropriate, which is why a framework specific to social science is necessary. In some areas of social science ethical issues are limited, but in others they raise significant challenges that need to be addressed at an appropriate point or points.
>
> (ESRC 2005: 1)

The ESRC presents six key ethical principles that it expects to be addressed, whenever applicable:

- Research should be designed, reviewed and undertaken to ensure integrity and quality.
- Research staff and subjects must be informed fully about the purpose, methods and intended possible uses of the research, what their participation in the research entails and what risks, if any, are involved. Some variation is allowed in very specific and exceptional research contexts for which detailed guidance is provided in the policy guidelines.
- The confidentiality of information supplied by research subjects and the anonymity of respondents must be respected.
- Research participants must participate in a voluntary way, free from any coercion.
- Harm to research participants must be avoided.
- The independence of research must be clear, and any conflicts of interest or partiality must be explicit.

Some researchers, however, such as Calvey (2008) and Guillemim and Gillam (2004) view research as 'ethics-in-practice', which is iterative, contingent and differs from the perceived frameworks of ethical review boards. They argue that ethical boards are not aware of the complexities of negotiating consent in certain research contexts and that ethics panels are rarely interested in the ongoing consideration of ethics, risk and consent.

> There is no direct or necessary relationship between ethics committee approval of a research project and what actually happens when the research is undertaken. The committee does not have direct control over what the researcher actually does. Ultimately, responsibility falls back to the researchers' themselves – they are the ones on whom the conduct of ethical research depends.
>
> (Guillemim and Gillam 2004: 269)

The ESRC is mindful of this contingent nature of social science research, however, stating that:

> Consent to participate is seen as an ongoing and open-ended process. Consent here is not simply resolved through the formal signing of a consent document at the start of research. Instead it is continually open to revision and questioning. Highly formalised or bureaucratic ways of securing consent should be avoided in favour of fostering relationships in which ongoing ethical regard for participants is to be sustained, even after the study itself has been completed.
>
> (ESRC 2005: 24)

It is not clear how the ongoing process should be managed but this acknow-ledgement of the 'open-ended' nature of research helps us to expand our understanding of ethics from the formal, procedural ethics of 'tick-box' pro formas and go beyond an 'ethics-in-practice' approach; to what Code (1995) refers to as 'epistemic responsibility', what it means to be really there and be really aware within the research process. This notion of 'epistemic respons-ibility' requires us to be aware of our intentions, our interpretations and our relations of power, before, during and beyond the life of the research project.

Feminist ethnography: researching rape

Studying 'deviants' or vulnerable groups, as seen in the research of Milgram, Zimbardo and Humphreys, as well as the work of the 'Chicago School', shows how sociology and criminology are particularly exposed to ethical dilemmas. Feminist researchers, in particular, were among the leaders in exposing the 'true' nature of social research and problematizing the issues of ethics, representation and power. Within sociology and criminology, much feminist research continues with such a focus by turning the ethnographic 'gaze' onto the sensitive issue of violence within women's lives. Second wave feminists began this work (for example, Brownmiller 1976; Firestone 1970; Millett 1972; Morgan 1970; Oakley 1974) and of real concern was how women's lives could be accurately represented through research that acknowledged their rights as participants in the research process. One of the foremost researchers in the late twentieth century on women's experience of sexual violence was Sue Lees (1996). She argued that:

> Asking women to reveal their experiences in such detail was under-taken only on the understanding that the results would be used to try and bring about improvements in the present situation where women are disbelieved and humiliated by the judicial system.
>
> (Lees 1996: 266)

Her theoretical position stemmed from a belief in 'standpoint feminism' (see Hill Collins 2000; hooks 2003): the idea that women's experience should be the starting point of research. It has been argued that it is only when 'detachment has been revealed as illusory and the stuff of privilege, we can dip into the question of stances' (Fine 1994: 16). Feminist theory highlights the importance of lived experience (Dobash *et al.* 2003; Fawcett and Hearn 2004) and Lees (1996) did not shy away from employing a range of research tools. Her methodology involved observation of court trials, listening to women's accounts of their experiences and analysis of police reporting practices. She also used her contacts with the police to collect police records on rape, attempted rape, buggery and indecent assault in order to approach these women to participate in her research, which might seem similar to the tactics of Humphreys (1970):

> Our letter asking whether they would be willing to be interviewed about their experiences was sent out by the police. This might have led to some confusion as to the identity of the researchers. Their confusion is understandable, since the letter was written on police headed note paper and this may have deterred some women from replying.
>
> (Lees 1997: 181)

Stacey has argued that 'discussions of feminist methodology generally assault the hierarchical, exploitative relations of conventional research, urging feminist researchers to seek instead an egalitarian research process characterized by authenticity, reciprocity, and intersubjectivity' (1988: 22). Lees (1997) contacted women who had made complaints of sexual assault, not to merely further her research, but also to find a way of giving their experience 'voice' and validating what happened to them as worthy of justice.

The notion of justice underpins much of the present-day feminist research on rape and sexual violence (Jones and Cook 2008). Nicole Westmarland is a central figure within this field and began her research life by researching 'female taxi drivers utilizing my personal experience as a night shift taxi driver' (2001). She argues that 'different feminist issues need different research methods', confirming Fine's assertion that while 'feminists vary in how we manage this treacherous territory; we manage it' (1994: 14). In this way, ethnographic research methods are part of a methodological toolbox rather than a single approach to gathering data. Just as a great deal of feminist theory emphasizes the context-specific, experiential, construction of knowledge; feminist approaches to ethnography acknowledge the importance of everyday realities for women. This is further justification for the necessity of ethical review boards to take a flexible approach to the context of any proposed research, particularly within the field of critical ethnography.

Critical ethnography: making a difference in the world

Critical ethnography (Thomas 1993) is a way of probing sites of injustice and taking on an ethical responsibility to those people involved in the lived reality of the research. The conditions of life within a particular context are held up for scrutiny but the critical ethnographer does more than report the surface level. The critical ethnographer drills down beneath surface appearances, questions received wisdom and disrupts the status quo. This process of unsettling assumptions by highlighting relations of power moves the reader from 'what we think we know' to 'what is actually happening', but challenging accepted wisdom is not easy.

An example of this is in the work of cultural criminologists engaged in 'edgework' (Lyng 2005), where structural dynamics are located within lived experience. Ferrell (2007) suggests this provides the critical researcher with another tool in the research toolbox to enable an examination 'from below'. This critical perspective ventures into realms often shunned by other researchers: the seedy worlds of the illicit, 'to conceptualize crime in relation to the many complexities of structured inequality and injustice' (2007: 92). Frequently researchers delve into worlds only imagined by the tabloid press, living with the people involved in prostitution, drug-use and gambling; such ethnographic studies provide valuable insights into worlds we know little of, worlds that most people make assumptions about and worlds that many 'respectable' researchers try to avoid:

> No matter how welcome, even enjoyable the fieldworker's presence may appear . . . lives, loves, and tragedies that fieldwork informants share with a researcher are ultimately data, grist for the ethnographic mill, a mill that has a truly grinding power. More times than I would have liked, this study has placed me in a ghoulish, and structurally conflictual relationship to tragedy, a feature of ethnographic process.
>
> (Stacey 1988: 23)

Burke (2007: 182) understands the dilemmas that appear in the complex relationships that emerge between researchers and researched: 'friendship and equality are pretty words, but they obscure the power that remains inherent to the researcher-participant interaction. We can reduce the differential; we cannot eliminate it.' Research into the night economy of private security staff in nightclubs (Calvey 2008), female drug dealers (Hutton 2006) or exotic dancers shows us a world where human beings, who are just like us, 'manage the stigma of their work as well as a host of dangerous and demeaning experiences when they work' (Barton 2007: 571). This research is not easy, it is not glamorous and it is often dangerous.

People living on the edges of mainstream society are often seen as exotic, dangerous and different and, where research has been conducted that is not of a critical nature, the theoretical understandings that emerge often utilize techniques of neutralization and denial to minimize the stigma of how such work is managed. Denial of stigma, denial of shame and denial of harm (Thompson and Harred 1992) are mobilized to suggest that these people are fragmented from society, dehumanized and different from 'us' (Condry 2009). By comparison, critical ethnography shows such narratives to be inadequate to secure a full understanding of the complexity of such lives. For example, Barton is able to show how 'the stripper reads her labor in a variety of ways . . . [and] perceives exotic dancing as a form of resistance to male power' (2007: 573). This subverts the conventional wisdom of her as victimized or desperate and represents her in a more ethical manner.

Representing others: a responsible ethic of care

Critical ethnographers enter into rarely glimpsed worlds to uncover injustice; however, not all such worlds are dangerous. Lack of scrutiny might be a result of mainstream researchers not deeming an area worthy of study. Consider the ethnographic research previously mentioned of Lees (1996) in uncovering the injustices faced by female rape victims or, to take a seemingly banal example, that of Ann Oakley on the sociology of housework in the early 1970s. Oakley was interested in the lives of ordinary women but was frustrated at the lack of attention that traditional sociological research had paid to them. She explains: 'A vast number of books have been written about men and their work; by contrast, the work of women has received very little serious sociological or historical attention' (1974: ix). What was remarkable about the research was its feminist perspective that believed women are worth researching. She travelled into the unreached and unobserved areas of women's lives to show the extraordinary conditions of their lives, and by doing so she helped to challenge much of the prevailing wisdom about the position of women within society at the time. Oakley demonstrated the dissatisfaction of British women in the last quarter of the twentieth century:

> 'Some women like it', goes the logic, 'and those who don't can do something else'. This contention ignores the shaping of women's identity by their social situation. It is not merely what a woman wants that is at issue, but what she is induced to want, and what she is prevented – by social attitudes – from believing she can have, or be.
> (Oakley 1974: 229)

Shining a light into the world of the housewife, Oakley heralded the social shift that occurred with the second wave of feminism and the challenges that surfaced about the dilemmas of research. Oakley was part of a new 'activist' turn, through which researchers positioned themselves politically. Fine (1994) has suggested that what emerged was a threefold model of qualitative research:

1 The ventriloquist stance: this is where the writer's interests are masked, requiring 'the denial of all politics in the very political work of social research' (1994: 19).

2 The use of voices stance: this is where the voices of those researched dominate, often leading to 'a subtle slide towards romantic, uncritical, and uneven handling' (1994: 22).

3 The activism stance: this is where the researcher enables an opening up of 'contradictions and conflicts within collaborative practices . . . [where] researchers, activists, informants, and other audiences are engaged as critical participants' (1994: 23).

The 'ventriloquist' approach of assumed objectivity based on the natural science model (which aims to produce replicable studies, where the social world can be predicted, measured and tested), is merely the opposite end of a spectrum from the more critical position of the 'activist', where the political position of the researcher is overt and stated. Critical, cultural and feminist researchers inhabit the 'activist' position, usually making clear their own political position. Refuting any truly 'value-neutral' research, they take ethical responsibility for their own subjectivity. Doing fieldwork is a personal experience and one that is often deeply emotional:

> I am a researcher who studies rape . . . I see up close and personal the devastation of rape over and over again. My job is to listen to women's stories of rape. Colleagues I have worked with for years, who know what I study and have even read my research articles, have never pieced this together. It has never occurred to them what it means to research rape, as a woman. They have not considered what it might feel like to do this research . . . There are words and images I wish I could forever purge from my memory, but cannot. I carry them with me, and try to make peace with them and learn from them . . . very little surprises me anymore, and very little shocks me.
>
> (Campbell 2001: 1)

It is only valid to put yourself through that, and put research participants through the pain of telling their stories, if you are going to do some good. Indeed, 'ethnographers often give back to the community via personal expertise' (Burke 2007: 191), but it remains emotionally demanding work. Many researchers discuss the emotional work involved in their research but it is often sidelined particularly if 'emotional relations develop between the researcher and the researched, but are left unexplained and often glossed over' (Calvey 2008: 911). Critical ethnography explores these sensitive aspects, negotiating the challenges and also finding a way to access one's own peace with the feelings raised throughout the research process:

My own notes attest to how intensely uneasy I was in strip clubs, how objectified I felt simply being in the space, how depressing I found it to watch beautiful, charming women dancing naked for men, how negatively I felt about strip bars while inside of them. I much preferred having a long, cozy conversation with a dancer over coffee in her home – on a comfy couch, with sunlight streaming through the window, I could much better perceive the positives of stripping. My own bias was obvious to me. I believed my informants' stories of the good and bad of stripping. I felt a strong ethic to be a vessel for their experiences, but nonetheless, I was personally repulsed by the inside of strip bars. I dreaded going. Ethnographic observation waned over time as I shifted to interviews as the primary form of data collection. As a researcher, this tension is something I have actively kept in the forefront of my analysis.

(Barton 2007: 578)

Centrally, this is about how subjectivity exists in relation to others. Within critical ethnography it is the interplay of the self with those within the research field. This makes sense because surely if it was 'all about me' it would be little more than a diary or an autobiography? Critical ethnography is more complex and includes multiple voices, multiple subjectivities and multiple meanings.

Too close to the research field or not close enough?

Researching the lives and stories of 'real' people can have consequences beyond our imagining. It has been argued that how people are represented is how they are treated (Hall 1997). Spending time in a location, and being with people in a space and trying to understand their lives, we interpret and record what we see. Embedded within this process are power relations, and sometimes we may not be aware of power issues or how they surround an ethnographic study; part of the developing skill of the researcher is to be aware and take steps to manage these relations.

An example from my own research history takes me back to conducting research in the magistrates' court. Every day for the whole summer of 1997 I observed the conveyor-belt justice of petty fines and conditional discharges until one day, a young woman, about my own age at the time, was presented for failure to pay the residue of a fine. The case unfolded against her and the details told of how she had initially been fined £200 for failure to buy a television licence. She had paid all but £25 because her circumstances had changed: her husband had left her and she was struggling to meet her bills and put food on the table for her children. The magistrates decided that a spell of two weeks in prison would settle the score. Before I fully realized it, I was on my feet demanding to be allowed to pay the fine. When I, the young woman and the officers of the court had all recovered from the shock, Julie ('the criminal') and I went for a cup of tea, which she insisted on buying. When I proudly told my research supervisor what had happened, she informed me that my research could be deemed to be ethically compromised as I had allowed myself to 'go native', I had identified too closely with my research 'subject' and therefore lost my objectivity. I am happy to report that I survived the experience.

This story is useful in illustrating the dilemmas facing researchers conducting ethnographic research from a critical perspective. Ethnographic research runs into issues of ethical review within university research ethics committees, where the risk of harm or exploitation of research participants is assessed. Obviously biomedical research or psychological research may involve complex issues of concern, but does social science research fit the concerns of such ethical review panels? Calvey criticizes the prescriptive notion of ethical standards: 'The guidance that professional associations and bodies offer their members amounts to a moral and methodological "frowning upon" covert research' (2008: 906). He also points to a statement within the newsletter of the British Sociological Association which is critical of perceived restrictive guidelines: 'The rise of ethical review should be understood as the latest in a series of legislative and institutional measures in which the state has restricted academic freedom and exerted greater control over social scientific research' (Travers cited in Calvey 2008: 907). Covert research which does not seek consent is supported in three ways. The first is suggested by Calvey (2008): that it is often just not practical or desirable to obtain consent in some contexts where it is risky to disclose that research is being undertaken. The second is the 'Hawthorne effect': the idea that people react differently if they believe they are being observed (Gillespie 1991). The third is where the research involves studying areas where reliance on the consent of research participants or promises of confidentiality may be morally wrong (Israel 2004). Frequently, research ethics is mediated by the feasible, and compromise may become one of the dilemmas of research.

Ethical struggles and responsibilities

Critical ethnographies are guided by concern for ethical sensitivities and have the capacity to represent the lives of others within the context of the competing demands of theory, politics, representation, ethics and activism. Ethnographers often form valuable relationships with research participants and can bring value to their lives, from the women who shared their stories of rape with Lees (1996), Westmarland (2001) and Campbell (2001), to the inhabitants of the night-time economy who provided insight to Calvey (2008), Barton (2007) and Hutton (2006). My own research (Jones and Cook 2008) has provided the rape crisis movement with a voice to government, which is informed by over a decade of ethnographic research. Each ethnographic researcher struggles with ethical considerations within fieldwork and this can take an emotional toll on the researcher and the researched. Ethical researchers have a responsibility to uncover injustice and challenge power. Research objectivity is an illusion and a potentially dangerous one at that. Critical ethnography allows a researcher to commit to uncover cultural accounts which may unearth further questions but which can achieve depth and richness that is often lacking in other, less immersed accounts.

Suggested further reading

Chambers, E. (2000) 'Applied Ethnography', in N. K. Denzin and Y. S. Lincoln (eds) *Handbook of Qualitative Research*, 2nd edn, Thousand Oaks, CA: Sage.

Fawcett, B. and Hearn, J. (2004) 'Researching others: Epistemology, experience, standpoints and participation', *International Journal of Social Research Methodology: Theory and Practice* 73: 201–18.

Hammersley, M. and Atkinson, P. (2007) *Ethnography: Principles in Practice*, 3rd edn, London: Routledge.

Israel, M. and Hay, I. (2006) *Research Ethics for Social Scientists*, London: Sage.

May, T. (2003) *Social Research: Issues, Methods and Process*, 3rd edn, Buckingham: Open University Press.

Walker, M. U. (2007) *Moral Understandings: A Feminist Study in Ethics*, 3rd edn, New York: Oxford University Press.

Reflective activities

1   In conducting ethnographic research on rape, consider which communities a researcher would be able to access (for example, victims, women's voluntary sector workers, police, prosecutors, etc.) and the potential difficulties that might emerge from seeking access and obtaining consent, through to dissemination of the research findings. In what ways might a researcher manage any potential emotional harm? Would these issues be the same in different geographical locations and what other issues might emerge?

2   You have been given £20,000 by the local community network to conduct research into the leisure activities of local youth. You uncover an 'informal economy' reliant on petty crime and the sale of illegal drugs. What ethical dilemmas do you face in conducting the research and in the dissemination of your findings?

3   In what research circumstances would a researcher breach confidentiality?

4   You want to conduct research on street prostitution. What sort of design would be best for this study? What previous research has been conducted in this area and what methods were chosen for those? What assumptions do you hold about the participants in this economy? Could you generalize from your findings? What dangers might you have to face from different groups (for example, women workers, the 'johns', the police)? To what extent are you willing to trust your participants?

4

'BUT IT'S GOT NO TABLES OR GRAPHS IN IT ...'

A legacy of scientific dominance in psychology

Sal Watt

This chapter takes a somewhat speculative approach that questions why ethnography is not more visible in psychology and, in particular, in contemporary social psychology. In its conception it was borne out of several comments made to me by my psychology colleagues. The first comment was more generally made around a disagreement concerning a qualitative psychology dissertation mark. The second marker questioned the validity of the dissertation and the mark awarded by the first marker. As part of the justification for this dissent, the above comment was made that it contained neither tables nor graphs. Relatively new to teaching in the psychology department, I was genuinely quite taken aback by this comment. Recruited partly for my expertise in qualitative research, it raised questions around what I was to encounter in respect of teaching qualitative research and the methodological direction of my new department.

Four years on, recently, another colleague asked me how this book was progressing and, taking a genuine interest asked, 'What exactly is ethnography?' When I outlined my philosophy of what ethnography is and how it generates rich data through a range of methods, my colleague looked thoughtful. Referring to a piece of work she had undertaken in America a year or two previously, I asked her whether she thought it might constitute as an ethnography. After a moment of reflection she conceded that 'yes', looking back she thought it was but had not thought of it that way. I agreed with her, because I believe her time working and researching in a particular subculture of society whose belief system in the paranormal was both unique and diverse was a perfect example of an ethnographic site. Her research and that of some of my colleagues could undoubtedly be categorized as ethnographic but for the fact that, as a concept, ethnography is neither familiar nor registers as a possible research option.

Without question ethnographies have and still are conducted in psychology and I will outline and illustrate some classic studies in due course. However, as Willig and Stainton-Rogers (2008: 1) point out, qualitative methods generally have 'until recently . . . occupied a contested space on the margins of psychology'. It is not surprising, then, that ethnography lies at the edge of this contested space as something of a quirky cousin. This chapter argues that ethnography is under-utilized in psychology, both in terms of the research we conduct but importantly also in our teaching. However, before arguing this point further, we need to explore and contextualize why qualitative methods and hence ethnography have traditionally been relegated to the margins of psychology. To do this we need to understand and contextualize the foundations on which psychology is built, and its predominant legacy of a scientific or positivistic methodology. I will then move on to illustrate that ethnographies are indeed conducted in psychology but question how visible these are. Finally, I will conclude that a broader understanding and engagement with ethnography would be highly advantageous if used more widely in social psychology.

Frustratingly quantitative

As a mature student when I commenced A-level study in psychology, I assumed, perhaps somewhat naively and based on lay knowledge of Freud and introspection, that psychology was about talking to people. It came as a great surprise to realize that right through to degree level I would spend the next four years surveying and experimenting 'on' people, producing statistics from which I could then infer whether findings could be generalized to a wider population. Over the years I have realized that I was not alone in my earlier preconceptions, and many of my colleagues and students have expressed similar thoughts and feelings.

Fortunately, my degree was also in sociology and it was this discipline that revealed a different way of undertaking research to me. I remember vividly sitting staring at the statistically 'significant' results of my third-year psychology dissertation and thinking, so what? What does this actually tell me about my participants' thoughts and feelings? It certainly did not tell me why I had found what I had found. Frustrated by an incomplete picture, at the eleventh hour, I decided to draw on my sociological methods training and chose to interview a sample of my participants. Willig and Stainton-Rogers (2008) suggest that qualitative psychology has gained ground over the last twenty or thirty years, but in that time question how many psychology students have been taught a balance of quantitative and qualitative methods?

Let's look back

If ethnography as a method is at the edge of qualitative psychology then first we need to consider why qualitative methods have been traditionally marginalized from mainstream psychology. Psychology gradually emerged as a discipline under the influences of Wilhelm Wundt, William James (1890, 1902) and later John B. Watson (1913; Watson and Rayner 1920). However, each of these influential thinkers approached psychology in distinct ways. In the latter case, Watson's influence was to have an immense impact on the research trajectory that psychology would take; one that would veer away from more qualitative methods of enquiry.

Ashworth (2008: 5) reminds us that psychology was defined as 'the science of experience' when founded in the latter half of the nineteenth century and that its methodology was to replicate 'as far as possible that of the physical sciences'. This of course follows on from the onset of the Enlightenment and modernity, when objective study in the natural sciences saw an explosion of knowledge that advanced our understanding of the physical world. Ashworth (2008: 5) makes the point that the objective was that psychology would complement these advances through the development of 'scientific under-standing of the inner world of experience' and that this would be achieved by objective experimentation that respectively brought together inner and outer worlds.

A science of experience that replicates scientific methodology is in itself problematic and this is immediately apparent in the work of Gustav Fechner. Ashworth (2008: 5) suggests that Fechner's publication, *Elements of Psychophysics* in 1860, can be said to be 'the founding publication of experimental psychology'. The idea of psychophysics was to investigate how individuals experienced different levels of brightness and relied on participant self-reports. However, the physical and mechanistic nature of how the participants experienced sensorial brightness highlights the difference in how experience was defined in a time and a context, which is clearly at odds with our contemporary qualitative understanding of experience. The emphasis placed on sensorial perception as experience illustrates perfectly how psychology, from the outset, was aligned with the scientific rigour of the natural sciences.

Wundt similarly applied rigorous laboratory controls and, indeed, in 1879, was responsible for setting up, in Leipzig, the first psychological laboratory (Smith 1998). Wundt trained medically as a physiologist but his interests were wide and varied; of particular interest to him was the topic area of consciousness. He believed that conscious mental states could be studied by experimentally manipulating variables, the effect of which could be followed by participant introspection. Rigorous training was undertaken before the introspection process commenced and so systematic was the process that not all candidates were considered proficient enough to proceed further. Wundt determined that sensations and feelings could be analysed introspectively through conscious experience (Ashworth 2008; Gross 1995). Wundt was regarded as the founder of experimental psychology, and we can see that his approach is both nomothetic (positivistic measurement of cause and effect across general dimensions) and idiographic (interpretative relying on in-depth 'thick' social narrative or description); in this respect there exists a tension which is problematic (Smith 1998).

Like Wundt, William James was 'concerned with meaning, culture and identity' (Willig and Stainton-Rogers 2008: 4). James, again, was medically trained and his initial academic and teaching interest lay in the relationship between physiology and psychology. However, psychology became his main focus and in 1890 he published his classic text, *Principles of Psychology*. James's contribution in furthering psychology is undisputed, but it should be noted that this contribution was that of a philosopher rather than a researcher (Ashworth 2008; Gross 1995). James was also interested in consciousness but, unlike Wundt, he considered this alongside awareness and notions of the self. James advocated that consciousness was a complex interaction whereby individuals do not become conscious of an entity or phenomenon in isolation. Instead we consciously become aware of something alongside previously learnt and/or experiential knowledge. James characterized knowledge as 'knowledge about' things, things that we learn or memorize, and 'knowledge of' things, knowledge that we acquire through our everyday life experiences and interactions (Smith 1998). We can see here then the direct link between conscious awareness and social interactionism. Our awareness is caught up in everyday interactions and experiences, and the concept of the 'self' and our own sense of self-awareness (Ashworth 2008). James advocated that conscious awareness comes in personal 'streams', which are then experienced and grounded in a wider framework that sees conscious awareness as ongoing, active, and that these 'streams' are informed by a wider and experiential knowledge base; one that includes the self. In other words, there is a direct interaction between the 'self', cognition, or thinking processes, and the social world. This complex interaction and the concept of the 'self' was later taken forward through, for example, the work of George H. Mead (1934), who distinguished notions of the self as between the 'I', the 'me' and the 'generalized other'. Later James (1902) was to go on to publish *The Varieties of Religious Experience*, which again focused on subjective accounts of individual perceptions and experiences of religion and God (Ashworth 2008). What is clear from James's work is that, in origin, psychology at this time was about the experiential and, as Ashworth (2008: 8) suggests, James's 'made a considerable contribution to the kind of thinking that lies behind qualitative psychology'. The question is why, then, when James was so clearly engaged in the 'self' and experiential thought processes, which align with qualitative methodology, did psychology become so subsumed in a scientific model? For the answer to this, we need to look to John B. Watson and the onset of behaviourism.

Changing direction

In origin then, Wundt and James's influence in founding psychology took a mentalist approach that looked to introspection as a means of exploring conscious experience. Of course, we can see the impact of introspection and individualism through the later work of Piaget (1932, 1950) and of course Freud (1949); but individualism and introspection as a method of enquiry was relatively short lived. The main thrust of psychological enquiry at the beginning of the twentieth century was overtaken by 'behaviourism'.

John B. Watson was highly critical of individualism. He viewed introspection as an unreliable method of investigation and questioned both the method and whether the topic of consciousness was worthy of study (Smith 1998; Willig and Stainton-Rogers 2008). In 1913, Watson published a paper entitled 'Psychology as a behaviourist views it', in which he criticized the subjective nature of intro-spection and enquiry into mental processes (Ashworth 2008). Watson determined that the study of psychological matters should be objective, that research methods should be rigorously controlled, reliant on observable and ultimately, quantifiable evidence. In short, a scientific approach should be used, that could emulate and coexist alongside the methodology of the natural sciences.

Thus, under Watson and later Skinner's direction, behaviourism came to dominate psychology, which emerged repackaged as the 'science of behaviour' (Smith 1998; Willig and Stainton-Rogers 2008). This scientific approach relied on observing behaviour in 'stimulus-response' experimental conditions. At this time then, mainstream psychology sidelined its original foundation of individualism and introspection, and jumped firmly into the paradigm of behaviourism. Behaviourism gained a lot of ground, particularly in America, and unquestionably from this scientific approach great psychological advances were made in understanding behaviour. This is evident through, for example, the work of John. B. Watson (1913; Watson and Rayner 1920), Ivan Pavlov (1927) and Frederick Skinner (1938, 1957) from whom we gained considerable knowledge as to how behaviour can be conditioned and modified. This kind of research is scientific or positivistic in approach, so, in trying to understand why psychology deviated so markedly from individualism and introspection, let us consider the impact of positivism a little further.

The challenge to common sense

Willig and Stainton-Rogers (2008) make the point that, in its conception, positivism originally set out to radically challenge 'common-sense' assump-tions; assumptions borne out of religion and metaphysical structures in society. The Enlightenment and modernity showed us new ways of being and under-standing the world. Positivistic thinking enabled us to challenge preconceived 'truths' about the order of things. Willig and Stainton-Rogers (2008: 5) draw on the *Concise Routledge Encyclopedia of Philosophy* (Craig 2000) to define the key ideas of positivism; the underpinning ideas are that:

> Philosophy should be scientific, that metaphysical speculations are meaningless, that there is a universal and a priori scientific method, that a main function of philosophy is to analyse that method, that this

basic scientific method is the same both in the natural and social sciences, that the various sciences should be reducible to physics, and that the theoretical parts of good science must be translatable into statements about observations.

(2000: 696)

When we consider this quote, it is not difficult to see how behaviourists such as Watson and behaviourism more generally engaged with the ethos of positivism. Through the gaze of behaviourism the key ideas in action meant that behaviour could be observed and 'tested' under replicable experimental or quasi-experimental conditions, generate quantifiable data, which could then be reduced deductively to generalizable truths or universal laws. In many respects, then, it is perhaps not surprising that – in keeping with the social, political and scientific environment of the time – 'behaviourism' and psychology more widely became so firmly established and, indeed, immersed in the scientific model. As a new academic discipline it sought to gain credibility and establish itself alongside the pre-existing disciplines of the natural sciences; those that, through modernity, were predicated on rationality, science and thereby positivistic in approach. This is a very brief overview but it serves to illustrate how individualism, introspection and more qualitative methods generally became overshadowed, superseded and indeed sidelined as 'soft/unscientific psychology' or, as Willig and Stainton-Rogers so aptly put it, relegated as the 'delinquent Other' (2008: 5).

The other side of the coin: interpretivism

Meanwhile, in sociology research was developing at the other end of the research spectrum, where 'interpretivism' was being embraced, particularly in German sociology of the nineteenth century. In keeping with some of James's original ideas, the epistemological root of interpretivism lies in the perception of being and is viewed through the subjective worldview of those being researched (Neuman 2006; Scott 2002). Dilthey proposed that two types of science existed: *Naturwissenschaft*, which is based on abstract explanation ('*Erklarung*') and *Geisteswissenschaft*, which is based on empathetic understanding of everyday life ('*Verstehen*') (Neuman 2006; Scott 2002). It was this latter concept that Weber (1949) extended still further through social action theory. He proposed that research necessarily needed to be embedded in empathetic understanding of the thoughts and feelings that underpinned individual agency. To that end, he extended the concept of '*Verstehen*' to include '*Acktueller*', by means of objective observation, and '*Erklander*', by means of reflexive and empathetic engagement (Weber 1949).

This approach emphasized hermeneutical understanding through the study of a phenomenon as a 'whole'. This was to have a significant influence in the field of interpretivism and ethnography as a method of sociological enquiry

47

(Neuman 2006; Scott 2002; Silverman 2001). At the beginning of the twentieth century the Chicago School was to harness some of the data collection techniques of ethnography, for example engagement in informal interviews and participant observation. Evidence of this can be seen through the work of Mead, Dewey, James and Whyte (Marvasti 2004; Neuman 2006; Scott 2002). In this respect then, the Chicago School were responsible for bringing together the philosophy of interpretivism and ethnography. Distinguished from early observational studies such as that of Booth (1902), the Chicago School embraced and appropriated the anthropological tradition of 'living' a culture. It was through this embodiment that they sought to engage with the research phenomenon at a social and cultural level.

The driving force toward this approach came largely from the direction of Robert E. Park, who advocated that researchers needed to 'get the seat of their pants dirty' when undertaking research in order to fully understand social issues and problems (Marvasti 2004; Neuman 2006). The Chicago School adopted an anthropological model of research, that advocated the principle that people should be observed in their 'natural' settings; should be engaged in direct interaction; and that social understanding gained should then inform academic theory. The Chicago School gathered momentum during the 1940s and into the 1960s. Interpretivism and, as a data collection method, ethnography, were popularized still further through the work of Becker (1963; Becker *et al.* 1961), Bulmer (1984) and in particular, through the accessibility and popularity of Erving Goffman's texts, for example, *The Presentation of Self in Everyday Life* (1959), *Asylums* (1961) and *Stigma* (1963a).

Today, as a methodology, ethnography is used across a wealth of disciplines, for example, geography, history and the social sciences, including gender and media studies, through to education, management, design and the law (Wacquant 2003). Yet its predominant use is maintained through social anthropology and sociology (Gray 2003; Katz and Csordas 2003; Wacquant 2003). But what of psychology? Unquestionably, there are ethnographies conducted in psychology, but how visible or prevalent are these? Let us now turn our attention back to psychology and consider the emergence of qualitative psychology and the use of ethnography therein.

A change of direction

So far this chapter has considered the foundations of psychology, its transition from introspection to behaviourism and therein its embrace of positivism and a scientific model of conducting research. In contrast to psychology; sociology meanwhile, although also a proponent of posititivism, explored interpretivism as a theoretical paradigm. In the introduction, I outlined the frustration I experienced as a psychology student as I completed my third-year quantitative dissertation that I perceived as limited in scope and failing to ask the 'why?' question. Willig (2008: 2), reflecting on her experience of being a student draws on a really good analogy; she viewed 'research methods as recipes'. In highlighting the mechanical process of following recipes she goes on to say that today she sees the 'research-process-as-adventure' (Willig 2008: 2). I totally agree with this sentiment.

However, setting out on the qualitative 'adventure' does come with some problems. Stepping back from the scientific model, from the tried and tested and venturing into uncharted ground, often takes us beyond our comfort zone. And this is made all the more difficult by unfamiliar phraseology. Hopkins (2008: 44) makes a valuable observation that, in psychology and more widely across the social sciences, we have constructed a 'maze of -isms' that makes the transition to qualitative research, all the more difficult. Textbook glossaries abound with '-ism' words, for example, positivism, interpretivism, empiricism, objectivism, subjectivism, feminism and on it goes. Taking this one step further we are similarly also not short of 'ology' words, such as, phenomenology, ethnomethodology, epistemology, ontology, methodology and so on. This wealth of terms can seem overwhelming and somewhat daunting, especially to students many of whom have in the main only experienced the scientific model. To make matters more complicated Hopkins (2008) quite rightly makes the point that across the social sciences often the wealth of terms we have are 'used interchangeably' and further that different texts define words quite differently. As a hybrid between two disciplines this was certainly my experience. To unravel the myriad of terms and their respective meanings is beyond the scope of this chapter but this brief account does serve to illustrate that embarking on the qualitative adventure can at first seem challenging to students and academic researchers alike. However, the 'adventure' is well worth the effort and perseverance so let us pick the story up with post-structuralism and psychology's 'turn to language' (Willig and Stainton-Rogers 2008: 7).

Let's talk . . .

Hard on the heels of behaviourism, psychology turned to 'cognitivism'. Cognitive psychology's interest lies in mental processes, to name but a few, those of attention, perception and memory. From such areas abstract models are constructed that map out cognitive functioning. Again, this approach focuses on the scientific model and experimentation. However, following socio-political discontent and the institutional challenges of the 1960s, qualitative psychology re-established itself in the 1970s as a challenge to the scientific model and in doing so its research focus 'turn[ed] to language' (Willig and Stainton-Rogers 2008: 7). This was a period that saw the rise of post-structuralism across the social sciences.

Post-structuralism is concerned with the ways in which language is used and how it describes reality. Michel Foucault, a French philosopher, was highly influential in theorizing the process by which knowledge is constructed and institutionally legitimized through power and authority (Foucault 1972;

Ritzer 2000). Foucault advocated that knowledge was constructed through 'discourses'. A discourse is a set of words or phrases that particularly relate to or encapsulate a way of knowing and understanding something. Such discourses can be positive, negative or discriminative. The best way to illustrate how this works is to ask you to think about what words or phrases come to mind when you think of the phrases 'binge drinking' or 'chav culture'. The chances are you will come up with a list of words that symbolize these contemporary subcultures, and that you may well have acquired these words and their related knowledge through, for example, the media. The basic idea is that a cyclic process is at work whereby knowledge (and therein power) is facilitated through discourses. The more these discourses circulate the more knowledge becomes embedded, institutionalized and thereby legitimized. Such discourses are known as 'discursive regimes' which we are exposed to, engage with and are perpetuated through their everyday circularity. Hence, if you have a particular discourse around 'binge drinking' or 'chav culture' ask yourself: where have I got these words and ideas from? 'Discursive regimes', then, give us a way of understanding our world, but they also tend to be self-serving in nature. Post-structuralism is concerned with deconstructing the discursive regimes by which reality is understood and, of course, identifying the potential institutional power with which they are underpinned.

Qualitative psychology, in turning to words and discourses, embraced various research methods and analyses. Discursive psychology, in common with other social science disciplines, engages in discourse analysis, Foucauldian discourse analysis and conversational analysis. Key in illustrating the power that can be embedded in discourse are feminist researchers such as Carol Gilligan (1990), Sue Wilkinson and Celia Kitzinger (1995, 1996), who have been highly influential in identifying the gendered nature of discourse in maintaining inequality (see Gilligan 1990 on moral development for a classic example).

The 'turn to language' allowed us to focus on individuals, their experiences and how those experiences were socially located; in short, it allowed us to focus on the process of social constructionism. The inequalities exposed by feminist researchers cast doubt on the supposed rigour of scientific study in psychology and instead gave insight into how reality could be constructed to support and institutionalize patriarchy (Haraway 1991; Harding 1991; Willig and Stainton-Rogers 2008). Social constructionism is concerned with understanding, questioning and challenging preconceived notions of reality (Burr 1995; Gergen 2009). Discursive psychology continues to make giant steps in understanding individuals, their experiences and social locations, and how language constructs reality.

Knowing me, knowing you

Currently the focus for qualitative methods in psychology has turned toward interpretation (Ashworth 2008; Smith 1996; Smith *et al.*, 2009; Willig and

Stainton-Rogers 2008). Ashworth distinguishes between two qualitative approaches: perceptual and constructionist orientations. He poses the question, 'What processes of construction have the researchers themselves employed in coming up with the findings they have presented?' (2008: 18). This is a good question and one from which it is possible to introduce IPA (Interpretative Phenomenological Analysis) in our expanding repertoire of qualitative methods in psychology. IPA builds on phenomenological and constructionist roots; it sees research as 'a dynamic process with an active role for the researcher in that process' (Smith and Osborn 2008: 53). Its concern is in gaining a deep understanding of the participant's lifeworld. Smith and Osborn (2008: 53) put it thus: 'the participants are trying to make sense of their world; the researcher is trying to make sense of the participants trying to make sense of their world'. This is known as a double hermeneutic and, as the IPA researcher attempts to access an 'insider view' of the participants' lifeworld, a questioning and empathetic hermeneutic is employed. In Chapter 8 I briefly outline the analysis process of IPA, but for a more in-depth account of IPA generally see Smith *et al.* (2009).

Coming from my hybrid background of two disciplines, the similarity and overlap between the two disciplines is both complementary and frustrating. I find myself increasingly substituting 'worldview' for 'lifeworld', I talk about the double hermeneutic instead of Weber's '*Verstehen*' and I have adopted the IPA analytic process in favour of a regular thematic analysis. The point is that, however frustrating qualitative methods terms are across the social sciences, with their confusion of 'isms', 'ologies' and interchangeable meanings (Hopkins 2008: 44), we are no longer bound by rigid scientific rigour and instead we seem to adopt a 'pick 'n' mix' approach that is adaptable to the circumstance and needs of the research question. So what of ethnography in all of this?

Where are you?

In 2006, the first newsletter from the newly formed 'Qualitative Methods in Psychology Section' (QMIP) of the British Psychological Society (BPS) was published. At the time of publication, membership had already exceeded 1,500 and the section had rapidly become the largest in the BPS. This is a clear indication that qualitative methods of enquiry are contemporarily very much alive and kicking in psychology. In 2009, I attended the inaugural conference of QMIP at Leeds. I have attended many conferences over the last ten years but the QMIP conference was the friendliest and most informative of them all: a forum of researchers all keen to share their qualitative methods experience. By way of a poster I canvassed the idea that ethnography was under-used or at least, at the moment, not as visible as it should be in psychology (Watt 2008). The feedback I received suggested similar sentiments, and the idea for this chapter was born. However, included in the proceedings was also a paper that encouraged the use of ethnography and narrative interviews (Paulson and Willig 2008). This paper was an excellent example of how ethnography can be used alongside narrative interview to research a subculture. I quietly observed the audience's interest as the speaker enthusiastically explained how immersion in a 'culture of dance' had afforded greater understanding of the group in question. So, with examples such as this available, why is it that ethnography is not more visible in psychology?

What's gone before . . .?

Before attempting to answer the question why ethnographies are not more visible in psychology, let us look back at some classic ethnographies so that we can appreciate the valuable contribution they have made to psychology and to our research repertoire. A significant contribution to social psychology was a study conducted by Lazarsfeld (1932) known as the 'Marienthal study'. This study focused on a small Austrian community formerly reliant on the textile industry which found itself beset with unemployment and associated social problems when that industry declined. Lazarsfeld's team employed a triangulated approach that collected data quantitatively but also through interviews and, importantly, naturalistic observation. Additionally they also became involved in the daily life of the community. This study was highly influential in understanding the effects of poverty both at a macro and micro level, and is a good early example of researchers living amongst those being researched.

A classic ethnography is that of Margaret Mead's (1943) *Coming of Age in Samoa: A Psychological Study of Primitive Youth for Western Civilization*. Mead's ethnography told of the seemingly easy transition of young Samoans as they progressed through adolescence and became sexually active. Mead advocated that the sexual freedom these young people enjoyed before settling down to rear children was in stark contrast to the transition of western adolescents, who experienced more problematic periods of adjustment. Although this work attracted much criticism for its radical views, it was a significant ethnography in understanding Samoan culture and the differences in adolescent transition between eastern and western culture.

Two further classic studies are those of Festinger *et al.* (1956) and Rosenhan (1973). Festinger *et al.* (1956) investigated a millenarian cult (that is, a religious group that believes the world will come to an end) who anticipate and look forward to a specified 'end time' date. Participant observers covertly pretended to be converts to the religious group. The study focused on how cult members intellectualized their belief system and, in particular, how they justified a specified 'end time' date once it had elapsed. They concluded that the millenarian beliefs of the group became more firmly embedded as they looked forward to a new predicted 'end time' date.

Rosenhan (1973), in what came to be known as the 'Rosenhan Experiment', involved eight participant observers who acted as pseudo-patients and who reported experiencing the typically schizophrenic symptom of 'hearing voices'. The pseudo-patients visited twelve hospitals and were admitted by eleven as patients with schizophrenia. The aim of the study was for the pseudo-patient to be admitted to hospital and then to see how long they would be confined there once they ceased exhibiting symptoms. The retention rate averaged nineteen days, but across the cohort this varied between seven and fifty-two days. As the common name for this study implies this was a field 'experiment', where the pseudo-patients were stimulating or manipulating the situation, therefore it possibly does not have quite the same resonance as a 'true' ethnography. On the other hand, the presence of any participant observer inevitably impacts on the context under investigation and, like Goffman's (1961) study before it, the researchers' relatively short period of confinement was highly informative in understanding the medical process of confinement and the process whereby the mentally ill are labelled and stigmatized.

In 1977 cultural theorist, Paul Willis published *Learning to Labour: How Working Class Kids get Working Class Jobs*. Conducted in the West Midlands of the UK, this ethnography highlighted the process by which working-class 'lads' fall victim to their own culture – culture where there is prestige in disengaging from school – the inevitable consequence being a working-class shop-floor job. Griffin (1985, 1986) similarly studied young women's transition from school to the workplace. Such transition, and indeed the workplace, itself is a perfect example of a social setting in which psychological ethnographies can be located. Contemporary examples can also be found in distinct areas of psychology, for example, health, counselling, and educational and even cognitive psychology (Ball and Ormerod 2000; Beck 2005; Henning-Stout 1999; Posada *et al.*, 2004; Taylor 1994). However, Shweder calls for a more distinct cultural psychology, that is the:

> [s]tudy of the ways subject and object, self and other, psyche and culture, person and context, figure and ground, practitioner and practice, live together, require each other and dynamically, dialectically, and jointly made each other up.
>
> (1991: 73)

This is a good way of defining cultural psychology, which in my experience has always seemed far more focused on conducting cross-cultural studies that look at difference and similarity. Shweder's definition makes perfect sense to me, although I concede that this is possibly because of my hybrid inter-disciplinary background. However, in respect of social psychology, Shweder's definition has the scope to encapsulate the key social psychological topics defined by the BPS, for example identity; group identity, behaviour and inter-action; conformity and obedience; and so on. It also therefore carries much potential for more ethnographic study within social psychology.

Where are we going . . .?

I would argue, therefore, that ethnography can bring much to the table, not just in cultural psychology, but also in social psychology, where it could be far more active. Griffin and Bengry-Howell (2008) highlight the fact that often ethnography is not included in psychology methods textbooks, which raise the question of why this is the case. Over the past few decades, we have come a long way in psychology in embracing qualitative research methods, but while ethnography is avidly conducted by some I would argue that it remains largely invisible for others. So let us consider some of the possible reasons for this. Taylor (1994: 34) suggests that 'ethnography is, perhaps, the original and quintessential qualitative research method'. Yet in psychology we seem to have appropriated its data collection techniques, for example interviews and participant observation, without fully embracing the values embedded in ethnography's ethos. In particular, we perhaps need to look to the legacy of positivism to understand this. Positivism and the scientific model that has predominated in psychology are reliant on an 'etic' approach, that is, one that is based on categorization, generalization and universality. Conversely, ethnography is steeped in an 'emic' approach, which values culture and cultural belief systems. In my own relatively short career, I have met with resistance from colleagues around the authenticity and usefulness of ethnography; for example, its application.

Such comments are clearly steeped in an 'etic' approach that are hypothesis, and probably research funding, driven. Having aligned itself alongside the natural sciences, where research funding is competitive and relies on a scientific approach, it is perhaps not surprising that ethnography's concern with culture might seem 'wishy washy' to the 'hardened scientist'. However, as some of the studies previously highlighted indicate, we cannot fully understand, for example, behaviour or attitudes, in isolation from culture. We need to understand the cultural values in which behaviour and attitudes are located and ethnography holds the key here – a key, which holds immense potential to inform social policy, as indeed many of the chapters in this book illustrate.

We have established that there has been rapid growth and interest in qualitative methods in psychology, but is ethnography just one step too far? Or is it perhaps a question of time? Fetterman (1998) suggests that ethnographic research typically takes six months to two years. This in itself can be problematic. For many of us, as researchers, the opportunity to undertake an ethnographic project of long duration is something that only arises for PhD research. On completion, the typical progression to lectureship manifests in teaching responsibilities that, for most people, obviates the possibility of undertaking a further, long-term ethnography. However, researchers and students should not be put off by this; ethnographic research, as Fetterman (1998) determines, can take place over shorter periods of time. I raise this issue because I have heard comments that there is little point in teaching ethnography in any depth because the modular system leaves insufficient time for students to undertake an ethnographic project. This is certainly not true at dissertation or Master's level, where a six-month ethnography (or even a little less) is perfectly viable.

Another obstacle can be the university ethics boards which are currently extremely vigilant in ensuring that social science codes of conduct are upheld. In psychology this is perhaps not surprising, given some of the studies we have conducted in the past, for example Zimbardo (1973) and Milgram (1974), but this legacy can in itself be another major consideration that students have to negotiate when trying to undertake participant observation or an ethnography. Both time and ethics can be negotiated and neither should be an insurmountable obstacle for students who wish to extend their research training.

Back to basics

This chapter has charted a brief history of the research methods psychology has adopted and I have questioned the visibility of ethnography in psychology and in particular social psychology. There is no question that ethnographies are being conducted in psychology, for example in the fields of counselling, health and developmental psychology, (Beck 2005; Paulson and Willig 2008; Posada *et al.* 2004) and, increasingly in sport and educational psychology (Palmer and Torevell 2008). In educational psychology, Anna Graham and Rosemary Kilpatrick's chapter outlines the exciting work they have respectively conducted using visual ethnography when working with children. The scope for utilizing ethnography is wide and potentially very exciting. Ethnography as Taylor (1994: 34) suggests 'is, perhaps, the original and quintessential qualitative research method'; we have appropriated its data collection techniques but let us not use them in isolation. We need to embrace the core values of ethnography and study experience and behaviour alongside the culture from which they emanate. Ethnography has much potential to enrich psychology and, importantly, to enrich our students' understanding of research.

Suggested further reading

Goffman, E. (1961) *Asylums: Essays on the Social Situation of Mental Patients and Other Inmates*, London: Penguin Books.

Griffin, C. (1985) *Typical Girls? Young Women from School to the Job Market*, London: Routledge.

Rosenhan, D. L. (1973) 'On being sane in insane places', *Sciences* 179: 350–58.

Willis, P. E. (1977) *Learning to Labour: How Working Class Kids get Working Class Jobs*, New York: Columbia University Press.

Reflexive activities

In a small group of two or three, consider how you could undertake a psychological ethnography:

1   Can you think of a 'safe' culture that interests you and that you have access to?
2   Now can you think of a social psychology topic area that you would like to study with that group, e.g. group interaction, conformity or compliance behaviour?
3   What ethical problems might you anticipate and how would you negotiate these?

In your group now consider how you could conduct the same research quantitatively. Discuss the ways in which an ethnography and a quantitative study would differ. What advantages do you think ethnography has?

Part II

ETHNOGRAPHY
IN CONTEXT

5

SENSE AND SENSIBILITY IN INTERDISCIPLINARY WORK

Designing and planning applied ethnography

Dave Randall and Mark Rouncefield

In this chapter, we will discuss the specific issues associated with 'working with others' and what makes that different from 'pure' sociological or social science research. Sociology, in common with the other social sciences, is characterized by an endless series of disagreements about methods, concepts, theories, commitments and so on. Even within the more narrowly defined 'ethnographic' project, we find the same disagreements. These are mainly about three things: issues of method; epistemological, moral and political issues; and conceptual and theoretical issues. It is not a part of this chapter to deal with those issues in any detail, but we do need to say that one of the things that characterizes ethnographic enquiry when done for sociological purposes is a commitment to the discussion of these issues; ethnographers agree, in other words, about what it is that they disagree about.

What we want to argue in this chapter is that, although we find these basic themes revisited in the context of applied interdisciplinary work, their specific character alters, because other interests are in place and need to be taken care of. Nevertheless, there is an underlying 'sensibility' that all ethnographers share, whatever their disagreements, demonstrated in their underlying agreement about what to discuss. We will further argue that this sensibility, even in applied[1] interdisciplinary work, remains largely the same, even if the way in which we deal with each of these issues as they arise might sometimes be quite different. When we look at work which is labelled as either 'interdisciplinary' or 'applied', we are still looking at work that is, in important senses, *sociological* or *social science*.

The point about this is that the ethnographic 'turn', as this book demonstrates, has become extremely fashionable in a wide variety of contexts. If it is the case that, in large part, sociology is a 'critical' discipline, then there is an obvious and rather important problem entailed in this kind of working and that has to do with whether 'critique' can, in theory and in practice, be its main focus, or whether such work entails a more abject 'service' role. Our purpose, then, based on our own experience of working with and for others in both the above senses, is to try to make sense of what difference it makes. In other words, how do the issues of method, analysis and ethics pan out in contexts where the focus of the enquiry is not determined entirely by the social scientist? We will examine this by referring to a number of studies we have undertaken both in organizations and for organizations, and with the intention of doing what is usually called, 'fieldwork for design'. We need to point out here that our interests are relatively specific, and have developed over roughly a twenty-year period. They have to do with new technology and its use. The studies we have undertaken, together and separately, have included organizations like an Air Traffic Control (ATC) centre (Hughes *et al.* 1993); a large UK bank (Harper *et al.* 2000); museums (Hemmings *et al.* 2001); software development (Hansson *et al.* 2006); community care (Cheverst *et al.* 2001); a 'smart home' (Randall 2003); wearable cameras (Harper *et al.* 2008) and so on.

The possible consequences of interdisciplinary work

We described the lines of discussion about ethnography as being largely threefold above, and we will describe the way they ramify in interdisciplinary work below in much the same way. At this point, we should describe the kind of work we typically do. Our work is usually thought of as 'design related' and, more specifically, to do with the design or evaluation of technology. This does not mean that our only focus is the way in which technologies get used; for we have learned over many years that it is nigh on impossible to sort 'technological' issues from 'social' ones. Indeed, our whole position is predicated on the indissolubility of the 'socio-technical'. Sometimes the work involves lengthy study of a variety of operations in a complex organization (see Harper *et al.* 2000). Sometimes the work is appreciably more focused, for instance when it involves one group of people using a specific piece of technology. Sometimes the work does not involve organizations at all, in the sense that our observations do not take place there (though organizational interests may have commissioned the work). For instance, we have worked on studies of mobile phone use, wearable cameras, technologies in the home and so on. What this means is that, although practical problems arise, they sometimes have a quite distinct flavour.

Practical problems: access

For the most part, access in this context turns out not to be terribly important in its conventional sense, if only because much of the work we are involved in is done at the invitation of, or at least with the collaboration of, the organizations we are studying. In practice, what problems there are turn out to be a group of fairly easily resolved difficulties which have to do with gaining acceptance. Our own experience is one of, in the main, finding the right 'sponsor' to smooth the way through various organizational interests. Even so, when invited into an organization, there can still be problems vis-à-vis different groups within the organization.

Organizations are complex and, in the worst case, it can be difficult to find someone who is able to take responsibility for a decision about access. The notion of the 'gatekeeper' is, of course, what we are talking about here, but this again can have a specific flavour in organizational work. The fieldworker will be spending time studying the activities of various groups of people and will depend upon their goodwill, so time spent informing them and reassuring them is not only a matter of courtesy but also likely to result in more effective relationships with them. It is important to remember that the process of gaining access is not simply 'something that has to be done' and 'something that is a bloody nuisance'. It can also be highly informative about the nature of the organization and tell one a great deal about the setting and its character. Harper (1998) talks of the way in which acceptance was a matter of going on 'a mission' in his study of the IMF and of accompanying police officers to a domestic disturbance in his study of police work (Ackroyd *et al.* 1992). He refers to the way in which interviewees were more forthcoming and materials became more accessible because what he was doing came to be regarded as 'serious business'. In our ATC study (Hughes *et al.* 1993), we felt it was necessary to work the same shifts as the controllers, so we could demonstrate that we 'really wanted to know'.

Some areas of an organization, we should remember, might be regarded as 'sacred' and off limits to the observer. Special difficulties arise when a research interest is generated by some issue that is newsworthy. Just as researchers might begin to take an interest in something like ambulance work as a result of a disaster, so might organizational members show understandable reservations for the same reason. Times of organizational transformation and political unrest make access more difficult. Another problem that can arise lies in another kind of organizational complexity, which has to do with different kinds of occupational role. Medical research, for instance, demonstrates the problem, in that hospital management, professionals and workers all have different but deeply felt interests in what is being studied. Oddly enough, we often see what can be called a 'reverse gatekeeper' function, where people being observed insist on determining your focus of interest on your behalf.

Timeliness: the pressure for results

To a certain extent (and we will not be popular with colleagues for saying so), academic enquiry is a relaxed affair. There are relatively few externally imposed deadlines and ethnographic enquiries can be undertaken over a long period of time (even if intermittently). Indeed, the classic anthropological approach to ethnography is dependent on some notion of 'enculturation': learning the language, mores, practices and values of a culture. It is no surprise that many ethnographies take years to finish. In contrast, the ethnography of cashier work undertaken by Randall and Hughes (1995) lasted approximately three weeks and that was because it was undertaken in three different settings to ensure some kind of validity. Here, the task was quite specific: to understand and assess the kind of problems that cashiers had working with technology when dealing with the public. The 'problem', that is, was tightly bounded by those who had commissioned the work. (Nevertheless, the ethnography subsequently 'opened up' and more work was done, lasting another six weeks.) The main reason for prolongation is that *in advance, for the most part, ethnographers have no clear idea what they will find*. Because there are in principle any number of aspects which may turn out to be interesting and any number of things which may be mystifying, it will take time to form a coherent view of what is going on. Nevertheless, ethnographic enculturation over time and a range of domains does rather suggest, on a commonsense basis, that experienced ethnographers will have some notion of what they are likely to see next time out. Clifford and Marcus (1986) is relevant here, insofar as 'multi-sitedness' at least reminds us that ethnographies can be done with varying degrees of intensity, over different periods of time, with the need for comparison (or otherwise) being one thing that underpins choices.

The communication of results to interested parties

Another practical problem, and one which is unlikely to be a major issue for the ethnographer engaged in 'pure' work, is that reports are not the same thing as the ethnographic record. Some kind of report, often in a 'house style', will be demanded by client organizations, as will presentations of results. A number of issues result from this. First, publication may not be possible for reasons of confidentiality. It is as well to establish up front what the limits will be. Second, what is contained in reports may be subject to 'censorship'. We have had the experience of being told that we cannot release a report because it was 'too negative' about the technologies in question. As our liaison said: 'I've been working on this for three years now, and I've spent a couple of million pounds of X's money. My career depends on what you say about this . . .' Third, the style of the report will have to suit organizational rather than academic needs. Again, this can be encapsulated with an example:

> Hi, Dave, have you got a minute?
> Sure, John, what can I do for you?
> Just got your report . . . it's really interesting . . . but . . . well, it's rather long, isn't it? [120 pages] The thing is, no-one will read it. You need to grab people's attention, so . . . could you reduce it to five bullet points?

The issue of 'censorship' is obviously rather more significant than the issue of 'style', insofar as it involves the clear implication that academics in these circumstances may not be free to say whatever they like. Our own experience, however, is that problems of this kind are rare and, when they crop up, can usually be resolved through goodwill. For the most part we ensure that they occur infrequently by encouraging our clients to read and comment, giving them a power of veto on work done in advance, especially for publication, and sometimes by including them as authors.

Ethical problems

Edles has summed up the problem of interdisciplinary enquiry (though not actually referring to interdisciplinary work) quite neatly.

> The questions were political, epistemological and methodological; who gets to say what about whom, and why? What are the interests and motivations behind alleged ethnographic 'realism'?
>
> (Edles 2002: 145)

As Edles suggests, sophisticated social scientific work, whether ethnographic or not, would reject anything that looked like naïve 'realism'; that the world is easily and unproblematically described in one particular way. One of the problems of working with organizational interests, however, is that their members, not being trained social scientists and having quite specific problems that they want solutions to, tend to see results in that way. In other words, they want certainty and they want definitive solutions. Now, if sociologists and others were willing to accept these constraints wholeheartedly then they would be guilty of adopting a mere 'service' role for other interests and managerial interests to boot. Most of us would regard that as an unethical stance. We do not believe that this is what ethnographers in these situations typically do, but we do accept that some 'negotiation' of the relationship is necessary.

Of course, there are some standard ethical positions, including the doctrine of 'informed consent', which social scientists accept as an ideal stance and we are no different. We have always tried to explain to people what we are doing wherever practicable, usually by asking to speak to them in a group. However, having said that, 'informed consent' turns out to be a difficult matter in the context of organizational life. The reason for this is that genuinely informed consent would require each organizational member to know a great deal about the structure of the organization in question, managerial objectives, and the processes of change management and design. Since, by definition, this involves some intervention in what the future will look like and since no one can 'design' the future in such a way that nothing unanticipated occurs, truly 'informed' consent is not possible. Indeed, the ethnographer cannot always know in advance what the results of his or her enquiry will be or the way in which results will be used.

A second quite pragmatic problem is that because people in organizations are actually busy doing jobs of work it turns out to be difficult in practice to get round to everyone. At the same time, it seems to us that there are some fairly straightforward procedures which produce a reasonable outcome, one which we can be comfortable with. These include guarantees of anonymity, clarifying the purposes of the work whenever asked and, above all, the simple injunction, 'do not lie'. Again, however, one should not assume that this solves all dilemmas. One of the authors has been put in the following position:

> So, X, tell us . . . what you do think of [ ] . . . we don't think she's very good . . . she's certainly irritating . . . I mean, you're interested in teamwork. . . . don't you think she's a problem?

Now it might be imagined that the simple and unequivocal response, given what we have said above, would be: 'I'm sorry, I have made a commitment to anonymity.' However, it happens that in this particular instance the ethnographer had been sitting observing a small team of people engaged in mortgage processing work and had been struck by the number of times that people in her team had approached the individual in question for solutions to work-related problems they had. And, further, how often she was able to provide highly detailed and specialized knowledge that no one else seemed to possess.

It is also true that ethnographers of organizations will come up against pre-existing, and quite formal, ethical demands. This is increasingly the case and, not to put too fine a point on it, can make life extremely difficult. Ethical problems take on a complexity when we are confronted with different kinds of occupational role. Medical research, for instance, demonstrates the problem in that hospital management, professionals and workers all have different but nonetheless deeply felt interests in what is being studied. This means that medical work is in some senses unique, insofar as it is one of those domains where 'ethics' becomes an explicit issue (and even more so when these issues, as they do from time to time, become 'newsworthy'). So much so, that research has to be validated through 'ethics committees' in most countries.

Similar difficulties can arise, for obvious reasons, where certain kinds of client group are involved. One of us quite recently had the experience of being told that while the observation of young children was acceptable (various bona fides having been given) in a school, the videotaping of their behaviour was not. At the time the ethnographer (a middle-aged man) was more than a little puzzled by this absolute ban, until he remembered that paedophilia had been something of a 'moral panic' in the British media in the preceding months. It is as well to be aware that ethical policy making has become something of an industry itself, and one which makes increasingly onerous (and sometimes impossible) demands on the researcher.

We cannot leave this topic without reference to a 'standpoint' problem. Honesty, a commitment to anonymity and so on would not prevent the researcher, if he or she were so motivated, from working for 'management' in an explicit and cynical way. That is, the ethnographer can still in principle take sides with the powerful. Remember that 'standpoint' sociologies make much of the idea that the researcher should be in the same 'critical plane' as the subject by identifying their own class/race/gender position. This turns out to be extremely important in the context of new technology and organizations because, time and again, we discover that the design and implementation of new technologies often omits to investigate the 'user'. It is well known how users confronted with new and potentially invasive systems find ways of preventing them from working. Resistance, in other words, is not futile. Conversely, it is also known that inappropriate and poorly designed systems (both technical and organizational) can often be made to look a great deal better than they actually are because 'users' have a set of professional commitments: they want to do 'good work' and so 'work around' poorly designed arrange-ments. Over the years this has led to an approach that can be loosely termed 'participatory design', which draws on a long-standing tradition of enquiry into work and organizational practices. Now such matters entail controversies all of their own and we do not propose to rehearse them here. Nevertheless, certain benefits do accrue from this commitment to participation. What we are, rather defensively, pointing to here is the casual assumption that 'applied' work is necessarily cynical. In fact, we would argue, we are for the most part on the side of the angels. In the end, of course, decisions about what is morally and politically acceptable are for the professional researcher to make, and a good rule of thumb is: 'If you think it's wrong, then don't do it.'

Conceptual/analytic problems

The purpose of ethnographic analysis is to produce sensitizing concepts and models that allow people to see events in new ways. The value of these models is to be judged by others in terms of how useful they find them . . .

(Hammersley 1990a:15)

Even professional social scientists will recognize that their discipline is jargon ridden and frequently opaque. We do not want to get into discussions here about whether 'technical' usages are useful or necessary in sociology or any of the other social sciences, but in the context of interdisciplinary work there will be various parties who do not understand it, do not see the point in it and seek clarity in some sort of 'ordinary language' sense. In other words, they will have a strong preference for the 'emic'.[2] The concepts that one might choose to deploy in interdisciplinary work are unlikely to be entirely sociological, in other words, but are more likely to be attempts to categorize experience and the similarities and differences to be found in our experience of working life. Our view is that going to the field is about looking in certain ways at certain things and analysing them with particular goals in mind, but not particular results. In sum, it is about looking in the right way at the right things with the right intentions. This means that fieldwork will have a different hue depending upon the purposes at hand; fieldwork for design is not the same as, say, fieldwork as a means of undertaking cultural analysis, or fieldwork used to explore feminist arguments, or fieldwork serving theoretical needs of any kind. Each is distinct. Getting to the relevant analytic concerns in an interdisciplinary context is a different problem because it is not the social scientist alone who decides what the relevant analytic choices might be.

Respecification

We have been arguing that one of the distinguishing characteristics of fieldwork for design is that the various responsibilities involved in doing fieldwork are shared. One particular feature of this kind of work, however, is the way in which shared responsibilities and interests do not necessarily result in similar ways of thinking about problems. A background question we have not yet addressed is: 'Why ask social scientists to do this kind of work?' We think there are good reasons, and they have to do with the way that (some) social scientists think. If sociology, as we argued above, sees itself as a critical discipline, then this critique takes or should take another form when applied to interdisciplinary working. For us, critique takes the form of respecification. There are any number of competing theoretical/analytical schemes that could be used to understand the way new technology works, or how organizations change, and there is, on the face of it, no reason to presume that sociologists or other social scientists generally have a better purchase on these problems than anyone else. In our view, the main danger with any analytical scheme is that its theoretical interests can determine the structure of the data from the outset. That is, in interdisciplinary working, the theoretical interests of sociologists, anthropologists and psychologists can easily take precedence over the practical business at hand, and can often dictate what is to be found. Instead, we take a strictly limited view of the role of concepts. We think that they should have, in our kind of work, no more than a 'sensitizing' role (Blumer 1956), making people aware of issues that they might otherwise ignore; that analysis should evolve from the particular problems that arise from the domain in question, not least because the theoretical auspices of the work are unlikely to be of any great interest to the client; and that whatever concepts turn out to be useful, they should be useful to all interested parties.

What we mean by 'respecification' is that too often research pays too little attention to the ordinary practical problems that people at work and elsewhere experience, and that any policy changes in relation to organizational change and new technology need to be based to some extent on that knowledge of the practical. Understanding the 'lived reality' of task, work, organization and political experience is just as important as (but does not replace) idealized conceptions of process and data (sometimes called 'plans') that one finds as well in the interdisciplinary arena. A way to see this is by looking at some of the things that were said about office automation:

> Once a clerk is told about a situation, s/he can consult a predefined procedure (formally or informally) to determine what action should be taken by the organization. The organization does not rely on the clerk to decide what to do; instead the organization provides a procedure which instructs the clerk how to react to the situation.
>
> (Zisman 1977: 98)

In fact, it turns out that the supposedly 'routine' nature of office work disguises some skilled, cooperative decision making and negotiation necessary to 'get the work done'. There appear to be important discrepancies between the formal office procedures that supposedly govern office work and practical actions as actually carried out by office staff. This was demonstrated in the ethnographic literature by focusing upon how workers creatively solved 'exceptions' and dealt with contingencies. These field studies showed how, in order to get the work done at all, it was often necessary to deviate from plans and improvise 'ad hoc' procedures in the light of the exigencies of some unfolding situation. The initial assumption we make, then, is that the world is '*socially organized*'.

This concept labels the fact that very little work in an organizational context is ever done in isolation. Even when the person doing the work is physically isolated, doing the work will normally involve an awareness of the work other people are doing or might do. To over-simplify, 'who's doing what' is an important organizing principle of working life. One might think that this is just a matter of looking at organizational charts or other plans, but it is not. Put very simply, the ethnographer might pay attention to the 'gap' between plans, procedures and processes, and the way things are actually done. This would include awareness of the influence of time constraints and knowledge constraints on how things get done; relations with customers; dealing with exceptional cases; the unfolding nature of 'planning'; sensitivity to participants' view of 'good' and 'bad' ways of getting things done; the role of organizational 'language' in the formulation and management of planning; issues of relevance that have moral implications (Harper *et al.* 2000).

If this is true, then it means we are justified in paying attention to the order in which people do things, the sequential and concurrent patterning of work and, along with that, how work can be said to '*flow*'; how decisions are made about what to do next, who should do it and when. That is, how people determine their own courses of action, in the here and now, by reference to what others are doing, as well as what others in the past and in the future have done and will do. There might be several different ways in which these things are manifested, and at various times we have in our work made reference to what we call, '*awareness of work*', or how work tasks are made visible to others, so that people in a workplace can 'see' what is or has been going on. As an example, the visible state of desks, where someone is in their 'heap of stuff', where they have got to in their pile of paperwork, furnishes information to others about what the person is doing and how far they have got to with it. Such information lets others update themselves on the state of all of their work (i.e. the team's), how it is going, whether 'we are behind', 'on top of it', etc.

The point about such aspects is that they represent arrangements which are used in the day-to-day 'doing' of work. They can involve any number of very practical ways of demonstrating what is going on, including writing notes on documents, helping solve problems by asking and answering questions, dealing with customers, allocating priorities, correcting mistakes and so on. The fieldworker, in other words, might be engaged in asking questions that workers might ask themselves, such as: 'What must I do next?', 'Who can I get to help?', 'Who dealt with this last?' and 'What is the easiest way of getting this done?' Such questions specifically draw attention to the way in which work may be interrupted; that things may be picked up and put down; the way that work may be left incomplete as more pressing matters have to be dealt with and so on.

In order to achieve these things satisfactorily, workers will need various *skills and expertise*. Skill is obviously dependent on the specific work context and it is difficult, not to say impossible, to generalize about the skills that are likely to be found in a given domain. Nevertheless, certain pointers are available in the literature, which can be used to orient the fieldworker toward aspects of skill which otherwise tend to remain 'invisible'. A study of breast screening conducted by Hartswood and Procter (2000; Hartswood *et al.* 2003) exemplifies this well. Here, the authors make use of the concept of 'professional vision' (Goodwin 1994). 'Professional vision' has to do with what being a competent practitioner entails. It invokes in particular, the ability to distinguish between 'normal' and 'abnormal'. Examples from their data include the following accounts of how experts 'read' mammograms in such a fashion that they can see more than is visible to the untrained eye and, in this instance, more than is 'visible' to a computer-aided detection system:

I'm having trouble seeing the calc it's picked up there . . . [pointing].
I can only think it's an artefact on the film [a thin line at the edge of the film].
   I'm surprised the computer didn't pick that up . . . my eye went to it straight away . . .
   This lady's got lots of little blobs everywhere . . . but they're not very interesting and I'm going to let her go . . .
   . . . just making sure there's nothing the other side [using fingers]
   . . . and there is . . . a bit of chalk but its harmless . . .

68

These experts are able to spot abnormalities within the films they read. Thus the positioning of an object in a particular area of the breast renders it more suspicious than if it had been elsewhere. At the same time, they note that certain areas within the mammogram are regarded as more difficult than others to interpret and professionals particularly orient to them in their examinations. The social distribution of expertise again becomes evident, as these professionals also frequently express the opinion that one or other of their colleagues is better at 'spotting' some cancers than others.

Some of these skills can be described as 'local knowledges'. 'Local knowledge' is a concern that entails studies of how knowledge is bound to the specifics of particular workplaces. Uncovering this 'local knowledge' can be important. Our own observations have shown that, for instance, even in environments where standard business processes are in operation, local differences almost inevitably arise. As one bank operative put it to us:

> [people] . . . carry these mortgage bibles around . . . and other policies . . . then there's products and handy info like the thing that's on your crib sheets . . . we want it all organized so you'll use it.

Observations of this kind raise important issues for knowledge use and retrieval, for they imply that 'at handedness' is important. There is also an important issue having to do with the formulation of questions. It certainly seemed to us at the time that having things 'organized so that you'll use it' had to do with the personal structuring of information resources such that problems of indexing, understanding titles, formulating questions in an appropriate way, etc. disappeared (Harper *et al.* 2000) and this goes a long way towards explaining why standardized help screens or manuals tend to be under-used.

Equally, it is a feature of 'local knowledge' that some people have more of it than others and it is often worth investigating how certain individuals are commonly recognized as 'local experts' to be used collaboratively, or, in contrast, how relevant knowledge can emerge out of a set of different and distributed knowledges deployed regarding a problem, as we saw in a study of emergency service work (Normark and Randall 2005). Another issue is a longer-term one and has to do with *the relationship between skills and organizational changes*. It can be seen in this example:

> The [expert] system I suppose has worked fine for the people who use it, although there are many that don't. You must have heard people talk about the problems there are with it, but for those that rely on it, it produces useful [insurance] quotes. However . . . some of the older underwriters . . . it is mainly the older ones . . . have always said, 'These people may know about computers, but they don't know anything about insurance.' And just recently, the last five months or so, I'm beginning to think they're right, because what we've

seen is a shift in the market. The market's gone 'soft' and the machine's throwing up quotes way above the going rate. It's losing us business . . .

These things can be thought of as *'normal, natural troubles'* (Garfinkel 1967), to use an ethnomethodological term. People assume that work, whatever it is, will be full of problems. The question is, how do they solve them and what effort is involved? In our case, the goal is to explore the ways in which *technology* and *problems of work* are interwoven, and whether the design of either the technology or the process or, attendant on that, the skills, 'know-how' and so on can be 'redesigned'. One of the things we have discovered is that, in their desire to 'get the job done', people often disguise the inadequacies of technology and procedures they have at hand by 'working around' them. Their skills often compensate for inadequacies of procedure or technology, without anyone outside the immediate work environment being aware of this. We ourselves have encountered more than one information system, which was deemed a success by some in a given context, when investigation showed that others thought the system in question a failure since it was hardly ever used to any great purpose.

Another analytic theme that comes out in studies of the workplace is that of *the role of artefacts*. Yates, for example (1989), described how in the late Victorian era memos, files, standard forms, etc. evolved to solve problems of 'distributed coordination', as organizations became larger and the problems of management and control correspondingly increased. A particular step change was enabled by the vertical filing cabinet, she argues, since it allowed easy storage and ready access to much more information than had been possible before. It allowed organizations to spread out, without the burden of having to increase the number of 'bureaucratic' centres.

We term this, *the 'ecology' of work*. What we mean is that work spaces can be thought of as *elegantly organized places*. Ethnographers in anthropology and sociology, of course, are interested in material culture, but here we are looking specifically at the spatial arrangements of things because it allows work *to be* done and is part of *how* work gets done. The first has to do with how things are arranged so that people can focus; the second is what they focus on. Examples of the kinds of descriptions appropriate here can be illustrated by how a fieldworker might examine a desk and the artefacts on and around it, or the particular ways in which paper can be used, and so on. We discover that the most commonly used artefacts are those kept 'to hand' in accordance with what we can call an 'economy rule', that is to say as reflecting an economy of action oriented to by 'users' (Lee and Watson 1993).

Though seemingly obvious, such an insight can be powerful. It takes attention away from the presumption that the functions of computer systems on the desk top are all encompassing, for example; it helps the fieldworker recognize that much 'work' goes on around the computer (rather than within it). This 'work' is undertaken through a myriad of often very simple artefacts, many of which have unique properties. It will lead the fieldworker to ask questions, for instance, about post-it notes, taped-up messages, notepads, certain kinds of documentation and the annotations they might contain, all of which are economically kept at hand, i.e. put in places where they can be seen easily, picked up readily, referred to in a moment. There will be other types of tool too: phones and calculators, and much else besides. There is always, an ecological arrangement of sorts.

In our work on the banks and building societies, we noticed the arrays of post-it notes, pasted documents on walls and sets of drawers in which different materials were variously kept without being sure at first what these artefacts were doing. Questioning practitioners about the reasons for the arrangement of these things led to answers with the flavour of 'Well, you can see the stuff you need straightaway, can't you?' As we reflected on this, we began to see that small details can often be important in understanding both larger processes and elements within processes; in being able to distinguish between the ways things enable work and the way they are sometimes the vehicle of work. Therefore, we began to examine and pay attention to how documents were frequently annotated, and this prompted further investigation into the typical kinds of information these annotations carried. We began to see more clearly the importance of having information 'at a glance'; how much it mattered that people needed to know who had produced information so that they could decide whether to trust it or not, and we saw how this could sometimes be a need that other techniques for gathering and organizing information failed to satisfy.

The commitment to collaboration

In conclusion, we have tried to show that subject-specific interest in the issues surrounding practical, ethical and conceptual matters does not exactly go away when interdisciplinary or applied work is done, but that their character takes on a certain cast. Things change. Specifically, these practical, ethical and conceptual issues have to be seen through the fact that the ethnographer is not the only, nor even the most important, individual involved in the work, but is trying to work effectively with a variety of other people who might include computer scientists, managers, workers, consultants, people from other academic disciplines and so on. We argue that taking interdisciplinarity seriously means forgetting entrenched disciplinary positions (much easier said than done, as the authors guiltily acknowledge), especially at the theoretical and conceptual level, but also in respect of the practical problems one has to contend with, and even the ethical decisions one makes. Forgetting disciplinary wars, however, does not mean forgetting the sensibilities acquired through disciplinary study, for they are what allows sociologists, psychologists and social anthropologists, among others, to claim to be providing a unique insight.

These sensibilities ultimately derive from a combination of our disciplinary origins and our interdisciplinary interests. The difficulty lies in marrying the two. How do we pursue the enquiries which we undertake, enquiries which depend heavily on our disciplinary sensibilities, in such a way that they are design-, or change-relevant but not purely 'servicing' specific interests? There is no easy answer. In the end, our own commitments to goodwill and tolerance, to recognizing the interests of all parties, to a broadly descriptive sociology and so on, work for us. They might be a starting point for others.

Suggested further reading

Cheverst, K., Cobb, S., Hemmings, T., Kember, S., Mitchell, K., Phillips, P. *et al.* (2001) 'Design with care', *Journal of New Technology in the Human Services* 14(112): 39–47.
Hughes, J. A., Randall, D. and Shapiro, D. (1993) 'Designing with ethnography: Making work visible', *Interacting with Computers* 5(2): 239–53.
Randall, D. (2003) 'Living inside a smart home: A case study', in R. Harper (ed.) *Inside the Smart Home: Interdisciplinary Perspectives on the Design and Shaping of Domestic Computing*, London: Springer Verlag.

Reflective activities

1   What do you think are the main differences likely to be found between doing 'pure' academic research and doing research with other interested parties? Are they likely to vary according to the particular kind of 'interdisciplinary' or 'applied' work being done? For instance, if one was asked to do a study of 'domestic life', or of the 'mentally ill', or of teenagers' use of technology, would there be special problems?

2   Is there any particular reason why ethnographers, of whatever kind, should be employed at all? Would it be better to ask someone who is actually an expert in the area to undertake a study? If not, why not?

3   What specific ethical problems might arise when the fieldworker is engaged in 'interdisciplinary' work?

4   Do you think that ethnographers have special qualifications for dealing with ethical problems, or are they easily overcome by simply saying, 'If it's wrong, I won't do it'?

Notes

1   The two are actually different in important respects. Interdisciplinary work is work where other *intellectual* perspectives are involved: that is, different assumptions, concepts, and theoretical commitments. *Applied* work is where other *interests* are involved, that is, where the outcomes of the research might be used for any number of purposes which do not necessarily have to do with sociology (although they might well relate to social policy) or any other social science discipline.

2   See Headland *et al.* (1990) for a discussion of this concept.

6

ACCESSING INSIDE

Ethical dilemmas and pragmatic compromises

Wendy Laverick

In this chapter, I will focus upon issues relating to accessing and conducting research within the institutional setting of the prison.[1] It will discuss particular issues raised in conducting prison research in general and then will go on to discuss the specific dilemmas faced in my particular research. The chapter ends with a reflexive review of the research process.

Conducting prison research

The prison has been viewed as 'an intense, risk-laden, emotionally fraught environment'(Liebling 1999: 163). Indeed, researchers working within this context emphasize emotional and practical burdens placed upon them, including ensuring personal safety and the risks of 'going native' (deMarrais 1998; Liebling 1999, 2001; Schlosser 2008; Sykes 1958).

It is perhaps necessary to make a distinction from the outset between 'prison research' and research conducted within prisons.[2] While both types may be subject to common methodological and ethical difficulties, 'prison research' may be subject to additional hurdles, which may need to be overcome. The former relates to research explicitly concerned to address the operational, procedural or personnel arrangements of prisons 'as institutions', and therefore may be subject to greater political ramifications and sensitivities than the latter, which does not (necessarily) take the 'prison' as the object of study per se.

Liebling (1999) raises a number of methodological issues with respect to research undertaken within the prison environment generally, which are useful in sensitizing potential fieldworkers to this precarious research setting. Prisons, of course, are not static. They comprise institutions with changing populations (both prison personnel and inmates), which react 'to internal and external dynamics or external political pressures' (Liebling 1999: 151).[3] One needs to reflect, therefore, upon the implications of such fundamental pressures upon research already taking place within such settings. A second issue relates to the impact of fieldworker presence (Liebling 2001) and the researcher–participant dynamics, influenced by variables such as gender, age and class – points to which I shall return.

As with all research methods, it is important to remain sensitive to the historically situated nature of ethnography. Ethnography has departed from an original faith in 'the transparency of reality' (Marcus 1994, cited in Liebling 2001: 475). Consequently, ethnographies broadly adhere to the goals of qualitative research, placing value upon reflexivity, subjectivity, involvement and the acknowledgement of perspectives as advocated by feminist research (see Bosworth *et al.* 2005; Carlen 1983).

If one accepts this position (namely, that the goal of objectivity and researcher distance from the research process is unrealistic and undesirable), ethnographic methods may be deemed advantageous, lending themselves as having special qualities suited to dealing with a whole variety of issues, including controversial topics in sensitive locations. However, such a position and alignment with reflexivity also renders a number of controversial methodological issues visible and subject to discussion, including the issue of allegiances, specifically the problem of 'taking sides' (see Liebling 2001).

Allegiances

All research (and by implication, any institutionally based research) is subject to issues of value neutrality and the extent to which political choices influence the outcome of fieldwork (see Becker 1967; Faraday and Plummer 1979). In obtaining access, for example, how might the researcher mediate the pressures and perspectives deriving from institutional personnel in contrast to the research participants themselves? Can sensitivity be maintained towards the needs and desires of the institution without undermining or distorting the research findings? The British Society of Criminology's (BSC) 'Code of ethics for researchers in the field of criminology', reminds researchers of a number of general responsibilities. Included within these are the responsibilities of the researcher to identify and seek to ameliorate factors which may restrict the development of professional competence and integrity. Liebling (2001) asks: 'is it possible to remain neutral and is it inevitable that we take sides?'

These questions reveal potential sources of tension between actors within the research endeavour (institutional personnel and gatekeepers, researchers, research participants) and serve to problematize the BSC's guidelines for researchers. The BSC Code, for example, reminds researchers regarding their responsibilities to protect intellectual and professional freedom; to promote free and independent enquiry; and unrestricted dissemination of criminological knowledge. The problem for research within particular institutional settings (such as prisons), is that power is ever present (Schlosser 2008), not only within the definition of reality, regarding whether the researcher favours officialdom or privileges offenders' construction of reality, but also in granting access, placing conditions upon fieldwork and on the dissemination of the research findings. Having obtained access to the research environment, fieldwork may potentially shed a critical light upon the institution or particular members of staff. This is not only an emotional issue – having been granted access one may not wish to disappoint gatekeepers – but it also has a direct bearing upon future access to such settings for other researchers and therefore is also a political issue.

This responsibility to retain professional competence and integrity sits alongside another responsibility, which, under particular circumstances, may mask a potential source of tension. Thus, in discussing researcher responsibilities and relationships with sponsors, the BSC Code explicitly recommends that researchers 'maintain good relationships with all funding and professional agencies' and 'avoid bringing the wider criminological community into disrepute with these agencies'. In practice, however, such advice largely ignores the emotional and research dilemmas that fieldwork produces.

'Taking sides', in addition to empathy, judgement and interpretation, while sometimes coming under fire as potential flaws (often labelled 'bias'), are also qualities deemed beneficial. While advocating close relationships, and identification with all the various participants within the research process, Liebling (2001) makes an important distinction between the fieldwork process and how the data is subsequently handled. The problem here is that, once the researcher forms an attachment to the research subject, pressure may be felt by the fieldworker at an emotional level to present participants in the most favourable light. Such feelings of loyalty and empathy are compounded and tensions created when researchers identify with multiple (contradictory) positions (e.g. gatekeepers and prison inmates). Analysis, after all comprises 'reflection, deconstruction, moral engagement and sensitivity to possible political consequences' (Liebling 2001: 482). The task remains, therefore, to acknowledge the existence of competing perspectives and the influence of sympathies without rendering research results invalid. The decision to acknowledge one's standpoint is consequently a research decision, one that aligns to particular research styles and therefore is dependent upon a degree of transparency and reflection.

Researchers' responsibilities towards research participants

In discussing allegiances, the previous section sensitizes the potential ethnographer regarding the possibility of unanticipated emotional responses entering into and influencing research decisions. However, not all perspectives are equal and the institutional setting of the prison raises a number of ethical issues regarding relations of power in addition to the particular vulnerabilities of prison inmates.

Burman *et al.* (2001) observe a potential contradiction contained within ethnography between feminist ethics and methods. Specifically, the key issue here refers to the inherent tension set up between the aims of research (to 'elicit information') and ethical concerns (to 'protect' those taking part) (Burman *et al.* 2001: 449). Ethical research is defined as that which safeguards the rights and feelings of those who are being researched. Assuring confidentiality, minimizing the impact of recalling and reporting stressful events, and avoiding deception are three components of any ethical expectation for social science researchers (Liebling and Stanko 2001). The guidelines provided by the BSC's Code recommend that research is based upon freely given informed consent. The BSC's guidelines also place a responsibility upon researchers to make clear that participants have the right to refuse permission or withdraw from involvement in research whenever and for whatever reason they wish. Thus participants' consent should be 'informed, voluntary and continuing'.

In summary, the guidelines emphasize the researcher's responsibility to protect the well-being of participants in order to ensure that they are not adversely affected by the research process. However, incarcerated offenders are potentially vulnerable on a variety of levels, because of their marginalized social, political and economic positions. Class, ethnicity, age and gender are consequently factors, which may need to be taken into consideration as offender populations are notoriously over-representative of certain social groups, which may have implication for vulnerabilities.[4] The researcher must therefore take care to consider any potential imbalances between the participants and themselves. Feminist researchers, for example, have directed attention to the significance of power within the research process, advocating involvement and engagement of active subjects in all stages of the research process and the rejection of research which treats research participants as objects.

These issues are compounded by the sensitivity of particular research topics, which may generate further ethical issues including the impact of disclosure of sensitive material (in terms of the participant's emotional well-being and personal safety). Burman *et al.* (2001) caution us with regard to the difficulty in predicting the effects of disclosure upon the research subject when undertaking research into interpersonal violence in particular: 'Violence research has the ability to revive old antagonisms and stir up latent harms not only in the fieldwork setting, but also beyond' (Burman *et al.* 2001: 451). Sensitive disclosures made during the course of research encounters may also run the risk of providing incriminating evidence, which may be legally used against the individual (Schlosser 2008). Therefore participants may become 'at risk' in the research relationship through the placing of trust in the researcher.

Having given informed consent, which includes becoming aware regarding the limitations of anonymity and confidentiality, participants should (in theory, anyway) be aware of the potential harm and consequences of disclosure. Burman *et al.* (2001) remind us, however, that it is still the responsibility of the researcher to renegotiate this consent throughout the research encounter and, in doing so, to minimize harm. Indeed, the extent to which a researcher can actually prepare their research respondents and/or anticipate the impact or consequences of the research process upon diverse individuals with their own specific (as of yet, unknown) life histories is by no means an exact science. Ultimately, measures taken by the researcher to adhere to research responsibilities as set out in professional codes of ethics comprises an element of risk, a subjective assessment and a degree of uncertainty which needs to be weighed up against the potential benefits of conducting the research in the first place. This calculation, while distasteful (and often unarticulated) remains implicit to any research encounter.

Rhetoric and reality: research in action

As the previous discussion has illustrated, guidelines are not prescriptive. The 'real' may diverge from the 'ideal', leading fieldworkers to feel uneasy and unsure, particularly when engaging in ethnographic research for the first time. This section will therefore detail a number of dilemmas faced while undertaking research into interpersonal violence, located within two prisons.

Liebling (1999) argues that any research is usually driven by personal curiosity. This is particularly poignant with regards to the rationale behind my own choice of research topic, which will be presented before moving on to discuss the key issues of obtaining access, building rapport and maintaining trust. During my undergraduate and early postgraduate experience, it became evident that traditional criminological theories tended either to ignore or sideline female experience, frequently employing crude stereotypes or remaining reliant upon unexamined gendered assumptions (Burman *et al.* 2001). Moreover, violence-related topics rarely examined both sexes together (Kirkwood 1993).

This realization became the driving force behind the eventual focus for the research discussed in this chapter. The research was to be fundamentally exploratory in nature. It was assumed that until research is undertaken with both male and female samples taken together, we cannot assume how men and women conceive of their own violent behaviour. The central part of this research was based on in-depth, semi-structured interviews. Male and female narrative accounts were examined in an attempt to identify human as opposed to 'gendered' traits, characteristics, values, attitudes and norms.

Why prison?

Why did I choose to undertake my research within the prison environment? In my case, initiation into the context of the prison involved a good deal of luck (gaining access to a male prison), contrasted with a long game plan, patience, negotiation and adaptation (particularly with reference to obtaining access within a female prison). Initial contact came through voluntary involvement in two student union community projects in 1999 (while undertaking a Master's degree in criminology). Participation in a prison sports project facilitated access to a voluntary classroom assistant placement, which eventually led to a PhD research proposal, institutional access and ESRC sponsorship.

Access, gatekeepers and trust

Wacquant (2002: 387) contends that in 'becoming simultaneously more bureaucratic and more porous to the influences of the political, juridical, and media fields, jails and penitentiaries have turned into opaque organizations that can be difficult and sometimes nearly impossible to penetrate'.

For myself, having already obtained a degree of access, a further (anticipated) technical problem referred to the issue of presenting the research to potential gatekeepers in such a way that permission would be granted. It was assumed that if the gatekeeper considered certain topics to be too sensitive, this would have implications for obtaining access, in addition to institutional restrictions placed upon the fieldworker. Care was required, therefore, when designing and presenting the research.[5]

From the research design, it was not important that the respondents had been convicted. What was important was accessing a sample of self-professed practitioners of violence. The prison setting was merely a convenient location. The study did not, therefore, comprise 'prison research' in the formal sense; it was not an attempt to examine the inner workings, dynamics or policies of prisons as institutions. This fact, it became apparent, had a central bearing upon the granting of access, and it also restricted the material to be included within the research findings. In order to secure access, it was the sample (offenders with established histories of violence) and not the location of the sample (prisons as institutions) that was to become the focus for the research. This focus placed a restriction upon dissemination. For example, it might have been interesting to report upon my experience of being accidentally locked in an area of the female institution and then subsequently mistaken as an inmate by an officer who treated me in, shall we say, a less than hospitable manner (until my true identity as a researcher was revealed by my interview participant). However, such material was beyond the remit of the original study and might have subsequently affected future access. Such a compromise regarding content was undesirable; ultimately I justified my decision to continue, however, by assuring myself that, without making such a compromise, the good-quality responses already obtained would be lost and that other researchers would be unable to study within this particular environment without additional hurdles to overcome.

Security checks and clearance for the male prison institution had already comprised part of a routine process upon acceptance into the community projects (thereby eradicating a potential hurdle from the outset). It was within the context of these voluntary schemes (and upon the completion of an MA course and acceptance onto a PhD course) that contact was made with the head of the prison education department. In discussing his own police research, Brewer (1990) recognizes two 'gates' or tiers affecting access: winning the support of senior managers, and accomplishing the same among ordinary members of the force. The latter posed a number of technical and practical problems within Brewer's fieldwork, resulting from the suspicion of ordinary police officers.

In my own case, within the male prison, gatekeepers included ordinary members of teaching staff within the education department, the prison governor, in addition to prison officers and, of course, the research participants themselves. Within the female prison, gatekeepers comprised the prison governor, members of the psychological staff, prison officers and research participants. Gatekeeper support, indifference, dislike or outright hostility to the fieldwork varied according to the institution and employment position, in addition to the degree of prior contact between myself as researcher and the particular individual involved.

Significantly, the attitude of the prisoners toward the staff supervising the researcher also differed by institution. In the male context the researcher was 'under the care' of the education personnel, who were either 'liked' or 'tolerated' and seen as essentially 'people who cared' or who were 'doing their job'. Education staff and prisoners expressed a relatively greater degree of informality toward one another, often joking together, and sometimes gaining advice. In contrast, within the context of the female prison, I came under the 'supervision' of the officers during the weekend sessions and the psychology personnel during the weekday sessions. Prisoners expressed a variety of attitudes towards the former, contingent in part upon the individual as opposed to their status as 'officers'. Several officers were viewed with contempt, some with dislike and others with affection. Introductions made by those held with contempt were more difficult and it is no surprise that the respondents who declined outright to participate in the research (I subsequently discovered) had been 'told' to participate by those officers (undermining completely the researcher responsibility to ensure informed consent and voluntary participation). Fortunately, after the completion of two interviews it appeared that one of the high-status prisoners had vouched for my intentions, making the sampling process easier. Such examples sensitize us to the subtle complexities involved in securing access, the power and potential impact of (and resistance to) gatekeepers and challenges, which may need to be overcome if trust and rapport is to be built with research participants.

In contrast, the psychological staff (based within the female prison), were held in high esteem. The psychology personnel were typically young, middle-class and female. It soon transpired in the interviews that many of the female respondents had a 'problem' with men generally, and particularly those in positions of power. Therefore, it remained unclear as to whether their dislike of the male officers was due to a generalized distrust of men or whether they had issues with individual male officers.

Prior contact and rapport with gatekeepers not only affected initial contact with research participants but also fundamentally influenced the ease with which access was granted (or not) in the first place. Having built up a good relationship with the education team (including obtaining trust) and gaining support from the departmental head within the male prison, a formal request was submitted (and subsequently granted) for access to conduct research at this category B male prison. This was a surprisingly unproblematic process; facilitated by a long period of contact with the education staff.

Access into the female prison was however, far more complex. A category B prison was approached in relation to conducting fieldwork. However, the application was declined due to concerns raised regarding the potential research overload of women offenders, perceived concerns regarding the lack of qualification or experience of the researcher, and the absence of 'necessary resources to pick up the pieces after you have gone'. Such a harsh rejection was very disheartening. However, over the next few months I decided to prove my commitment and qualification by completing four counselling courses, including counselling women survivors of rape and child sexual abuse. This attempt to demonstrate how seriously I took the governor's concerns, and the steps taken to meet his recommendations, proved successful. Access was granted for a limited period during which the research interviews could be conducted. Fieldwork consequently commenced earlier within the male prison than the female institution.

While undertaking the role of a voluntary teaching assistant within the male prison, permission was obtained to conduct focus groups by approaching the head of the education department. The pilot study was arranged swiftly and comprised four focus group sessions with four male prisoners over a period of four weeks in 2000. While these were organized without difficulty, as will be seen, gatekeeper issues – including access constraints and concerns for security – impacted upon each stage of the research process.

During the focus group phase, issues of safety placed several restraints upon the setting in which the activity took place. The education personnel, in collaboration with the prison officers on duty, decided that it would be safest for these to be conducted within the wing's refectory area. This was a decision taken beyond my control and therefore entailed a compromise. The location was within clear view of the prison officer's office. While reassured at the steps taken to ensure my personal safety, the location raised the possibility that the research participants might have become inhibited in their responses. Thankfully, although subject to observation, the prison officers and education staff did not intervene or obstruct the groups unnecessarily. The groups were given relative privacy and intervention only occurred on occasions when excluded inmates attempted (in vain) to join the group.

The focus group sessions were relatively informal and comprised discussions around a variety of subjects. A list of themes and issues had been produced arising from a preliminary review of interpersonal violence literature. These included expectations, attitudes, values, experiences and behaviour. It was initially decided not to tape record these sessions as it was thought that it would become too difficult to differentiate the voices during transcription. It was decided that note taking would be sufficient. However, it soon became clear that the presence of pen and paper served to obstruct the flow of the sessions with participants eager to 'help' by stopping talking (to allow me to catch up), and on occasion attempting to take the notepad so that they could write for themselves what they wanted to say. Subsequently it was decided to tape-record the remaining sessions with minimal note taking to aid in the transcription process.

At the final interview phase, all of the prisoner interviews were conducted on a one-to-one basis and were tape recorded with the prisoners' written consent. It has been argued that the mere presence of a tape recorder threatens to totally destroy not only willingness to participate in research, but also rapport between the researcher and respondent (Sharpe 1998). Once assurances (and the limitations) of anonymity were discussed this was not found to be the case. Not only did the participants cite countless potentially incriminating events but they also disclosed an enormous range of sensitive revelations. Together such revelations indicate the degree of trust and rapport built up during the course of these interviews.

Methodologically, it is impossible to be absolutely certain that ethnographers have gained trust. Brewer's (1990) research illustrates that once obtained, gaining trust is never a simple matter of being forgotten about. The fieldworker's legitimacy had to be earned continually and skilfully, and trust was gained as a result of a progressive series of negotiations (Brewer 1990: 585).

Surprisingly, the focus group sessions elicited a great deal of spontaneity and candour from the participants. The group sessions allowed group norms, common knowledge, consensus and conflict to be identified. From these discussions, a pilot interview schedule was produced. Four prisoners were interviewed in order to test out the validity and the functionality of the schedule in terms of its ability to capture the opinions, values, attitudes, and experiences of the respondents, and the relationship, if any, of gender identity to violent behaviour. This was important, since it was believed that the presence of other prisoners may influence the types of information disclosed within the focus group context. This was found to be the case. Relatively few participants disclosed personal or emotional topics within the context of the focus groups. Overall, the participants appeared to prefer to discuss cultural pressures and expectations in contrast to painful personal events or experiences. This focus contrasted sharply with the one-to-one interviews for both the male and female respondents.

Each pilot interview lasted for approximately two and a half hours. Furthermore, each was subject to follow up visits in order to clarify issues and themes, which arose during the course of the interview. These were tape recorded and transcribed within a day of the interview occurring. The sample size of the pilot study was kept to a minimum due to time and access restraints (both to the researcher and to the prison staff). This process was repeated in 2001 with four female prisoners from a Category B prison. This was essential in order not to extrapolate from the male interview data, factors that may, or may not be significant in the lives of the female respondents. From this relatively small number of interviews (8 in total) a wealth of information was compiled regarding the factors deemed significant by the respondents themselves in the commission of their violent behaviour. The information obtained from the focus group sessions and the pilot interviews were not included in the research findings of the study, rather they formed the basis for the interview schedules.

The physical setting of the final interviews differed by institution. Due to security concerns and staff shortages, the male prison personnel were unable to allocate a private room in which the interviews could be conducted. Through a process of negotiation, a quiet area was eventually found in full view of the officers on duty. This was far from ideal in that such a positioning aroused a considerable degree of interest from the other men on the wing creating a potentially distracting environment.

Initially I had been concerned that discussions of sensitive and potentially emotional issues would be 'contaminated' by such an environment. However, this was not usually the case, bar a few exceptions in which the researcher was offered tea and tobacco, or where the interviewee became subject to remarks designed to embarrass. I remain confident that the interviews were successful in eliciting informative responses regarding a variety of sensitive and evocative topics. These included disclosures of sexual and physical abuse, and experiences of bullying.

To minimize the trauma of recounting such experiences I sought written consent from the respondents prior to interview. During this time, I outlined the objective and content of the interview, emphasizing that the interviews were to be anonymous and that the respondent need not disclose anything with which they felt uncomfortable. Furthermore, I informed each interviewee that they had the absolute right to terminate the interview should they wish to. No prisoner took up this offer. However, a concern for 'aftercare' was raised with prison staff. Unfortunately, at that time resources for counselling were nonexistent within both these institutions and the interviews themselves revealed that, for many of the subjects, unless counsellors were 'independent' of the institutions, many would have difficulty confiding in anyone. These were real concerns; however it was hoped that the research process might prove to be a cathartic experience for many of the respondents.[6]

Significantly, virtually all of the interviewees within the research expressed a desire to be heard; some explicitly described the interviews as a unique opportunity to discuss issues never previously disclosed. As one inmate, 'Larry', noted:

> I think that's like the first time I've ever expressed how I feel in life; like I say, I'm thirty eight years old, I've never really explained any of this to anybody, nobody's really asked me before, I don't know, I don't know how comfortable I am. I couldn't go to anybody.

A number of the participants discussed undisclosed incidents of sexual, physical and/or mental abuse, self-harm, previous suicide attempts and current suicidal thoughts in addition to desires for revenge upon release. Such disclosures created ethical dilemmas regarding whether it was appropriate to pass on information about potential self-harm by research participants to third parties (such as psychology personnel, prison officers and/or education staff). In such instances, it was decided to remind the participants regarding the limitations of assurances of confidentiality (particularly where disclosures might be incriminating). Where participants seemed distressed and/or disclosed suicidal thoughts, the individual involved was asked how they wished for the researcher to respond, including whether they desired any third party contact and/or support. Perhaps unsurprisingly, all such offers were declined.

Ultimately, the effect of the research process upon the respondents will remain unknown. It is hoped that the steps taken to minimize harm, including strategies such as informed consent, the right to terminate the interview and the explicit instruction not to disclose anything that the respondent felt uncomfortable with, would suffice to these ends.

The interview setting in the female prison was more adequate in the sense that a private room was designated in which to conduct the fieldwork, with access to an alarm if the need arose (it did not). This environment was important since limited access restricted the ability of the researcher to become familiar with the women, who often expressed suspicion regarding the motives of the research prior to its commencement. Furthermore, the initial sample selection was performed by a member of the education staff, who selected six individuals on the basis of his own subjective impression as to who would be relevant for the research, directed by the criteria of 'established history of violent behaviour'. This of course was not ideal and reflected a pragmatic compromise faced by the fieldworker when confronted by the reality of institutional restrictions, safety considerations and gatekeeper intervention. Later on in the process, it became possible to select with a relative degree of freedom who would be included and who would be excluded.

Both the male and female samples were selected to reflect the variety of offences included within the legal category 'violent offences' (including individuals convicted of murder, manslaughter, armed robbery, GBH and kidnap). The only significant difference was the inclusion of rape within the male sample. However, it should be noted that there existed a large overlap of individuals committed for several types of violent and non-violent offences, and two respondents (one male and one female) who had only committed one offence (attempted murder and murder respectively).

My experiences within these two research settings differed considerably. In part, this was due to the familiarity between the researcher, education staff, officers and prisoners within the context of the male prison, and the contrasting absence of relationships within the female prison context. An interesting and frustrating feature of the experience was that the prison officers were generally less receptive than the education and psychology personnel were to researcher presence in both contexts. Officers expressed frustration at what they considered to be an imposition on their time and staff resources. This attitude was reinforced by a string of redundancies within their institutions. Several officers also expressed a dislike for research within their department, remaining suspicious as to the research objectives. However, that said, these officers were in the minority.

Personal characteristics of the researcher and impact upon research

It is commonly acknowledged that the personal characteristics of researchers affect research outcomes. Brewer (1990: 584), for example, discussing police ethnographies, contends that 'being female brings its own problems'.[7] Preconceived ideas regarding female researchers, while comprising potential hurdles to be overcome, may also bestow a number of advantages, however, as the literature reviewed by Brewer (1990) indicates: young female researchers have been variously viewed as 'acceptable incompetents' and 'non-threatening'.

During the interviews, I adopted a variety of roles, attempting to take advantage of preconceived ideas as identified within this literature regarding the perception of female researchers. In some instances, I adopted the role of the 'acceptable incompetent', presenting myself as naïve and unthreatening. At other times I adopted an informed stance, partly reflecting upon my own familiarity with lower-class environments. The former worked particularly well with respondents who had well-established careers in violence, and those who expressed distaste toward 'know-it-alls'. The latter role was employed to encourage security and common ground, and overall worked well.

This concern with gender, age and background differences between researchers was deemed significant within Liebling's (1999) research in relation to the gender dynamics of her research team. Within my own research data, 'Larry' (introduced previously), had expressed his desire to be heard. However, he explained that his previous attempt to confide in male 'friends' had resulted in far from satisfactory outcomes, leading to 'pisstakes' and mocking. Within the confines of the individual interviews, 'Larry' revealed that as an adult, his wife was:

> The only one that knows anything about me, apart from you now. She's the only one. I don't know, talking, whether I thought it would be wimpish I don't know.

However, even some topics of conversation were withheld from his spouse. 'Larry' went on to disclose that an unknown male, had sexually assaulted him as a child. He described the incident in the following way:

'Larry': When I was a kid like, we used to play in the woods, eh, I can remember this guy coming one day, I've seen him in our town an' all. He pinned me and one of my mates down and he made us play with him when we were young, and it sticks up in here you know [points to his head], that that bastard did that to us like that, I didn't even dare tell me mum, I don't know what my mum would of thought of me you know.

Interviewer: Have you talked about this to anyone before?

'Larry': No, you're the only one I've ever told. I can remember holding it, I can remember like seeing his face, thick glasses and I don't know. I've often thought about it, I remember it clear as day me. I just thought it was the right thing, if he did it to us it was right you know, he never touched us in any way but he made us touch him. I see him about; I know for a fact it was him. I see him, I said 'I know you'; he said 'Who are you?' I said my name and I said I'm sure you used to knock about near the woods and he's like 'No, no wasn't me, wasn't me', and he backed off like. My wife's gone like 'Who was that?' and I'm like, 'Nobody'. How many years has that can of worms been shut? I don't know, I don't know if it will ever help me to talk about it, I think that's why I've got such a big hiccup with sex offenders and, you know, what they've done to children.

An important point to note from 'Larry's' account is that he was later convicted for assaulting a suspected paedophile. 'Larry' reported that he had never talked about his experience with anyone before.

Safety is also a key issue, which remains bound up with issues of gender, as my own experience attests. A considerable degree of negotiation was demanded between the researcher and institution staff prior to access. In the male prison, an alarm and appropriate dress code was seen as compulsory, and it was further necessary for the researcher to be accompanied at all times or within observational distance of an officer or educational staff. In the female prison, there was less concern with security, enabling greater freedom within the institution's grounds. Access to an alarm button within the interview room was deemed sufficient.

A reflexive review

I consider that empathy is important. The capacity to feel, relate and become 'involved' is, I believe, an essential component of the research task. However, acknowledging the significance of such involvement places an additional requirement upon the researcher to consider a variety of methodological and ethical issues during the course of the fieldwork, which remain invisible within older ethnographic accounts. The dilemmas faced within my own research decisions reveal uneasy compromises made to facilitate access, maintain relationships and build trust, which necessarily impacted upon the location of the fieldwork, strategies to minimize harm and the conditions imposed upon the material to be included and dissemination.

During the course of the interviews, for example, I experienced an ambivalence between a stance of empathy towards the experiences of the respondents, many of whom I liked very much, and a real abhorrence of many of their crimes and a degree of sympathy for the victims. This was regardless of whether the respondents themselves may have seen such actions as 'justifiable'. Ultimately, it was considered that attachment to those being interviewed enhanced the validity of the data obtained, challenging a charge of superficiality posed by those who 'do not get close enough'.

Gathering detailed material is demanding and emotional. I was initially unprepared for the exhausting and emotional consequences of the interviews, particularly the often terrible experiences faced by the respondents within the context of their lives. Towards the end of the data collection phase of the research I found it hard 'to let go'. Although forewarned of the potential experience of 'going native', in practice I found this process to be more difficult than anticipated.

Emotional fatigue was again encountered in the 'transcription' phase of the research, when faced with two months of re-hearing the emotional accounts of the respondents. This occurred once again, at the 'writing up' phase of my doctoral thesis and its subsequent publication. Editing decisions regarding how much of the graphic detail of the accounts was to be included in the dissemination process brought up further dilemmas. Would the inclusion of descriptive accounts of sexual and physical abuse risk a degree of voyeurism on the part of the audience? How would it be received? How much filtering and selective presentation of the data collected was desirable and or necessary? Moreover, how much detail could I bear to report? Could inclusion be conceived as faithful representation or exploitation in the furtherance of career aspirations?

This chapter has served to sensitize the potential ethnographer to some of the challenges of undertaking research on sensitive subjects within challenging environments. Thinking reflexively about the dilemmas and decisions involved has raised my own consciousness regarding the impact of my own experiences upon the data collection process and the data produced. By remaining brutally honest and transparent, ultimately I hope to have done justice to those involved.

Suggested further reading

deMarrais, K. B. (ed.) (1998) *Inside Stories: Qualitative Research Reflections*, Mahwah, NJ: Lawrence Erlbaum.

Liebling, A. (1999) 'Doing research in prison: Breaking the silence?', *Theoretical Criminology* 3(2): 147–73.

Schlosser, J. (2008) 'Issues in interviewing inmates: Navigating the methodological landmines of prison research', *Qualitative Inquiry* 14(8):1500–25.

Sykes, G. (1958) *The Society of Captives*, Princeton, NJ: Princeton University Press.

Reflective activities

Consider how you might resolve the following ethical dilemmas:

1   A prison interviewee expresses hostility towards the recipient of violence in the incident for which he/she was subsequently incarcerated. The interviewee states that the victim deserved 'what they got' and expresses the intention to seek revenge upon release. Are there any limits regarding the confidentiality of the research participants?

2   During an interview located within a prison, the research participant is overcome with emotion. He/she explains that they have attempted suicide on numerous occasions prior to their incarceration and explicitly states that 'life is no longer worth living'. You leave the interview fearful that the interviewee may harm themselves. What should you do?

3   At the start of an interview with a violent offender located within a prison, the participant discloses personal information, including home address, family details and offending history. You feel that the interview is progressing well, including rapport and trust with your research participant. The interviewee asks you to disclose personal information including where you live and your relationship status. To what extent is the disclosure of personal information permissible? What are the implications for refusal? How might you diplomatically resolve this request?

4   During the course of your prison fieldwork, you observe a prison officer verbally abusing an inmate. Your interviewee expresses that this is not an uncommon occurrence with this particular member of staff. What are your responsibilities to (a) the institutional gatekeeper; (b) the research participant; (c) the prison population; (d) the discipline of criminology?

5   A prison interviewee reveals information regarding the presence and trade in illicit drugs and mobile telephones within their particular wing, including names, details of concealment and methods of transportation. What ethical issues are raised by this revelation? How might you have prevented such a disclosure?

Notes

1   This chapter is based upon research conducted by the author at one female and one male prison in the north of England (for a discussion of the findings see Laverick 2007).

2   Sykes (1958) and Clemmer (1940) are widely credited for establishing prison sociology as 'prison research'.

3   For example, this might include the recent changes in jurisdiction from the Home Office to the Ministry of Justice, or the implications of sentencing reforms upon prison numbers and issues of overcrowding. Cavadino and Dignan (2007) provide a particularly good introduction to these issues.

4   In relation to gender, see for example *The Corston Report: A Review of Women with Particular Vulnerabilities in the Criminal Justice System* (2007) and the Fawcett Society Report (2007) *Women and Justice*.

5   For a discussion regarding 'getting a foot in the door' and overcoming access constraints within prisons see Schlosser (2008: 1510). Wacquant (2002) also provides a good discussion regarding obstacles to prison research, including questions of access, funding, the policing of knowledge claims and the (mis)use of the military metaphor of 'collateral damage'.

6   A sentiment shared by the respondents in Schlosser (2008) and Bosworth *et al.* (2005).

7   The 'problems' of being female, contained within Brewer's quote, include reference to female fieldworkers' experiences of sexism and paternalism while conducting research on the part of male respondents, gatekeepers and organizational staff alike.

7

UNDERSTANDING CHILDREN'S EDUCATIONAL EXPERIENCES THROUGH IMAGE-BASED RESEARCH

Anna Graham and Rosemary Kilpatrick

Contemporary social science research is increasingly focusing on the need to research the lives of individuals, especially children, from their own perspectives. Studies seek to capture and make visible the diversity of children's lives, but this requires that researchers explore methodologies that enable participants to tell their own stories. In recent years, the growing sense of urgency to uncover the realities of children's worlds (Christensen and James 2000), has been accompanied by the growing recognition of the need to fully engage the child in any research process that involves them (Green and Hogan 2007). This has been paralleled by a renewed interest in visual ethnography (Banks 2001), prompting second editions of certain key texts such as those of Pink (2007) and Rose (2007). Clearly, visual methodologies allow researchers the possibility to enter children's worlds in very immediate, yet creative ways using techniques such as drawings (Kilkelly *et al.* 2004), video diaries (Haw 2008) and photography (Ewald and Lightfoot 2001).

This chapter builds on these bodies of literature by focusing on the use of photography as a means of engaging children in research and allowing them to have greater control of the research process. However, even in the literature on the use of photography (Banks 2001; Prosser 1998; Rose 2007) several different uses or approaches are described, such as photo-documentation and photo-elicitation. The latter has been defined as a method: 'to encourage interview talk that would not be possible without the photos, and the photos and the talk are then interpreted by the researcher' (Rose 2007: 239).

Within photo-elicitation there are again different methods, including either the researcher using a bank of photographs to trigger dialogue or the participants being given cameras to take photographs themselves. Both methods have been used with children (see, for example, Thomson 2008), but the current chapter draws on two case studies where the researchers gave children the cameras with sufficient time and space to choose how to represent their lives and experiences and thus they determine the context for the ensuing discussion.

Children are 'vulnerable subjects', and while these methods are accessible and can embrace notions of participation and empowerment within the research process, they also present significant challenges for the researcher. Of particular importance here are ethical concerns regarding the ways images are created and disseminated, both in terms of the practical considerations surrounding the use of cameras and the ways in which the image making and sharing process can impact on the participant–researcher relationship. From these issues stem critical questions of privacy, disclosure and the sharing of this information with wider audiences.

This chapter looks at some of these questions from the perspective of two researchers and their very different projects. The first is Anna Graham's ethnographic study of poverty and social exclusion in 'Wratton View',[1] a declining social housing estate sited on the edge of a small town. The second is Rosemary Kilpatrick's longitudinal study of an intervention programme for school children in a disadvantaged inner city area. These separate, and in some ways contrasting studies chronicle how the use of image-based research can generate rich and vibrant data to illuminate children's lives. They explore how the methods used within their respective studies allowed the children to reveal new insights into their social worlds and reflect on the dilemmas arising from the process. However, together, they highlight the ways image-based methods can offer tantalizing glimpses into the private domains of children's lives, but provoke heightened vulnerabilities for participants. They explore the ways visual methods require researchers to employ a rigorous, reflexive approach and a critical engagement with new ethical debates about the possible unintended consequences surrounding the production and dissemination of the images.

Education and children's life chances

Sociology of education has long determined a relationship between social class, educational attainment and children's life chances (Floud *et al.* 1956; Goldthorpe and Jackson 2007; Halsey *et al.* 1980; Shavit and Blossfeld 1993). Despite three decades of broad social and economic change, and an unprecedented period of radical education reform,[2] there has been little empirical evidence of the ways dramatic changes in the family, new patterns of employment and the increased spatial concentration of poor and marginalized groups shape children's educational experiences. Understanding the different social, economic and cultural contexts in which children negotiate schooling has taken on renewed significance in the light of government commitment to challenge poverty and social exclusion in the UK.

Schools, specifically those sited in areas of concentrated disadvantage, have been positioned at the very heart of a plethora of policies designed to build social capital, emphasize family responsibility and reinvigorate communities suffering from social, economic and environmental decay. Initiatives heralded by Education Action Zones (EAZs) and consolidated within 'Sure Start' and community regeneration programmes, have sought to combine educational interventions with new inter-agency collaborations to improve educational performance, while simultaneously challenging the underlying processes of social fragmentation, disaffection and exclusion (Sparks and Glennerster 2002). However, while such strategies acknowledge that educational failure is deeply rooted in family, school and community contexts, education and welfare professionals charged with their implementation rarely live in the areas in which they practice, or witness – beyond the confines of the institution – the ways such interventions either address the problems of target groups or impact upon established survival strategies. Without empirical evidence that explores educational policies and practices in relation to wider social and cultural constructions and political and economic interests, there is a risk that schooling, and its broader welfare concerns, may become dislocated from the lived realities of young people and their communities (Gamarnikow and Green 1999).

Anna's study: schooling in 'Wratton View'

Schooling in 'Wratton View' focused on the education experiences of the young people involved in the study and is therefore used as the primary example in this chapter, with the findings being explored in depth.

Background

'Wratton View' is the last and the largest of five London overspill estates built on the western periphery of 'Trenton'; completed in the late 1970s, the development of 1,200 houses had its own community centre, parade of shops and middle and infant schools. Settled initially by young families relocating with their employers from south and east London, it rapidly entered a spiral of decline. Successive economic recessions and prolonged under-investment throughout the 1980s and early 1990s resulted in major job losses, a deteriorating housing stock, few viable local amenities and a reputation in the local area for overt drug use, vandalism and car crime. As a predominantly low-skilled workforce, residents were dependent on low-waged temporary contracts or part-time shift work in nearby light manufacturing and food processing plants. With little prospect of full-time work, many established families returned to London and 'Wratton View', with its high levels of youth unemployment, and lone-parent and low-waged households became an unpopular estate. This had a significant impact on its schools. By the late 1990s, 'Wratton View Middle School', had a school roll of 160 children, under half of its maximum capacity. Low levels of educational attainment, poor pupil behaviour and a demoralized staff led to a failed Ofsted inspection. Despite comprehensive Local Education Authority (LEA) support and radical improvements by a new and charismatic head teacher, the school was 'named and shamed' by the tabloid press as one of the poorest performing in the country. After a further inspection two years later, the school emerged from 'special measures' but remained a fragile institution with a fluctuating roll, acute staffing problems and Statutory Assessment Tests (SATs) results significantly lower than the national UK average.

This study was designed to generate data in discrete stages to build a comprehensive understanding of the dynamics of poverty as they operated across community–family–school contexts from the multiple perspectives of those who lived and worked in the estate. Throughout the work with the community and the families, the research followed a traditional ethnographic approach involving participant observation and interviews, with each stage carefully designed to triangulate the data. From the outset, residents were wary of engagement with, and interventions by, statutory and voluntary agencies, and sceptical of the possibilities advocated by the planned programme of regeneration, including the much-heralded, Education Action Zone. Mindful of the low levels of social trust, and anxious to avoid any speculation about association with the multitude of agencies involved with the estate, interviews were conducted off-site with police officers, social workers, health and educational professionals, before building links across the community through involvement with the tenants' association and local playgroup.

During the second stage, six mothers, each with children in the Year 5/6 class at 'Wratton View Middle School' were accessed through the community and thus detailed case studies of their family lives were constructed. During months of interviews conducted in kitchens, sitting rooms and gardens, as children played and meals were prepared, women spoke about their relationships with their families and partners, confided their fears about their children's futures, the problems of managing money on a low income and the regular battles fought with benefit agencies, welfare professionals and the school. These insights lent particular poignancy to mothers' stories of their interactions with teachers and the ways professional assumptions around their maternal competence left them and their families vulnerable to the machinations of institutional power. This was especially true as they described their struggle to meet the economic priorities and caring practices demanded by the school and welfare agencies.

Children's educational worlds

It was against this background that the final phase of the research began. This sought to investigate children's experiences of school and their understandings of the ways family material circumstances and the parts played by their peers, teachers and the community shaped their educational experiences. In order to fully engage the children and allow them to determine the direction of such conversations it was decided to ask the children to take photographs with the instruction 'tell me about your life', thus allowing them to have some degree of ownership over the research.

The emotional intensity of the images children captured and the serious intent with which they used their photographs to represent their lives was powerful. Snapshots of places, people, pets and possessions had been expected, but instead children produced carefully framed, sharply focused portraits and unpredictably posed pictures of themselves in staged scenes. Frequently these pictorial narratives acknowledged and refuted adult, and specifically teachers' representations of themselves as resistant to school aims and values. In commenting on a picture of herself cross-legged reading her book on her bed 'Janie' (aged 10 years) commented: 'I love reading, I'll read anything I will. Look at them books on me shelf. I've read all them.'

'Janie' was not alone in her desire to assert her identity as a 'good' reader. 'Lawrence' took a photograph of the head teacher's cupboard, which prompted his discussion of the contents he found there. He went on to reveal that he would wait with his friends while workers removed the household effects of empty or repossessed properties in the estate and rummage through the skips to find discarded books and toys. His animated description of his favourite 'treasure', a book on spiders and the effort required to forage for it and to carefully dry out its tea-stained pages, was in stark contrast to his class teacher's portrayal of him as a 'nice kid but totally disengaged – a non-reader'. Through his photograph, 'Lawrence' revealed a real commitment to and enjoyment of learning that had hitherto remained hidden in the school context. The 'secret world of learning' discussed by 'Lawrence' was shared with other children. Pictured by her mother in an armchair, expertly balancing her baby sister on her knee and surrounded by her six siblings, 'Kylie' spoke about her household chores that left her little time for 'playing out' or homework. She delighted in going to bed and explained:

> Don't tell no-one I'm in STARS, right? [the special educational needs group] – but when I go up I practise me spellin's. Don't laugh [I wasn't] I write poems too, yeah honest. I love me poems, I do – and me readin' . . . I'm doin' good in school now.
>
> ('Kylie' aged 9 years)

Many of the children's photographs were taken in their bedrooms, a private space that few adults outside the family would have access to. While children used this room to illustrate their favourite possessions, it also prompted discussions about children's interior worlds as a place where they could think and reflect about their lives and relationships. Discussions around these photographs revealed that, for many of the children in the study, school could be an emotionally demanding and turbulent place.

Pupil behaviour was the defining aspect of school life in 'Wratton View Middle'. After angry and occasionally violent confrontations with staff, children regularly stormed out of lessons and rampaged through the school. Support staff funded by the new Education Action Zone, who were sent to impose calm and retrieve distressed pupils, were regularly seen in the school corridors. Managing poor behaviour, its impact on teaching and learning and inconsistencies in the application of the school behaviour policy, dominated staff room discussions. Whereas teachers' explanation for children's outbursts focused on tensions between families on the estate, chaotic households and inadequate parenting, a number of children used their photographs of the empty art, science and music rooms to challenge these representations of family and community life and to put forward alternative explanations.

> This is the art room. We ain't been in there since Mr Johnson left. See them planets [*papier mâché*-covered balloons] we did them. That was good that was. They ain't finished though. I dunno why we don't do art no more. I think it's 'cause we're not good but when we done them no-one acted up. Not even Aiden – we was quiet, 'cause we was concentratin'. It's like PE we ain't done that for ages, nor cooking. I mean we go to do it but then we're naughty and Mr Churchill [new teacher] takes it away and then the kids just wanna act up more.
>
> ('Luke' aged 9 years)

Children used their photographs to speak with a genuine sense of grievance about the denial of their full curriculum entitlement and their teachers' reluctance to allow them opportunities for their own investigation or play. The wistful account presented by 'Luke' of the ways creative and less easily managed aspects of the curriculum were withdrawn by teachers unwilling to risk unruly behaviour, was echoed by 'Sean' (aged 9 years) in his angry description of his photograph of the music room.

> We ain't never been in there – 'cept one time when Mr Churchill banged on a drum. We got took out 'cause we all started banging the instruments, makin' a racket. They int supposed to do that is they? Take away the good stuff – 'cause how you gonna learn?

'Sean' was not alone in his frustration. The children spoke vividly of the boredom and sense of powerlessness that pervaded their learning. With photographs of their classroom they raged against the pedagogical shortcomings of their teacher; highlighting the tedium of copying information from the blackboard, the long rows of desks that minimized group work or social interaction, and the lack of basic resources that frustrated every task.

> I 'ate 'im [his teacher] – he's always shouting you through the wall and back. The other day we 'ad to do these sums in numeracy and I didn't 'ave no pencil so I kept askin' everyone if they 'ad one and

no-one did. So I got up to ask 'Rachel' and he [teacher] told me off
for talking and put me on the behaviour list. It ain't fair. I asked him
why we ain't got none but he didn't say nuffink.

('Aiden' aged 10 years)

The regular competition for pens and pencils and the teacher's reprimands that
followed, fuelled rivalries and resentments. Tensions built throughout the day,
culminating in afternoon sessions punctuated by aggressive outbursts towards
each other and teaching staff. 'Stacey' described her photograph of her
classroom.

We 'ad just come in from dinner play and I took it [the photograph]
coz it was a laugh. Lonie's chucking a chair at Mr Churchill coz he
'ad detention for gobbing off in the morning but it was Aiden's fault
– he nicked his rubber. . . .

('Stacey' aged 10 years)

Children's photographs also explicitly linked their school experiences with their
family lives. 'Alan' discussed his picture of his mother sitting at the kitchen
table reading his school report, dressed in her work clothes; he spoke about
the long hours she worked as a cleaner to support the family as a lone mother
and his desperation not to disappoint her.

I gotta do good an I? Mum says she don't mind working so long as
we do good at school and we get decent jobs an that. She gets us books
and stuff to 'elp us. Most kids, their Mum's don't do that, they don't
care but mine, well – um, she wants us to learn good.

('Alan' aged 9 years)

The importance of maternal work to the family finances became a familiar
theme. Mothers worked long hours, often cleaning in the early morning
followed by other jobs late into the evening. Children spoke about missing the
time they could spend with their mothers and having to remember the complex
childcare arrangements involved in taking or picking them up from school.
'Sean' described the picture of his mother pushing his sisters' buggy across
the precinct to get to his grandmother's house.

I remember this – it was a Thursday. I know that 'cause on Thursdays
we have to be at Nan's by seven 'cause Mum starts at eight and Nan
takes us to school. Look she's got [her work] uniform on.

('Sean' aged 9 years)

Other pictures brought forward thoughts and feelings other than that suggested
by the subject matter. The photo that 'Rachel' took of a lone pot plant on the

kitchen windowsill generated a discussion of her family's hardship. Like many other children in the estate, 'Rachel' had rarely left the town and her family found it hard to provide the educational opportunities and experiences that could support her learning.

> I ain't never been on holiday. Mum and Dad are trying to save but there's always somethin' else come up. We might go to the sea next year – get a caravan. I ain't never been to the sea. . . . We did it in literacy though so I know all about it . . .
>
> ('Rachel' aged 9 years)

Despite the enormous strain of living on a low income, the problems of family breakdown and constraints imposed by a community suffering the chronic problems of disadvantage, children's photographs also portrayed caring loving families. 'Mark' took a picture of his sleeping elder sister, simply because he 'loved her' and 'Aiden' created a portrait of his family on the sofa, now reunited after a period of marital disharmony and separation:

> That's me Mum and me Dad and Casey. Me Mum let me Dad back [home] so it's them all together. That's Jake and Alex behind the sofa . . .
>
> ('Aiden' aged 10 years)

These intimate and often very moving photographs revealed the struggles of 'Wratton View' families, the school and the community it served with simplicity and candour. Children articulated their thoughts, feelings and experiences in ways that shed new light on the realities of schooling; the demands on parents to reconcile their educational responsibilities with the pressing economic priorities of paid work; and the stresses of professional practice in areas of concentrated disadvantage. The photographs taken indi-vidually created a platform for children to share their stories, but collectively they formed a rich seam of evidence of the local expression of current government education and welfare policies on the lives of those who lived and worked in 'Wratton View'.

Rosemary's study: life on 'Wenchater Estate'

Rosemary's study is ongoing and has as its focus life in an inner city estate originally built in the early 1950s as part of the 'solution' to tenement living. Over the decades the estate became one where poverty, social exclusion and drugs were predominant facts of life, reflected in the high unemployment statistics and levels of crime and ill health. Regeneration attempts in the 1970s and 1980s were poorly received by the local community, and the social conditions continued to deteriorate and haunt the estate until the new millennium. Renewed attempts at rebuilding the community and government initiatives led to a task force and local community initiative proactively working together to influence politicians, with a resultant second and extremely successful regeneration plan whereby all the old flats were to be knocked down and local residents rehoused in new homes on the same estate. This regeneration plan is now completed and living conditions and community spirit have significantly improved.

However, not surprisingly there are still marginalized families and young people who are emotionally vulnerable and struggle with their attendance at school. It is the lives of eight such children, aged 9–11 years, which are the focus of this case study. These children have been described by the school as coming from 'problem' families and have been referred through their school 'because of emotional and behaviour problems' to an intervention programme delivered by a practitioner who visits the school once a week on a long-term basis.[3] The research is designed to follow these children as they progress through the programme and to provide insight into their experiences and progression to secondary school. The research is still in its first phase and initially time was devoted to negotiating access with the school, getting to know the children, introducing the idea of the research to them, and ensuring they understood what was involved. With this being a collaborative piece of work between the researcher and the practitioner who had been invited into the school, much of the groundwork had already been done and the permissions required were most probably more readily acquired due to the existing relationships that had been established. The focus of the first phase of this study was to explore what was important in the children's lives from their perspective; it therefore did not focus on school unless the children themselves brought this into their discussions. As with Anna's study, there was a desire to give the children control over the research process and explore with the researcher 'what was important to them in their lives' in a way that would be non-threatening and empowering for the children; it was with these aims in mind that the use of photographs, supported by conversations with the children exploring the images, was the chosen method.

What was immediately striking was the range and variety of the photographs, combined with the careful thought and planning that had obviously gone into them. The importance of the environment in which the children were living was abundantly clear, with numerous photographs of the new housing and others which reflected the sense of community. For example, 'Cathy' had taken a photograph of a keyring with a heart on it and explained:

> The heart; we got it when 'Wenchater' was being knocked down. . . .
> I've lived in 'Wenchater' for most of my life and when they knocked down the flats and we moved into the houses they gave us two hearts and we buried one in 'Wenchater' and we kept one.
>
> ('Cathy' aged 10 years)

There were numerous photographs of the children's school, which was set in the heart of the community, and invariably the children told of how their sisters and indeed mothers had gone to the same school (and brothers to the boys' school across the road). Photographs of classrooms and teachers were also common, as were photographs of the practitioner who was working with the children, because 'she helps us' and 'I like when she comes – we do lots of good things with her' and 'I can talk to her when things ain't right for me.'

While some of the children talked about their struggles with their school work, there was a strong sense of being supported by their teachers. Related to this were the photographs which several of the children had taken of the building in which the 'After School Club' was held, and there was much talk about the activities and help gained from staff there. While some talked about the support for understanding and improving school work: 'they just help you – it means that I can keep up – I do my homework there – I can't do it at home 'cos I can't think there', others, like 'Kate', talked about the social activities and excitement generated by these:

> 'They took us into the City – we went to the funfair – and I went on this here ride and it was scary – I was almost sick but . . . oh it was just great and then I was home really late and me ma, well she was cross 'cos my wee sister had been waiting for me, but she was asleep so I went and gave her a kiss 'cos I love her.
>
> ('Kate' aged 9 years)

For all those children who had lived on 'Wenchater' for most of their lives the sense of community, and school as part of that community, was unquestionable. Unfortunately, this was not the case for 'Dorota', a Polish child with no siblings, who had been living in 'Wenchater' for just over two years. 'Dorota' (who spoke good English despite it not being her first language) appeared isolated from her peers at all levels, and this came across powerfully in her photographs. All of these were taken in a Polish social centre and, despite the fact that 'Dorota' told me this was a 'party', there was a sense of them being static, isolated and unconnected with the real world.

As with 'Wratton View', many of the photographs the children took in 'Wenchater' revealed family stories and intimacies that needed to be managed with sensitivity and respect. Sorrows were talked of, sometimes in a matter of fact way, which might have disguised the hurt but for the long pauses and thoughtful moments in the conversations. However, over-riding all of this was an extremely strong sense of a community in transition, with pride in a shared history and a school that played a central role through supporting vulnerable children in their learning.

Using photographs in a research project

These two case studies illustrate how the use of photographs taken by children, combined with accompanying narratives, can challenge the stereotypical accounts of dysfunctional families presented by the children's teachers. They further demonstrate how photographs taken by the children themselves can provide a rich context for discussion and new insights, while still giving children choice in how and what they reveal about their lives and experiences. Photographs are powerful images that enhance the credibility and authenticity of children's stories. They communicate meaning to audiences by liberating children's stilted and often disjointed dialogue, and provide visual impact and emotional intensity to the voices of the least heard. However, it is the intensity of the stories that emerge that leads to the need for caution when using photography, or other creative visual methods, especially with children. Leitch (2008) points out that such techniques require emotional sensitivity and inter-personal awareness, which are not always taught as part of the repertoire of conventional research training, and argues that: 'As interest in creative research methodologies expands it is worth considering the value of specialist research guidance being developed to ensure safe, ethical and child-centred practice in their application' (Leitch 2008: 55).

Stages of photo-elicitation research

Given the above cautionary notes and with the proviso that those intending to use this approach should have demonstrated a required degree of empathetic understanding, it is then necessary to think about the processes involved in using photo-elicitation as a method of data collection. Rose (2007) outlines five stages which she suggests are common to most of the various studies using this technique and in adapting these stages for work with children the authors suggest that the following would be a useful framework for developing projects that intend to use photo-elicitation where the children take their own photographs.

Stage 1: Initial interview; gaining consent

In the initial interview(s) it is important to explain to the participants what exactly the research is about, why you are doing it and what you and the participants might get out of it. The photographs are not the focus of the initial interview stage, but written consent will need to be sought from the children themselves, their parents and the school (or other gatekeepers) for participation in the research. It should also be made clear that, even if initial consent is given, the participants can withdraw at any stage of the research process.

Stage 2: Distribution of cameras and instructions for use

The children are then given a camera (usually disposable), with instructions as to its use along with any personal safety and/or privacy issues. The brief for the photographs is also given at this stage. Thus, for example in Anna's study, each child was given a disposable camera for a forty-eight hour period, instructed in its use and given the brief, 'tell me about your life'. Each child was allowed ten exposures, this being both an economic measure (to reduce the costs of development) and a way of ensuring that, through exercising choice, children thought about the relevance and significance of the images they wanted to take and share. Mindful of the risks to young children of walking around with an albeit inexpensive camera, and the possibility that their photographic activities could intrude on the privacy of others not directly involved in the research, personal safety issues, privacy and the rights of individuals not to participate were discussed. To preserve confidentiality the returned cameras were taken some distance from the fieldwork site and two copies of the photographs were developed; one for the child and one to be retained as part of the data set.

Rosemary's study followed a similar pattern in terms of instructions, privacy and safety issues, though the numbers of exposures used and instructions differed. In this research, the children were given digital cameras with 28 exposures and instructed in their use (including taking practice photographs in the school). At this time it was also made clear to the children that they should always ask permission of someone before they took their picture and if photographs were taken in people's homes (including their own) they must seek the permission of the owner (or in the case of their own home the permission of their parents/carers). The children were given the cameras for a week and asked to take photographs of what was important to them in their lives. The cameras were returned the following week (though one child forgot hers and it had to be collected later in the week), and two sets of the photographs developed. A week later (i.e. a fortnight after the children had received the cameras) the eagerly awaited packages of photographs were given to each child who opened them with the researcher. Both sets were retained by the children, though the researcher also had a set scanned into the computer (about which the children were aware).

Stage 3: Viewing, selecting and exploring the photographs

A follow-up interview (or interviews) is then held with the participants to discuss the photographs in detail and clarify what the photographs mean to the individual who has taken them. These interviews invariably cover sensitive issues and the location is therefore important; privacy and some guarantee that there will be no unnecessary interruptions should be a high priority. It is extremely helpful if these interviews can be recorded (for which, of course, consent must be given), and where this is possible then it is important for the researcher to ensure that there is some means of identifying which photograph is being discussed.

It is usual for the packets of photographs to remain unopened until each child had been given the opportunity to open them in private with the researcher close to hand. Thus, in Anna's study, the researcher identified quiet places around the school where she sat with each child individually as the packages were opened and prompted by the question 'Can you tell me why you took that picture?' explored each photograph in turn. In Rosemary's study, the opening of the packages of photographs took place on an individual basis in a small, quiet room in the children's school. All the children, except one, had taken a full set of 28 photographs; some of which were duplicates 'just in case it hadn't come out' and some of ceilings, floors and unidentifiable objects, which were clearly taken by mistake. After having sorted through the exposures and removed the ones that the children identified as duplicates and 'mistakes', the children were asked why they had taken each photograph and to select six that represented what was most important to them in their lives; these final six were then made into a collage. In this way, and through conversations regarding why certain photographs should be included and others excluded, the children narrowed their selection down while at the same time exploring what they perceived as most important to them in their daily lives and why that was the case.

Stage 4: Interpretation

Interview material and photographs are then interpreted using traditional social science techniques, possibly using data management packages for qualitative data such as NVIVO or by the individual researcher determining the approach as in Anna's study. It is also quite common to find content analysis being used with photographic material. While not used in Rosemary's study, there was potential to do this, the photographs clearly dividing into those of people (self-portraits, brothers, sisters, families and friends), places (the school, houses in the estate, shops in the city centre, churches), and things (televisions, diaries, plants, posters, even a chocolate fountain!). This procedure has been used recently by Lee (2008) in a study of second-generation Chinese children living in Northern Ireland and their sense of cultural identity, which then led to examining individual differences in identity using Identity Structure Analysis (Weinreich and Saunderson 2003).

Stage 5: Final report

Generally, the final report will be written in such a manner that the dialogue takes precedence over the photographs themselves, and indeed there are occasions where the photographs have not been used, as is the case in Anna's study. From the outset of this study, it had been intended to use the photographs merely as 'trigger material', enabling children's narratives to be turned into text. In this respect, it had been assumed that the value of images would diminish once the narrative had been transcribed. However, the photographs were visually stunning and provided a powerful means of chronicling the impact of poverty in contemporary childhood as well as illustrating the findings of the study, thus the decision was not taken lightly. After all, the parents had given their permission for the photographs to be taken and had often assisted their children in making them. However, it was felt that they were unaware of what exactly they had captured; the empty beer cans discarded on the living room floor, black bin bags lining stairwells, shabby furniture and untidy homes, all of which vividly captured the stark realities of the families' lives on the estate.

In contrast, in Rosemary's study it had always been the intention that the photographs would be used as part of a school display of the lives of children on the estate: it was to be a celebration of the school's achievements in the community and the children were anxious to use the photographs, which belonged to them, in this manner. This permission had to be negotiated and discussed with the parents/carers, who could, at any time, say that they did not want certain photographs to be used if they so wished; though it was interesting that there was no such vetting and all the six photographs that each child had chosen to be used remain in their collage. Such permissions do not negate the necessity to seek the agreement of both parents and children should the researcher wish to use any of the photographs in any further reports and/or publications.

Ethical issues

The use of photographs in research, and particularly with children (and other vulnerable groups), raises specific ethical issues which have been discussed and debated in the key visual ethnography texts including those by Banks (2001), Pink (2007), Prosser (1998) and Rose (2007), as well as those exploring visual approaches when researching with children and exploring childhood such as that of Thomson (2008).

Walker *et al.* (2008) draw attention to the fact that the Economic Social Research Council (ESRC) in 2006 defined ethical research as having six key principles, including those of integrity; quality; providing full information about the research to all concerned; voluntary participation; avoidance of harm to participants; and independence of the research with conflicts of interest being made specific. There is also one principle on confidentiality and anonymity which specifically refers to the use of photographs as follows:

> All information supplied by informants should be confidential and all
> informants guaranteed anonymity (in the case of photographs, this
> would entail ensuring that no individuals were identifiable, by blurring
> faces digitally for example.
>
> (ESRC 2006: 1)

Additionally, the increasing awareness of research ethics has resulted in the development of government research ethics bodies, such as the Office of Research Ethics, and a growth of university ethics committees. The former in particular generally want to know the exact nature of any vulnerable group's involvement, which includes children, and where photography is involved they want to know what the photographs will be of and how they will be used – often something which is difficult to define. How such guidance and the ESRC principles sit with participatory research where the children themselves may decide what to photograph; where they may own the photographs; where disclosures of potential harm may make confidentiality difficult to uphold, has not really been debated and these two issues are further explored below.

Confidences and disclosures

There is an increasing requirement by ethics committees for participants to be told that what they tell the researcher will remain confidential, unless they disclose information that makes the researcher think that they are at risk of being harmed or of harming someone else. However, whether this is fully understood by younger participants is debatable and it may not always be possible to remind children of this clause before they have disclosed certain information. Furthermore, the fact that children have the undivided attention of an adult who values and respects their perspectives can give them space and confidence to disclose more than what is immediately apparent in the photograph.

For example, in Anna's study, take the discussion that resulted from the picture that 'Lawrence' took of the head teacher's cupboard. This photograph showed a collection of 'freebies' she had collected to reward children for good behaviour. After discussing the drawing books, pens and pencils, he focused on the miniature pots of jam often provided with hotel breakfasts. His discussion swiftly turned from his ambition to collect enough good behaviour points to earn the jam as a prize, to revealing that he had only recently returned to his family from foster care.

'Lawrence' described how after months of little food (other than jam sandwiches) and regular smacks from his stepfather, he and his siblings had run away to the police station and were taken into local authority care. Despite his assurances that everything was fine, since he had returned home, he went on to disclose that people regularly called at their house 'to get tobacco'. In an estate with a high incidence of substance misuse, a credible alternative explanation of this story was that his mother might have been dealing in marijuana. Clearly, this sort of activity could place him and his siblings at risk. However, to report this to a third party would have breached his trust and that of the families and jeopardized the integrity of the research as a whole. In view of his happy demeanour and the fact that there was still active and ongoing social services involvement with 'Lawrence' and his family, it was decided not to take the matter further.

Disclosures did not present such a problem in Rosemary's study since this was being conducted in collaboration with a practitioner whom the children knew well. Where disclosures did occur in this study, the researcher (with the child's permission) was able to ensure that the practitioner was aware of any risk for the child. Drawing from this is the idea that a useful addition to the notion of consent could be that the child nominates a 'trusted adult' outside of the research to whom the researcher or the child can turn if disclosures are made that warrant further intervention or investigation.

Privacy and publication

The power of photographs has been adequately demonstrated in Anna's study, but this and their potential for chronicling the impact of poverty in contemporary childhood presented the researcher with a dilemma, and despite having the relevant permissions to publish the photographs, the researcher in this instance has remained reluctant to do so. This unwillingness stems from the manner in which the photographs were taken and the lack of informed consent about the ways in which the pictures, uncoupled from the children's narratives, were open to the possible misappropriation and reinterpretation by a wider audience. In sharing these images (and those invited to view them) the participants' homes and families would be exposed to the intrusive gaze of the uninvited guest, allowing those with limited knowledge of participants' circumstances to become a voyeur; a 'spy in the home'.

In Rosemary's study, and despite having the relevant permissions, there was still a feeling of unease in wishing to use the photographs for a presentation to an invited audience. This resulted in a personal debate as to why exactly the photographs were being used and whether there was a potential for misusing or misrepresenting the children's stories. Following extensive discussion with the practitioner involved in delivering the programme to the children, and sharing with the children the manner in which their stories would be told and the photographs to be used, a decision was made on the grounds that the research was collaborative, reflexive and that permissions had been sought and granted from those who owned the photographs and therefore the copyright (Rose 2007). Finally, it was agreed that the children would receive feedback from the practitioner on how their stories had been portrayed and received by the audience.

Walker *et al.* (2008) argue that standard ethical procedures do not work in an age where digital and video cameras, mobile phones and computers provide easy access to children's lives, and where instant delete buttons give children a greater degree of control over the images they wish to capture and share:

> In a digital environment, the rational plans of conventional research that separate researcher from subject, plans from practice, involvement from consent, collection from publication, shrink often to vanishing point.

... What is needed, we argue is an approach to ethics that steps back from procedures and returns to principles then reconnects principles to methodologies. This has significant consequences for researchers because it returns the basis of trust to the area of professional judgment and to the actions of the researcher-in-action.

(Walker *et al.* 2008: 172)

They go on to argue that the heart of the problem lies not in the new technology but the need to acknowledge that, in participatory action research, there is no role of subject as we traditionally understand it and, by its very nature, participation in research 'includes the right to have a voice in terms of research ethics' (Walker *et al.* 2008: 173) – an argument that resonates strongly with the two authors of this chapter.

Working with and respecting children

Increasingly researchers are seeking to engage children collaboratively in their research to become active participants. The search to allow children's voices to emerge is made more practical by the availability of new technology, which provides children with an ability to engage in participatory research based on a more equal collaboration and allows them to shape the parameters of the research as 'real' participants. However, while photography is a powerful medium that can elicit new understandings of children's lives and perspectives, it is a method that challenges the legitimate scope of research and conventional ethical procedures. The ability to produce and instantly transmit data electronically around the world creates new risks to privacy and demands that researchers adopt measures to rigorously safeguard children's physical images and comply with both data protection and child protection legislation. However, ethical considerations also extend to a closer scrutiny of the researcher/child relationship and the kinds of assurances of confidentiality that can be offered. Negotiating and managing children's responses require researchers to acknowledge with their respondents at the outset the scope of the enquiry and the ethical guidelines by which they are bound. Image-based research with children is a powerful method for generating rich contextual understandings of children's experiences and perspectives. However, researchers need to be mindful of the ways it is disseminated. Issues of ownership of the photographs and the ways in which they can be used, exhibited or published, need to be determined before fieldwork commences, and child or parental rights to withdraw material at any stage respected. While the data yielded from interviews allows respondents to demonstrate cultural competence, that is, the interview itself invites participants to account for their actions and behaviours in ways that reflect the social structures and dominant discourses surrounding the sphere of investigation, the power of an image alone to represent and interpret the social world is limited by the subjective gaze of the viewer and the context in which the image is viewed. Therefore, while the interview process can discern through interrogation explanations for social behaviour that can determine social actors' motivations and intent, the capacity of the image alone to communicate meaning is constrained by questions of credibility and authenticity. In this respect, narrative text derived from children's own photography and used in conjunction with the photographic image can provide greater illumination of children's lived realities and new visual pathways for adult understandings of children's worlds.

Suggested further reading

Ewald, W. and Lightfoot, A. (2001) *I Wanna Take Me a Picture: Teaching Photography and Writing to Children*, Boston, MA: Beacon Press.
Pink, S. (2007) *Doing Visual Ethnography*, 2nd edn, London: Sage.
Prosser J. (ed.) (1998) *Image-based Research: A Sourcebook for Qualitative Researchers*, London: Falmer.
Rose, G. (2007) *Visual Methodologies: An Introduction to the Interpretation of Visual Material*, 2nd edn, London: Sage.

Reflexive activities

This is a paired exercise that needs to be undertaken sensitively by both partners. From your own collection of family snapshots, select four photographs you are willing to share of a celebration such as Christmas or a birthday party.

1   Ask your partner to look at the photographs and decide what is the key subject matter?
2   What story or moment did the photographer seek to capture?
3   Now ask your partner to let their gaze move from the central image and focus on the periphery of the snapshot and explore what else the photograph tells them. For example: who else is in the photograph?
4   What emotions can they infer from their expressions?
5   What can they assume about the family from the image: the way people are dressed, the room décor or the garden?
6   Could there be another story emerging that was not the original intent of the photographer?
7   Discuss why you chose those photographs to share and how you feel about your partner's comments.

Notes

1   In accordance with established research practice, pseudonyms have been used to protect identities.
2   For a comprehensive discussion of educational change in post-war Britain, see Tomlinson (2001).
3   The practitioner works with a small group of children to broadly build confidence, motivation and enjoyment of learning.

8

LET'S LOOK INSIDE

Doing participant observation

Sal Watt and Julie Scott Jones

This chapter will explore what we mean by participant observation; defining different types or levels of observation that researchers and, in particular, ethnographers engage in. It will draw on two case studies of participant observation: the first an overt study of organizational change in the British Civil Service and the second a covert study of a Christian fundamentalist group in Midwest America. This chapter concludes that each site brings with it its own practical and ethical dilemmas; dilemmas that are often difficult to anticipate in the design and planning stage.

What is participant observation?

Paul Willis (2000: viii) suggests that ethnography is the 'eye of the needle through which the threads of the imagination must pass'. As observers then, what we see through our eyes, how we see it and how we represent what we see, is crucial in constructing as true a picture as we possibly can of the research culture we are privileged to study. We inevitably have an immense responsibility to record accurately not just what we see but also to locate our observations contextually; culturally, socially and importantly, politically (Breakwell *et al.* 2006; Hammersley and Atkinson 2007). Behar (2003) writes passionately that we must capture the 'really real', that our observations must not be caught up in our own preconceptions, but instead give a true or 'real' account of what we observe. Further, that our observations are reflexively accounted for alongside our own socio-political location and standpoint, and how these might impact or influence what we see and how we see it in the first place. However, before exploring this important issue further we first need to briefly contextualize the origins of observation and ask where does this tradition of observing people in their natural and social location come from?

From anthropology to the social sciences

Ethnography and qualitative methods more generally have been highly informed by the work of social anthropologists. The work of Bronislaw

Malinowski (1922, 1929) A. R. Radcliffe-Brown (1952) and Margaret Mead (1943), and their accounts of living among indigenous peoples, learning first-hand of their lives, had an immense influence on early fieldworkers (Angrosino 2007; Neuman 2006; Ritchie and Lewis 2003). Testament to this came at the beginning of the twentieth century, when the Chicago School started to harness some of the data collection techniques of ethnography through, for example, informal interviews and of course observation. Evidence of this can be seen through the work of Park (1915; Park *et al.* 1925) and Whyte (1955). Distinguished from early naturalistic observational studies such as that conducted by Charles Booth (1902) into London's poor, the Chicago School embraced and appropriated the anthropological tradition of 'living' and participating in a culture (Neuman 2006; Scott 2002).

Under the direction of Robert E. Park, social researchers were encouraged for the first time to get out of their armchairs and to 'get the seat of their pants dirty'; to embody and immerse themselves within their research culture in order to fully understand it (Breakwell *et al.* 2006; Silverman 2004). In this respect, the Chicago School set about a programme of naturalistic social research that investigated marginalized Chicagoan people afflicted with social problems (Marvasti 2004; Neuman 2006). By the mid 1960s naturalistic and participant observation was firmly established within the Chicago School and, through the gaze of symbolic interactionism, the focus shifted to understanding how people made sense of their social environment and how they constructed order in their social lives (Ritchie and Lewis 2003; Scott 2002). This is evident through the work of Mead (1934), Becker (1967, 1971; Becker *et al.* 1961) and Bulmer (1984) and in particular, through the popularized work of Erving Goffman (1956, 1959, 1961, 1963a, 1963b).[1]

The research tradition established by the Chicago School has had an immense influence in sociology and more widely the social sciences. In embracing the concept of fieldwork our legacy is an array of appropriated ethnographic data collection techniques, such as participant observation, that provide a rich and valuable insight into people's lives.

Let's get dirty!

As we have seen, 'getting the seat of [our] . . . pants dirty', getting to know and living among the people we want to know more about is the key aim of any ethnography. Throughout our lives, our behaviour has to varying extents been driven and contextualized by observing those around us (Bandura 1965, 1973; Goffman 1959; Willis 1977). Some of you will probably readily identify yourself as a 'people watcher' and, when we watch people, we tend to interpret someone's action or behaviour, dress, accent and so on. In doing this, our interpretation is often based on former experience and 'common sense', and usually results in us forming some kind of judgement or opinion.

However, while 'people watchers' might well make good ethnographers, as researchers, we need to be highly mindful of Behar's (2003) concerns about observing the 'really real'. As social researchers and ethnographers, we constantly need to be reflexively aware of how our own thoughts and feelings hold the potential to influence our research interpretation. Therefore, we need to be very clear about the distinction between everyday or casual observation and observation in empirical social science research by adopting a far more formal and systematic approach in our observations (Angrosino 2007).

Definitions abound for social science research, ethnography and participant observation; here I draw on Wacquant's definition that fuses these together well:

> Social research is based on the close-up, on-the-ground observation of people and institutions in real time and space, in which the investigator embeds herself near (or within) the phenomenon so as to detect how and why agents on the scene act, think and feel the way they do.
>
> (Wacquant 2003: 5)

The purpose of ethnographic field participant observation, then, is to observe people in their natural surroundings, their everyday behaviour, interactions, routines and rituals, along with the artefacts and symbols that bring meaning to their lives, while of course, conversing and listening to their narratives (Angrosino 2007). The criteria around what to observe are not exhaustive. However, what makes ethnographic observation distinct is that the field researcher engages in observation over a sustained period of time (Fetterman 1998). Fetterman (1998: 35) suggests a period of six months to one year as an appropriate time to engage with the language, observe 'patterns of behaviour' and allow the researcher to 'internalize the basic beliefs, fears, hopes and expectation of the people under study'. Angrosino (2007: 53) echoes this, stating that 'ethnographic research is predicated on the regular and repeated observation of people'. Fetterman (1998: 35) also makes the point that, in the early stages of observational research, the process can seem 'uncontrolled and haphazard' and only becomes clearer the longer the researcher is in situ and gains experience of the research field. As I will explain in the next section, this was certainly my experience.

If, as Wacquant (2003: 5) suggests, we are to engage in the 'close-up, on-the-ground observation of people and institutions in real time and space', the first quandary to negotiate when entering the field is what and where to start observing. Depending on the research question and the duration of the research project, potentially I would advise initially observing anything and everything, and to 'write up' field notes as soon as is practicable. Clive Palmer, in Chapter 10, gives sound guidance and advice about 'writing up' and coding field notes; but I would just make the point here that often something seemingly insignificant or inconsequential can at a later point prove highly meaningful.

When we talk to people, it is not uncommon for them to leave gaps or silences in their narrative. People sometimes have a tendency to sanitize or censor, to tell us only what they want us to know; they tell us a version of a story. What people say, and what they actually think, feel or do can be quite different. This can create gaps or silences in the data and sustained participant observation can help in filling in these gaps or contradictions. As noted earlier (Fetterman 1998), in the early stages the data collection process can seem somewhat haphazard and uncontrolled, but later, if gaps or contradictions appear in the data, comprehensive or 'thick' field notes can be immensely helpful to fall back on throughout the research period and, of course, the analysis.

Getting to know you

Participant observation is a key characteristic of ethnography and it is reliant on the researcher being accepted by the research group and becoming immersed in its culture. However, if becoming immersed relies in the first instance on being accepted, it must not be assumed that acceptance is easy, or, indeed, an automatic right. There are several issues here that need to be considered. First, in order to become accepted researchers need to build up rapport with group members, and to do that, they need to possess the necessary interpersonal skills to get along with people and earn their trust (Neuman 2006). Angrosino (2007) sums up these skills well; first, the ethnographer has to have a keen eye for detail, a good memory, possess good language skills and, to reiterate Behar's point (2003), have the ability to represent those under observation accurately, fairly and with sensitivity. Such skills become honed and enhanced over time. However, most budding ethnographers are likely to have had some previous research experience that will help here, and the level of experience is likely to inform the type of participation and level of observation to be engaged in. But, as O'Reilly (2009) points out, the process can be difficult as the researcher adopts two identities: that of the participant engaging in everyday activities and interaction, and, at the same time, also that of the objective observer. The balance between the two can be problematic; on the one hand, one is trying to blend in with the group, to become accepted and privileged with an 'insider' view, while, on the other hand, remaining the objective observer or 'outsider'. The tension between the two identities can be difficult to handle and mesh together on a practical level. O'Reilly (2009) puts it well when she highlights the 'instrumentality' of our participation, because in most cases our participation ends when the research draws to an end. However, as the final chapter in this text illustrates, although the research practically and physically ends, psychologically it stays with us and often the experience can leave its mark. So let us move on and consider the different participant and observation roles we can adopt.

Participant observation roles

Generally it is agreed that Gold's (1958) classic typology of participant roles has helped us to define different levels of participation (Angrosino 2007; Angrosino and Perez 2000; Dallos 2006; Flick 2009). The four participation roles are: the *complete observer*, the *observer-as-participant*, the *participant-as-observer* and, finally, the *complete participant*. So let us briefly look at each of these in a little more detail.

The *complete observer* remains detached from the researched cohort and strives for complete objectivity (Angrosino 2007). In this role the researcher is located covertly in the research field, with the group under observation unaware they are being observed (Bryman 2008; Flick 2009). However, there can be ethical concerns with this kind of observation, and ethical guidelines laid down across the social sciences by the respective disciplinary bodies, for example, the British Psychological Society (BPS), the British Sociological Association (BSA) and so on, should be fully considered and adhered to as much as possible. The issues of ethics and covert research will be explored later in this chapter.

Bryman (2008) suggests that we see these roles on a continuum of detachment and involvement, and this is quite a useful way of conceptualizing the different roles. If the *complete observer* remains detached and unknown to the research group, then the *observer-as-participant* would share similar alignment on such a continuum. While in this role there is detachment from the research group, at the same time there is a degree of participation. The *observer-as-participant* may observe in the research field over brief periods of time. Angrosino (2007: 54) highlights that this provides the opportunity for the researcher to 'set the context for interviews or other types of research'. The status of the researcher is overtly known to the research group, but the researcher boundary is acknowledged and maintained by both parties (Angrosino 2007; Bryman 2008).

Moving along the continuum, there is some similarity between the *observer-as-participant* and the next role type, the *participant-as-observer*. Again, the researched culture is aware of the researcher's status but in this instance the researcher openly engages with the research group and builds up a relationship that is both 'friend' and 'neutral researcher' (Angrosino 2007). On Bryman's continuum, this role errs on the side of involvement. However, while fusing together the two roles of participant and observer, this type of participant observation does not lose sight of the research focus and acknowledges the researcher's role in this respect.

Finally, the *complete participant* observer becomes completely absorbed in the researched community, engaging and fully participating in the group's everyday activities. In this case, the research may well be covert and the research agenda may never be acknowledged to the research group. There are pros and cons here and the risk of 'going native' exists. On the one hand, complete participation can be said to be advantageous because it opens the window completely to an indigenous population. While on the other hand this type of research can be fatally flawed if the participant researcher's standpoint has influenced or compromised the research objective and outcomes (Angrosino 2007).

However, a more contemporary view on observational research is that of membership roles. Adler and Adler (1994) suggest a three-membership role typology: *peripheral, active* and *complete membership. The peripheral membership* role entails the researcher engaging with the group and establishing an 'insider' identity. Adler and Adler (1994: 380) suggest this is 'vital to forming an accurate appraisal of human group life'. However, despite observing and interacting with the group in this role, and although the researcher attains an 'insider' identity, there is no participation in the group's core activities.

In the *active membership role*, according to Adler and Adler (1994: 380), the researcher is 'more involved in the setting's central activities, assuming responsibilities that advance the group, but without fully committing themselves to members' values and goals'. These two different membership roles will be explored later in this chapter. The final role is that of *complete membership* and in this instance it is highly likely that the researcher is already a member of a particular group or will become a 'full' or 'complete' member of the group and identify fully with its values and beliefs. In Chapter 9, John E. Goldring discusses the pros and cons of assuming this membership role.

As you can see then, the way in which, or the extent to which we can undertake participant observation is varied. Which role we assume can be determined by several design choices. For example, it might be determined by how much experience and confidence the researcher possesses. Access issues and reliance on gatekeepers might well be another factor that determines the role assumed. Importantly, ethical considerations will without doubt play a major part in the design process; will the research be covert or overt? The chances are that all student research will be overt because university ethics boards will be highly active in determining this (Helen Jones talks about this in Chapter 3). Perhaps the best way to bring these roles and considerations to life is to illustrate them through our own research.

Sal Watt's overt participant observation in the Civil Service

When I try to categorize the participant role I took when undertaking my PhD research in a department of the British Civil Service I find it quite difficult. What kind of participant observer was I? At the outset, I need to tell you that for twelve years I was a Civil Servant, so in terms of role membership it could be argued that I identified strongly with the culture of the researched group. During the years of the Thatcher government, the drive for downsizing gave me the opportunity to take voluntary redundancy. I chose this because I had become frustrated by what I perceived as years of chaotic change in the Service.

Every day I was caught up in what seemed to be change for change's sake and the bigger picture eluded me. Studying for my first degree in sociology and psychology, my research projects always pulled me back to workplace issues. So it was a natural progression that my postgraduate study would focus on organizational research and, in particular, the mechanisms that communicate change. Not surprisingly perhaps, my choice of research site was the Civil Service.

Since its formalization over 150 years ago, the call for change has been ongoing in the Civil Service amid continued criticism of its cost and efficiency (Drewry and Butcher 1991; Pyper 1995). While the Thatcher government set out to redress this and provide 'value for money', New Labour and the Blair government continued with the project of 'modernizing government'. Six years on, and based on my own experience, my research focus took an ethnographic 'bottom-up' approach that investigated how change was contemporarily communicated, interpreted and experienced by Civil Servants at the turn of the twenty-first century.

Let me in . . .

Most Civil Service research is undertaken 'in house' by the Home Office and I was expecting difficulty around access. However, with the help of a gatekeeper I approached the headquarters of my former department and I was surprised and grateful that a divisional manager welcomed me into his division of 'the department'. I should emphasize that I did not research in any of the areas I had formerly worked, or with any of my former colleagues. My research was overt and underpinned initially by the somewhat loose research question: 'How effectively is change communicated in the Civil Service?' While I had anticipated difficulty in accessing 'the department', in fact it was more problematic recruiting participants. Fortunately, two volunteers were interested in my research and from them my sample snowballed as people grew confident about me, my research and what it involved.

I took a 'bottom-up' approach and, as such, my research question, although initially somewhat vague, was exploratory in nature. With two cohorts of 'key' and 'peripheral' participants, the aim was to spend considerable time with the small cohort of six 'key participants'. The questions that I would pose to the wider cohort of 'peripheral participants' would be informed by the various data collection techniques I employed. These were: secondary research of 'the department' and its internal policies and strategies; shadowing and participant observation, and semi-structured interviews and conversations with the 'key participants'.

The data was then triangulated, being drawn from various sources, and the intention was that this would build in validity and reliability. In total, I spent fourteen months going in and out of the 'department' as and when teaching commitments allowed. During university vacations, I would spend extended periods of time, first of all investigating its intranet and government internet sites more widely, noting the ways in which change was communicated to the workforce. As to my six 'key participants' – I spent varying but long periods of time shadowing them. By this I mean simply sitting beside them, working the hours they worked; sometimes these were very long days, for example, on one occasion one of my 'key participants' worked an eleven-hour day to ensure a task for a customer was completed. I observed what they were doing or working on, I asked questions or sought clarification about their respective roles and experiences and, of course, I socially conversed with them and the colleagues with whom they worked.

To cut a long story short I concluded that it was the 'department's' human resource management strategy that underpinned and drove communication on departmental change (see Watt 2005, 2007). While this conclusion emerged over time, what I observed immediately was that, since leaving the Service six years before, a new discourse of 'professionalism' had become prevalent in the 'department's' literature, internet and intranet sites, and common in the narratives of the people I interacted with. Underpinning this word, and embedded within the appraisal system, was a set of 'behaviours': 'behaviours' that for the most part are 'common sense' and what might be expected, or indeed be typical of many organizations. For example, drawing inclusively on a 'we' discourse, two examples are: 'We are honest and open', 'We embrace creativity and innovation'. Some of the workers described these 'behaviours' as patronizing and objected to the implication that formerly, before their introduction, they had not been honest and open. These 'behaviours' were disseminated across 'the department' frequently through various modes of communication. For example, by plasma and PC screens, mouse-pads, calendars and so on. All seemed to prominently drive home or remind the workforce of the need for 'professionalism'.

Like many large organizations, the Civil Service possesses its own glossary of acronyms and the usage of these was a practice I was very familiar with. To be able to use a string of initials representing a much longer phrase or name saves a great deal of time and becomes, of course, both ritualistic and meaningful to members of a group or organization. However, I quickly noticed that the glossary of acronyms had changed radically in the intervening years since I worked in 'the department'. In order to be able to integrate and become accepted I needed to embrace the new acronyms as quickly as possible. One of the necessary qualities of a participant observer that Angrosino (2007: 57) identifies is that of 'cultivated naïveté', that is, not being frightened to ask naïve questions that might seem obvious to the listener. In this respect, regularly seeking clarification of the Civil Servants' shared language helped me several ways. When I came upon a new acronym, I immediately took a note of it for the glossary I was building in my field notes. However, to the participants I think it also showed a keen interest in their work and my engagement. As time went on I observed the participants quizzically looking at me pondering

114

whether I knew the acronym they had just mentioned. Without even asking, they tended to assume I would not know its meaning and automatically clarified it for me. In this respect I often felt that they were 'watching me, watching them', and that they played their part in taking responsibility for my ignorance by leading me through a dialectical maze rather like a child developing a wider vocabulary.

There were other instances where my lack of knowledge or experience was assumed and one of these was around tea making. The common joke about Civil Servants is that they consume vast quantities of tea. Truth be told, their habits are no different from those I have experienced or observed in other organizations. However, tea breaks are highly ritualistic and, as a participant observer, I thought this a ritual in which I could, or so I thought, at least make myself useful. I spent considerable time with one section in particular and for this section, a tea break was an opportunity for everyone to take fifteen minutes 'out', to look away from their PCs and to share their news, what they had watched on TV the previous evening, what they were doing that evening or weekend or to discuss family matters. Given their generosity in allowing me to share their space and time, I thought a valuable recompense might be that I could at least take my turn in making their tea or coffee. Their response was to say that it 'was a very nice thought but the tea club order was complex' and it took some getting used to. I did not push the issue in this respect because this was in the relatively early stages of the research and I was aware that I was still 'the researcher' and as such positioned as the 'guest'.

However, as time went on and the cohort got to know me, I observed their interaction and response to me change. The corporate speak I had listened to and observed over previous weeks started to fade. While their behaviour and output remained unquestionably 'professional', as time went on I noticed increasingly that I was being allowed to see 'backstage' (Goffman 1959). Despite the complexity of 'milk no sugar, lots of milk, two sugars, toast lightly done but with Flora not butter', I was, in time, allowed to make the tea, coffee and toast. In terms of membership, this had clearly been a process of negotiation. Yes, I had been generously allowed to observe this group in their working habitat but initially I had not been fully accepted around participation. This was a right that I had to earn as I came of age in the membership stakes.

The point of recounting this simple example of group acceptance is to illustrate that when we start observational research, it can be really quite difficult to define the type of observer we will be. We might anticipate a particular role but to an extent how successfully we achieve this is in the hands of the group. As a consequence, how we define ourselves is often retrospective, and writing this chapter has been part of that process for me. As ethnographers, our participatory observation relies on us engaging with the research setting and context, and possessing good interpersonal skills that allow us to build rapport with those people who then 'may' allow us into their lives. If I had to define the type of participant observer I was in the Civil Service research, it would first depend on whether I was talking about my 'key' or 'peripheral' participants. Drawing on the typologies mentioned earlier, under Gold's (1958) typology, I would identify myself in the 'participant-as-observer' role with the 'key' participants, but conversely with the 'peripheral' participants, as an 'observer-as-participant'. I find it much easier to identify with Adler and Adler's (1994) idea of membership. With membership comes the idea of flexibility and the possibility that membership can be seen as fluid, on a continuum that ebbs and flows depending on how immersed or accepted we are at any given time. As outlined, my research was clearly overt, but there are some cultures and 'closed' communities that would be impossible to access through an overt approach. So let us move on and explore this further through an example of covert participant observation.

Julie Scott Jones's covert participation observation in a religious community

The previous section of the chapter focused on observer roles generally and overt participant observation specifically. This section will explore covert participant observation drawing on my fieldwork in a small religious community.

What is covert research?

Earlier in this chapter, we discussed Gold's (1958) four field roles that a researcher conducting observational based research can adopt. His *complete participant* role is a covert position. Most ethnographers assume *participant-as-observer* or *observer-as-participant* positions within their research predominantly for ethical reasons, as field subjects can give fully informed consent, and also for practical purposes – being open about your observer role allows you to ask new questions or change data collection techniques when needed. Covert research is when researchers hide their role and identity as 'researchers' and assume a role/identity that allows them to fit fully into the field setting. As with all observer roles, there are advantages and disadvantages to this approach.

Covert participant observation has a long history within ethnography, examples of which include Festinger *et al.*'s (1956) study of an apocalyptic UFO cult; Goffman's (1961) and Rosenhan's (1973) studies of life in mental health institutions; Humphreys' (1970) study of gay sex in public toilets; Fielding's (1982) study of far right-wing groups; Holdaway's work on police 'canteen culture' (1983); Fountain's (1993) work on drug dealers; Scheper-Hughes' (2004) study of organ traffickers; and Calvey's (2008) research on night club bouncers. This is a disparate list of topics but there is one common denominator that provides insight into why these researchers chose this research technique: they were all researching 'closed' or 'hidden' social worlds.

Gaining access to such groups, whether closed religious communities, individuals involved in illegal activities or other forms of hard-to-access organizations, is the key motivation for doing covert research. More often than not, covert research is the only way the researcher will be able to investigate that social world. This remains the main attraction of a technique that, Calvey (2008) contends, has become 'stigmatized' due to the growth and power of the 'ethics industry' that has emerged in the social sciences over the past thirty years (the emergence and growth of the 'ethics industry' is discussed in Chapters 2 and 3 of this book).

I chose to do covert research because I too sought to access a 'closed' community, in this case 'God's Way' community[2] a small group of fundamentalist Christians living in isolation in the Midwest of the USA (Scott 1996, 1997, 2001). The group are apocalyptic and believe that they are specifically the 'chosen' people of God who will survive the coming and eagerly anticipated end of the world. 'God's Way' try to minimize contact with the world around them, restricting entry to the community's ranch to prospective members and only leaving their home for economic necessity (they did contract farm work for local commercial farmers). Therefore, the only way to access this group was through covert research. However, why choose such a difficult field setting when it poses such ethical and practical challenges? The simple answer is intellectual curiosity to explore a specific social world that is interesting – the reason most researchers would give for their subject choice. If we did not do covert research, we might argue, important subcultures and groups would remain 'hidden' from view and understanding. I chose 'God's Way' because I wanted to explore how a small group of Christians can maintain the belief that they are uniquely 'chosen' by God and that the end of the world is coming. This is an extraordinary worldview to uphold, maintain and, like Festinger et al.'s study (1956), I wanted to explore how this belief is constructed and reinforced through everyday life; not to mention what happens when the planned end of the world does not happen and has to be rescheduled.

Gaining access

One of the central problems facing the covert researcher is gaining access to their field setting. 'Closed' groups have clear boundaries and barriers to 'outsiders' that make gaining entry difficult. How researchers negotiate such barriers is the key to successful access. I came across 'God's Way' by accident; I had been writing to the leaders of a variety of religious and ethical communities in the USA, some 'closed', some open to 'outsiders', for the first five months of my doctoral studies. These letters introduced who I was and I gave my background as a student researcher interested in their community and belief systems. Thus, at this stage, my research was overt, but it should be stressed that I included a note of ambiguity into my introduction by presenting myself as a student but also as a 'seeker' of alternative ways of living.

Therefore, I presented a dual identity; this was not a deliberate lie, as at that time I was interested in seeking out a new way of living.

I received a variety of replies and invitations to visit. My initial intention had been to explore the nature of communal living and how communities that are intentionally founded construct their belief or meaning systems. However, I soon began to become more interested in the religious groups and a letter from the leader of 'God's Way', which outlined their belief system, interested me enough to want to visit. 'Isaac' the group's leader wrote several times outlining their belief system and in my replies, I stressed an interest in visiting but also played-up my 'seeker' role. 'Isaac' passed my correspondence on to 'Rachel' his niece and she became my new correspondent from the community. We wrote to each other for the next six months during which it became clear that the group was interpreting my interest as a 'sign' from God and that I was a new member to be 'brought from overseas'. I went along with this deception, as it was clear from 'Isaac's' initial letters that only potential members could visit the community. Gatekeepers are a common feature of most forms of research (Bryman, 2008) but covert research particularly means that the researcher will have to work with a gatekeeper, whether it is a gang leader or a cult leader; this individual is the key to 'getting-in'. Gatekeepers are useful in that they have the power to grant you access into and within a social group; they can provide an important overview of the group. However, they are problematic in that over association with them may make other group members suspicious and also they have the power to withhold access. 'Isaac' was my gatekeeper; as the group's leader, he alone had the power to grant access and he was the key figure in my construction as a new member who was 'God sent' which got me 'in'. 'Rachel' played the role of my 'key' informant who gave me enough information, through her letters about the group, to be able to construct a convincing role as a 'new member' and whilst living in the group I shared a room with her which allowed us to form a close friendship and further facilitated my entrée into the group. We genuinely became friends during my fieldwork and my later 'coming out' as a researcher was precipitated by my desire to no longer lie to someone whom I considered a friend.

Playing a role

The other key problem facing covert ethnographers is the fact that they must hide their 'true' identity as a researcher and assume and perform a 'new' social identity and role. This is challenging on several levels. First, the identity must be convincing to allow the researcher to 'pass', which means trying to find out as much about the group as you can beforehand; I was fortunate in that my correspondence with them allowed me to build a picture of their basic way of life and how best I could fit into that. I was also lucky in that in the role of 'new member' I was allowed 'role failure', i.e. to make mistakes, as that would be expected of me. Indeed 'failing' was a useful technique to extract further information at times.

Playing a role is not that difficult on one level, as to an extent all of social life involves role playing and most social actors assume that the person in front of them is who they say they are (Goffman 1959). That said 'performances' must be convincing enough and that is stressful on two levels; first, you are always anxious as to whether people will find out who you really are and, second, you rarely have an opportunity to 'relax' your 'performance'. My anxiety about being found out was at its highest during my first month at 'God's Way', when I was hyper-sensitive to every situation and rarely felt relaxed; this was stressful and exhausting. I would dream about being found out and I constantly thought through what I would do if they did find out. My most anxious moment was when I discovered that 'Rachel' had been looking through my things to check which version of the Bible I had brought with me; this made me realize that some checking was being done on me and made me worry as to whether I would 'pass' the test: I did.

Ethnographers often experience 'testing' by participants as a way to see whether they 'pass' into the community; ethnographers might have to think through how far they want to go in 'passing': does it involve illegal activity (Humphreys 1970), expressing views you do not agree with or being involved in acts you disagree with? 'God's Way' expressed deeply racist and homophobic views and, in order to 'pass', I found myself echoing their views despite being appalled by them. On a more mundane level I faced the early 'test' of showing my enjoyment of the community's nightly meal of gritty refried beans and sauerkraut, which had to be eaten with relish and joy despite being close to inedible. Assuming a covert role puts additional pressure on such 'tests', as to fail them or refuse to participate in them threatens to reveal the 'true' identity of the researchers. There may also be situations where ethnographers' 'cover' is threatened in unexpected ways, for example, Calvey's covert identity as a 'bouncer' was almost 'blown' on several occasions when his students recognized him (2008).

The inability fully to 'relax' your identity or be 'backstage' (Goffman 1959) is very challenging on both practical and emotional levels. Practically, it means having to be innovative in recording field notes; I adopted the tried and tested route of 'writing up' in the bathroom (Ditton 1977), as it was the only room in the community where you were left alone without question. Consequently, the others began to worry that I had developed 'tummy troubles'. Writing field notes in a bathroom means you face time constraints and also you have to find a way to conceal the notes once written. I concealed my field notes by posting them back to friends in the UK, after checking that 'Isaac' did not read the mail that members sent; although all mail did go through him he assumed that my letters 'home' were just that.

Emotionally, maintaining a 'false' identity is very stressful and draining; I had not anticipated this as a problem, which was incredibly naïve in retrospect. At times I felt a sense of personality dissonance. My central coping mechanisms were to relish the quiet moments that community life offered:

living in a community without any internal doors (bar the bathrooms) and where you were never alone (bar the bathroom) meant that noise and interaction were never far away. I seized on quiet times to escape into my thoughts: lying awake in bed before sleep overtook me; daydreaming while doing the repetitive farm labouring outside the community; gazing out of the windows of the communal bus as we journeyed to and fro between farm work and 'home'. Going 'into my head', as I would put it, was how I de-stressed and I found myself focusing on what I would do when I left the community; often it would be on seemingly little, inconsequential things, like my recurring fantasy, while doing the hot and dusty labouring, of the anticipated delight of an ice-cold can of fizzy pop (the community only drank water) as soon as I left.

The other opportunity I had to escape the stresses of my role play was in finding a kindred spirit with whom to share 'quiet' downtime; this was 'David' one of the group's single men who loathed the constant noise of the group and constantly sought solitary activities around the ranch. I soon realized that 'David's' way of being in the group, yet emotionally 'taking a break' from it, was in long sessions of chess each evening while the others talked, sang or watched Christian TV. Despite an inability to play chess well, I soon persuaded 'David' to let me join him on the proviso that neither of us spoke. Those nightly games of chess were a useful 'escape' but brought with them an unanticipated and unexpected problem that would facilitate my departure earlier than I had planned; a point to which I will return.

I judged my role performance successful through the fact that I was quickly accepted as a provisional member and assigned to the social category of 'adolescent', which included all single community members, all the teenagers, uninitiated, and any others who were not married with children. Marriage and children brought status and authority in this community; without them you were deemed an eternal teenager, low in the social hierarchy. I was single and uninitiated and so found myself as a 'teenager' again, but this status suited me as it gave me greater licence to make mistakes without damaging my role performance. For example, following the communal evening meal all the dishes were washed by the 'teenagers' (supervised by the older women) in cold water. The water was not heated as it was deemed 'pure' as it came from the communal well. However, using cold water without soap meant that the dishes were rarely truly free of food or stains. My endeavours to fully clean the dishes were seen as 'typical' behaviour of an uninitiated teenager with lots still to learn. I therefore had two field identities to balance: new member and 'teenager'.

Exit strategies

The conclusion of this book makes the point that ethnographers rarely fully leave the field in an emotional or spiritual sense: however, they usually physically leave it at some stage, often never to return. In overt research, leaving the field is physically and socially easy, if emotionally difficult. However, in covert research, where one has been living for some time in a different identity, departure needs careful consideration. Again, naïve as I was, I had not considered my exit strategy before starting my research: I had been so focused on 'getting in' that I omitted to think how I would 'get out'. If you are planning to do covert research such naïveté should be avoided. While living in the community I began to think through my departure. My initial plan had been to stay until I neared my initiation ceremony (it took a year to get to a stage of being ready for initiation) which would make me a 'full' member: I planned to say I was having 'doubts' and needed to leave the community for a short time to reflect. 'David' had told me that his sister 'Martha' had done this (although she did return) and 'Isaac' had accepted it as 'God's will'. I, of course, planned not to return and instead would write to 'Rachel' explaining my doubts.

However, as can happen in field research, events overtook me very quickly. I had been in the community for ten months and was in the midst of preparing for 'initiation' with some of the other 'teenagers', when I suddenly found myself engaged to 'David', my chess partner. Our months of nightly chess had been interpreted by the community's senior members as a 'sign' that we wanted to marry each other; why else would we set ourselves apart? It needs to be noted that the community did not allow outward signs of affection between couples, so any form of romantic courtship between the sexes had to be opaque. I had not anticipated that our behaviour would have been viewed in this light: 'David' welcomed the 'engagement' as he had given up hope of achieving the 'adult' status of married man, as there were no women on the community that he was not related to either by blood or marriage and new members rarely joined. The 'engagement' was my signal to leave the community as quickly as possible.

I constructed a 'family emergency' that necessitated me leaving as soon as possible, with the intention of returning. I did this through arranging via mail for a friend in the UK to phone the community in the guise of a relative. The deception worked and I left 'God's Way', promising to return as soon as I could; I did not. I wrote to 'Rachel' in the months following, continuing to pretend that family illness kept me in the UK; then 'Rachel' left the community. She had expressed doubts to me during my stay about living long term in 'God's Way'; she wanted a family life and did not see living in the community as able to give her that. She had thought about leaving and joining her estranged father at his religious community, where there was an opportunity for an arranged marriage of sorts. She wrote in a letter that my departure had encouraged her to leave; that my behaviour had influenced hers. The significance she had placed on our friendship made me question my continuing deception and I wrote to her explaining that my main reason for living at 'God's Way' had been to do research to understand their way of life. Although shocked by my revelation we continued our correspondence for several years until it suddenly stopped.

One condition of our continuing friendship was that 'Rachel' insisted I write to 'Isaac' telling him everything. It was the hardest thing I have ever had to write; his reply was to send the most quoted passage from their sacred scripture, written by their founder (and 'Isaac's' father): '*God sees dust*'. The phrase is used in the daily life of the community to illustrate that not only does God see everything (even dust) but also that the community is like 'dust' in terms of significance to God. 'Rachel' later revealed to me that 'Isaac' had come to view me as 'fallen' but with the potential to be 'saved' if I returned.

Going under cover: behind the 'glamour' and against the myth

Students always find the idea of covert participant observation 'glamorous' and 'exciting', but in reality it is far more mundane and lacking in glamour; I found it dull and monotonous most of the time. It is also very stressful and can be dangerous. But then again, so can overt research. Covert research should only be done when there is no other means to access that social world. Many myths circulate about the wrongs of covert and the rights of overt observation. Access for both can be problematic; in both cases you might need to work with gatekeepers and you will certainly have to build relationships of trust with 'key' informants. You will face 'tests' of your suitability to be a member of the social world in question. Often students think that covert research will give a more 'truthful' picture of the field setting, as the participants will act 'naturally'. This is a myth, as your presence will affect the field setting, whether you are role playing or not, and how are we to really know what 'natural' behaviour is anyway? All forms of participant observation allow the researcher to really experience life in that social world. Overt researchers have more space to relax their role and take 'time outs', but all forms of participant observation are stressful and emotionally draining. Covert researchers may be more at risk from 'going native', as they are more likely to experience personality dissonance, but there are plenty of cases of overt researchers doing so too, as Helen Jones notes in Chapter 3 of this book. Perhaps covert researchers are more likely to be sensitive to this issue and plan against it happening.

The biggest issue that remains about covert versus overt participant observation is the issue of ethics. Several infamous cases of covert research have raised the issue of ethics, for example, Festinger *et al.*'s (1956) team actively encouraged the apocalyptic beliefs of the cult in order to see what would happen when their predicted apocalypse did not happen. Humphreys (1970) not only participated in illegal activity but also violated participants' privacy by tracing their home addresses via car licence plates. Both these cases show a blatant disregard for any form of sensitivity to participants' emotional, legal or human rights. But covert researchers do not necessarily seek to abuse their informants and usually safeguard them in a variety of ways, from using pseudonyms to ensuring that their 'voices' are heard. That was my strategy and I stepped away from encouraging any beliefs beyond what they already held.

Most professional ethical codes caution against covert approaches, for example the British Sociological Association states:

> Covert methods violate the principles of informed consent and may invade the privacy of those being studied. Participant or non-participant observation in non-public spaces or experimental manipulation of research participants without their knowledge should be resorted to only where it is impossible to use other methods to obtain essential data.
>
> (2002: 6)

The central issue is that of informed consent: covert researchers cannot obtain this because to do so would 'blow' their 'cover'. However 'informed consent' cannot always, guarantee that research is fully ethical, as the nature of fieldwork means consent is a fluid concept at best. As Burgess (1984) notes, to what extent is consent sought from every member of a field setting? Practical reasons – such as an organization being too big to get consent from everyone (Punch 1994) – may make this impossible. Does this make the research semi-covert? Similarly, as research evolves, the consent given at an earlier stage may not be sought for new lines of enquiry; does that make the research covert? Lugosi (2006), among others, makes the point that, even with consent sought and given, researchers still conceal information or aspects of identity, and ultimately choose what data is or is not used. To an extent, most field research requires a more flexible or situational approach to ethics, and it is naïve of any researcher to assume that an overt role, combined with signed informed consent forms, means that research is fully ethical.

That said, there is a moral case that covert research is wrong as it involves deceiving people in a deliberate and sustained fashion. To me, covert research brings with it tremendous guilt that is hard to come to terms with: trusted friendships were built on lies and deceiving honest and decent people is not something to be proud of. Myself and most other covert ethnographers would make the case, however, that this form of research is vital to allow us to access social worlds which might remain 'hidden'. It could be argued that the insights provided by covert work – such as that of Wallis (1976) and Barker (1984), that challenged stereotypes of religious groups; or Goffman's (1961) and Rosenhan's (1973) work, that raised awareness of the treatment and stereo-typing of mental health patients; or the insights into racism provided by Fielding's (1982) study of far right-wing groups and Holdaway's (1983) study of the police – outweigh the broader ethical or moral arguments.

Inside out

In this chapter, we have defined the different roles and memberships that researchers can adopt and, inherent within those, the question of whether research should be overt or covert. As outlined by Helen Jones in Chapter 3, for most researchers the decision will be quite straightforward, in that ethics and, in particular, university ethics boards will be highly influential in determining the level of participation we are 'allowed' to undertake. Our respective research experiences discussed in this chapter have highlighted both overt research in the British Civil Service and covert research conducted in a small religious group in the Midwest of the United States: two very different settings and two very different groups. Reading this chapter, your interest may well be caught up in the intrigue of the covert researched group, whereas the overt research may well seem quite pedestrian. However, both serve to illustrate that the role of the participant observer requires much thought and planning. We have both acknowledged that, in various respects, we approached our respective researches with a degree of naïveté and, similarly, we both made mistakes. Neither role is easy, but covert participation, in particular, is very difficult, stressful and certainly not something to be entered into lightly. However, having said that, there are some groups whose identity and activities are not fully known and so it can be argued that the only way to extend knowledge and understanding of such groups is to enter via covert means. In reconciling this approach, there is an argument for 'means–ends justification', which is basically what it sounds like: can the means by which something is learned justify the methods used to learn it? Bearing in mind ethical codes of conduct laid down across the social sciences, for example by the British Psychological Society, the British Sociological Association and so on, researchers have to take responsibility for the design decisions they make and, as this chapter has illustrated, these are not easy decisions and they are not taken lightly.

Suggested further reading

Adler, P. A. and Adler, P. (1994) 'Observational techniques', in N. K. Denzin and Y. S. Lincoln (eds) *Handbook of Qualitative Research*, London: Sage.

Festinger, L., Riecken, H. W. and Schachter, S. (1956) *When Prophecy Fails*, New York: Harper Row.

Goffman, E. (1961) *Asylums: Essays on the Social Situation of Mental Patients and Other Inmates*, London: Penguin.

Humphreys, L. (1970) *Tearoom Trade: Impersonal Sex in Public Places*, London: Duckworth.

Whyte, W. F. (1955) *Street Corner Society*, Chicago: University of Chicago Press.

Willis, P. E. (1977) *Learning to Labour: How Working Class Kids get Working Class Jobs*, New York: Columbia University Press.

Reflective activities

1 With a partner, design a small piece of participant observation that you can conduct together for a duration of 30 minutes. The observation must be overt and it must follow social science ethical guidelines. There are several advantages of conducting an observation as a pair: you can design this together, ensure you look out for each other at the research location and you will be able to see if you observed similar or different things. Choose a public social location that you have access to and one where your observation will not be intrusive to the people around you. Consider the following:

   a First, where will you conduct your observation? For example, a shopping mall, sports event, theatre, café etc.?
   b What ethical considerations do you need to be mindful of?
   c Where will you situate yourself? Together or separately? Why?
   d How will you take notes of your observation? What will these notes look like?
   e When you have conducted your research, sit together and compare your field notes. Are there differences or similarities?
   f Either together or separately, analyse your field notes, what themes have you come up with? How would you write these up?
   g What would you do differently next time? Discuss with your partner what worked and what did not.

2 Again, this is a paired exercise. In this chapter, you read about overt and covert participant observation. With your partner discuss:

   a Whether you think that in some field settings there is an argument for 'means–ends justification' in relation to covert research?
   b If you do not think there is an argument for 'means–ends justification', what other methods could be used to generate data to learn more about, for example, an unknown subculture or 'closed' group?

Notes

1 See the end of this chapter for suggestions for further reading.
2 A pseudonym.

9

BETWEEN PARTISAN AND FAKE, WALKING THE PATH OF THE INSIDER

Empowerment and voice in ethnography

John E. Goldring

The purpose of this chapter is to explore the challenges and constraints that arise when taking an emancipatory approach to conducting ethnographic research. Emancipatory, liberatory or critical approaches to research are not merely concerned with increasing knowledge about specific issues. Rather, at their core is an unequivocal desire to challenge the taken for granted social injustices faced by marginalized groups within society (Kincheloe and McLaren 2008). I will draw on my experiences of conducting my doctoral research, which included participants recruited from a self-help group for men who are in relationships with women, but who are sexually attracted to other men ('gay married men'). The irony is that an unintended consequence of the improving social and legal climate for gay men, since the decriminalization of 'homosexuality' in 1967 in England, will be the increased need for such groups to support those who entered into seemingly heterosexual relationships and are now beginning to question this decision. These are not your 'typical' gay men – 'out and proud', exuding confidence at the local gym or while walking arm in arm with their lovers through city centre gay spaces. They do not fit the gay stereotype of the middle-class, affluent, hedonistic, young, single male, 'up' for a good time and anything he can get. This population quietly goes about their business, trying their best to go unnoticed, invisible in every respect. Many come from a generation exposed to derogatory images and symbolism of what it was to be gay, having been brought up at a time when homosexuality was viewed as morally questionable, deeply perverted and routinely punished. They have never demanded equal rights, joined a 'Pride' march or challenged injustice for fear of drawing attention to themselves. It has been easier simply to avoid addressing the issue of sexual orientation in the hope that it might go away. However, the late modern social climate that exists in the UK has meant that, to some degree, being gay is much less of an issue. Gay men are now much more visible and vocal in all walks of life. It is under these improving social conditions that a generation of older gay man has started to explore their sexuality anew.

I will be calling this group of men 'gay married men' for reasons of convenience rather than accuracy. There is no need to identify as 'gay', 'bi' or 'straight', nor to be married in order to be part of this population. A more accurate description would be 'men in long-term relationships with women but who are sexually attracted to other men'. But this somehow has less impact when conjuring up what this group of men represents. These are a silent minority within a minority. What connects them is their invisibility and their lack of meaningful control in many areas of their lives. Little is known about this group of men, yet some estimates suggest that around 20 per cent of gay men have been previously married (Alessi 2008).

Empowerment through ethnography?

The focus of this chapter will be the 'process' of ethnography, not the product or actual accounts from gay married men. This is quite a 'messy' process, which will be 'sanitized' for the sake of the chapter. What I will focus on are the tensions that surface when blending research in an applied setting with an emancipatory agenda. The claim is that ethnography has the potential to empower and improve the social conditions of minority groups (Goodley 1999; Truman 2000). What is less clear is just how ethnography does this. Fawcett and Hearn (2004) regard the empowerment agenda of social research as having the potential to constrain as well as facilitate. Further, what is meant by 'empowerment' within the social sciences also reveals a lack of clarity (Cheung et al. 2005; Rissel 1994). At an interpersonal level, the common theme the literature highlights is that of 'control' (or lack of control). For instance, Rappaport (1981), a key theorist on the subject, suggests that empowerment relates to the increased possibility for people to control their own lives. Perkins and Zimmerman suggest empowerment is 'a process by which people gain control over their lives, [and] democratic participation in their community' (1995: 570). For Maton and Salem, empowerment relates to 'the active, participatory process of gaining resources or competencies needed to increase control over one's life and accomplish important life goals' (1995: 631).

Another challenge faced by ethnography surrounds the adequacy with which the stories of those who occupy less powerful social positions are represented or reconstructed (Fawcett and Hearn 2004; Olesen 2008). The vexatious question of how to 'give voice' without exploiting or distorting has been a feminist dilemma for some time now (Olesen 2008). With the 'crisis of representation' it is unclear if the 'voices' we give our subjects are the ones they would necessarily choose for themselves (Fawcett and Hearn 2004; Hammersley 1990a; Olesen 2008). What is clear in contemporary research is how the participants are central to all stages of the research process (Olesen 2008; Truman 2000). What this actually means seems to vary enormously from researcher to researcher. I will therefore be using members of the self-help support group as a critical case to explore the grandiose claims made for ethnography.

The research context

The chapter draws on my doctoral research, conducted between 2001 and 2007 in Greater Manchester. Manchester has a highly visible gay scene called the 'Gay Village' that has featured in TV dramas such as *Queer as Folk* (for more on gay Manchester, see Hindle 1994, 2001). The general theme of my work explored gay intimate relationships, social capital and health in the gay community. Ethnography has a long tradition of researching intimate relationships. I found Bott (1971) and Cornwell (1984) particularly useful as they presented grounded and approachable accounts of the norms and practices of 'typical' family life. Of course, their research was carried out at a time when the social and legal climate made it very difficult to research any issues related to gay men. More recently there has been the growth of research projects exploring lesbian and gay relationships. An especially approachable and thorough book is by Weeks *et al.* (2001), who, among other things, explore the growth of 'families of choice'. Their research, in common with that of many others, has tended to focus on the more visible factions of the gay communities. The approach I took when conducting my fieldwork was not to rely on the 'Gay Village' as the main source of recruitment. While this would have been the easy option, it would have resulted in a highly restricted sample lacking the diversity of experience needed in this exploratory study that was intended to expand our understanding of what it was to be a gay man. I therefore started looking beyond the 'gay scene' at the 'hidden' populations of the gay community. Getting off the 'beaten track' (Wood and Duck 1995) revealed a somewhat 'awkward' field of exploration. The diversity that existed was astounding.

An insider's perspective

Quite early into the research I made contact with a 'disgraced' vicar who had been 'defrocked' after 'coming out' as a gay man. He indicated that he might have an interesting story to tell, as he had also been married and was now running a self-help group for other gay married men which at the time was called 'Options'. Adopting the ethnographic principle of immersion, or Whyte's (1955) notion of 'being there', I quickly immersed myself into this group and began building trusting relationships with the membership. However, matters became complicated when, in 2003, the principal volunteer could no longer commit to running the group. This left me with a choice. Either I would also have to leave, which would have led to the group's demise, or I would have to run the group myself.

At this point it seems sensible to declare my interest in this group. I was once that gay married man. As a working-class man, growing up in a working-class mill village in Lancashire, marriage was not just 'normal' but expected. Clearly, my background and past experiences influenced how I came to work within this group. In the first instance, my 'insider knowledge' provided me with access into the 'hidden' worlds of gay married men. It is questionable whether anyone can claim to speak for others deemed 'similar' in their oppression or discursive construction (Fawcett and Hearn 2004). Yet it seems plausible that my shared sense of marginality influenced my decision to include the accounts of gay married men in the original research. Therefore, in presenting the accounts of this group of men, I make no claims to objectivity, neutrality or expertise in this matter. Commenting on such notions, Denscombe contends that:

> research that sets out to promote the interests of a particular group or individual – which seeks to empower them – does not claim to be impartial, neutral or open-minded about the topic of inquiry, the notion of 'partisan research' has been challenged as an oxymoron – a figure of speech which combines contradictory terms so as to create a new notion.
>
> (2002: 165)

Objectivity is therefore an illusion (Fine 1993; Foley and Valenzuela 2008). Within feminist research, there is a view that objectivity relates to male dominant values (Fawcett and Hearn 2004; Olesen 2008). I would go further to suggest that, disguised in the notion of 'scientific objectivity', is the dominant heterosexual bias that historically positioned gay and bisexual men as deviant 'Others'. I therefore offer no apologies for my thoroughly partial account. It is nevertheless important to stress that this is not my story as an ex-gay married man. This chapter explores the issues that I encountered when working as a researcher with this group. Faced with the choice of leaving the group or running it, I decided to stay and I am still there today midway through 2009. The group has since been renamed the Gay Married Men's Group (GMMG).

There are many levels at which the group offers support to its members:

- Supportive and safe social setting: twice monthly, face-to-face meetings where members can work through their problems, share experiences and 'feel comfortable in their own skin'.
- Access to knowledge and information via literature and through other group members.
- Peer support and friendship where members are encouraged to interact outside of the group setting.
- Online support via a dedicated webpage and MSN forum called 'gaymarriedmen', which has over 700 members.

There is a great deal of work that goes on 'behind the scenes', such as telephone calls, email and other electronic messages, and liaising with other similar groups. We tend not to get bogged down with labels that could limit the opportunities of the membership so while the group's name uses both 'gay' and 'married', neither are necessary preconditions of joining. The primary goal of the GMMG is to offer peer support and friendship in a positive and empowering setting (be it online or face-to-face). Here members are encouraged to explore issues around their relationships, and how their 'fluid' sexual orientation complicates their social lives. One of the main aims of the group is to promote personal growth, which is achieved by members taking control of their own destinies. It is not the intent of the group to 'persuade' members of their sexual orientation or the superiority of living a gay lifestyle. Nor is it to suggest they leave or 'cheat' on their wives and families. We offer little advice, but encourage the exchange of stories in the hope that, in this way, others are able to explore the options open to them.

The invisible man

What became immediately noticeable when building up a picture of this group is how there were no 'typical' members. A diverse range of people have attended the group: middle-class professionals, working-class labourers, members with various physical and mental disabilities, or from different ethnicities and religious backgrounds, including Evangelical Christians, Catholics, Muslims and those of us with no religion. What they have in common is that, despite improving social and legal conditions for gay men, their social and relational infrastructure continues to silence and disempower them.

The commonly shared experience is that of utter despair. Many of the members talk of their sense of social isolation, feelings of guilt, shame and worthlessness. Gay married men face multiple disadvantages. Their lifelong attempts to conceal their sexual orientation make them feel their lives are precarious. However, because they exist in a kind of 'no man's land', neither in the 'gay' or 'straight' world, their unique needs are easily missed. Their general lack of self-worth or esteem can lead to, among other things, drink and drug problems. The necessity to conceal their sexual orientation means it is difficult for this population to directly vocalize their needs in terms of health and well-being. Their level of disempowerment goes unrecognized, partly because of the hidden nature of the group and partly because, as seemingly heterosexual men, there is an assumption that they are without need. Their 'traditional' social networks (wife, close family and friends) cannot be utilized as to do so would raise difficult questions. In some instances, they are also unable to call on the medical profession for help because, again, this could 'out' them as gay to the family doctor, a risk that many simply will not take.

It is clear that being in this position places great strain on their psychological and emotional well-being. Many experience severe mental health issues and, as a consequence, pose a serious suicide risk (Alessi 2008: 195). There are instances of prolonged periods of illness, and early retirement due to ill health (Goldring 2007). Those who have been through the medical and psycho-therapeutic process have often received less than professional treatment. A recent article by Bartlett *et al.* (2009) found that even in today's social climate, a 'significant minority' of mental health professionals were still willing to 'help' lesbian, gay and bisexual clients become heterosexual, despite there being no evidence that such practices actually work. Coupled with this is a general lack of understanding from the mental health professionals, who either miss the significance of sexual orientation, or suggest that the men are to 'blame' for their and their families' situation, or offer inappropriate advice that they either 'commit to the marriage or leave it' (Alessi 2008: 195).

Alessi (2008) recounts his professional encounters with several gay married men. As a gay therapist, he reflects how he misjudged the complexities faced by those struggling with their sexual orientation in long-term relationships with women. In what he termed as 'counter transference', he relates instances where he thought it would be in the best interest of his clients to persuade them to leave their wives and live as gay men. Through professional supervision and reflection, he now acknowledges how this would have had catastrophic consequences for the men in question. This illustrates how even those profes-sionals who are themselves gay know so little about men in this situation. It seems that the oppositional discourse establishing gay rights struggles to include those considered 'still in the closet'. They seem to be treated as in a state of flux, or as potentially 'happy homosexuals'. The assumption is that gay married men simply need help finding the firm ground from which to make the leap into the gay world. However, some gay married men do not want to leave their wives or adopt a gay identity.

There also seems to be a lack of sympathy for them because of the assumption that they must have known they were gay before getting married and, as such, are responsible for their plight. This reactionary attitude neglects the enormous societal pressures to conform to heterosexuality and marriage. It is a powerful discourse that positions the men as the 'villains of the piece' and their spouses as the 'victims' of a massive lie. Potentially, the reality is that they have both become victims of a heterosexist society that validates and valorizes heterosexual relationships while devaluing all 'others'. However, this moralizing blame culture creates a lack of social justice that situates the gay married man in a vulnerable position and open to excessive claims in divorce cases where they are willing to sacrifice almost everything to reduce the feelings of guilt. They too are victims of the blame discourse and often consider the situation 'to be their fault'. There are no simple answers to the problems faced by this group of men. The reality for this population is that they are 'excluded' from both the 'gay' and 'straight' mainstream.

The great pretender: I'm a fake!

Upon immersing myself in the group, one of the main issues I had to readdress were the ethical protocols I had set in place regarding my research. They seemed suitable for a more predictable style of research, where notions of confidentiality, anonymity and 'do no harm' are most salient. However, entering into the world of the gay married man made my ethics look woefully inadequate. How, for instance, would I address issues of protecting participants from potential harm when taking part in the research? This was, after all, a particularly vulnerable group. The Social Research Association (SRA 2003) guidelines suggest that what needs summing up is the 'equation' between risk to the participant in taking part in the research and the possible benefits that the research could bring to society. This was not quite as simple as when conducting participant observation with more 'traditional' groups. Nor was it straightforward to access, recruit, interview and withdraw. The marginal social status of gay men in general had led me to an ethical position of caution over the strong desire to collect data. Yet in relation to gay married men, 'being there' had greater potential of harm that went beyond confidentiality and anonymity. The power imbalances between the group members and myself required further consideration.

Superficially, we looked like social equals: equally powerful/powerless. However, the social cleavage between us had considerable potential to disempower. Consider for a moment my personal circumstances. My gay married man status was from some time in the past. Before 'coming out' as gay, I was crippled with self-doubt and lacked any sense of self-worth. Nevertheless 'coming out', leaving my wife, and immersing myself in gay culture was the defining moment in my life. I felt a surge of clarity that put me in control of my own destiny and from which I was able to reconnect with all of society's structures. I went into full-time education, first at college, then university and later embarked on a PhD. To say I am 'evangelical' about this would be something of an understatement. Therefore, to some extent, acknowledging my presence, cultural legacy and biography is more than a methodological issue but can be seen as an ethical matter as well. Method-ologically, it appeared relatively easy to present myself in several meaningful ways with which the group members could identify; 'John the former gay married man'; 'John the journeyman'; and 'John the volunteer', 'researcher', 'interested party', etc. Adopting these strategies when in the field can help 'normalize' the presence of the researcher in the group, as Mahoney points out: 'the more I revealed about myself in these settings, the easier it was for other group members to get to know me better and make judgements about my character – and vice versa' (2007: 587). Mahoney was conducting research on aspects of the UK gay community from the position of being a Canadian. His dual identities positioned him as both 'insider' ('gay') and 'outsider' ('foreign'). Presenting his various identities helped him to position himself as a 'trusted insider'. I also found it necessary to present to the group members what I was not: 'John not a counsellor'; 'John not a social worker'; and 'John not a potential boyfriend'. It was not necessarily about constructing boundaries between us, but rather defining the limits of my experience: what I could and could not do. Therefore, while on the surface, it was relatively easy to present myself in meaningful ways from which it would be possible to build up a trusting relationship, the ethical considerations of how my presence could affect the group members needed careful consideration.

For instance, could my status as an 'out' gay man in a long-term relationship have the potential to disempower those still struggling with their sexual orientation? It was not possible for me to step outside or disguise my biography and past experience as, without them, it would not have been possible to access this group. It would also be 'dishonest' and not good research governance. Ribbons and Edwards have previously addressed this dilemma and asked where the limits of 'self revelation' are set. They suggest that:

> If we reflexively make ourselves visible within our research as embodying and constituting those edges, we may run the risk of muting the voices of our research participants. Yet on the other hand, if we do not do this, we perpetuate the illusion that we are not actively present in the data collection, analysis and writing of our research.
>
> (1998: 204)

In my case, being too 'evangelical' about my biography could be viewed as either inspirational or oppressive.

I therefore needed to consider the degree of disclosure I would make to the group members. Good research governance suggests honesty, but this is not as straightforward as it at first appears. Fine (1993) presents three degrees of honesty that researchers can adopt. 'Deep cover', he suggests, is where the researcher's role is not made clear, making this approach akin to covert participant observation (or dishonesty). At the other end of the continuum is where the researcher is explicit about the goals and hypotheses of the research, but there are concerns over the extent that this could affect the research (too honest?). There is a middle ground which Fine termed 'shallow cover', which is where 'the ethnographer announces the research intent but is vague about the goals' (1993: 276). The exploratory nature of the research meant I could be quite candid about the broad aims and objectives of the research.

Through my 'insider' status and 'shallow cover', I quickly immersed myself within the group and was able to position myself as friend and trusted confidant. I began to build up a picture of the issues the members faced. In the initial stages, the high levels of distress the members experienced led me to question the legitimacy of 'being there'. Was I developing my academic career on the misery of others? It would have been procedurally easier to observe the group members' interactions, 'write up' my field notes, interview those I felt offered the most to the research and then withdraw. This felt exploitative and akin to 'knowledge rape'. Classical ethnography has a somewhat torrid history of past abuses of power that put the research above the well-being of the researched.

For instance, reflect on Laud Humphreys' (1970) *Tearoom Trade*. This ethnographic research adopted 'deep cover' and covert means by which to observe men engaging in sex with other men in public 'restrooms'. Not only did he deceive his research subjects and conceal the real purpose for his 'being there', but he also traced them back to their homes via their car number plates. The potential harm that could have come to his research participants is incomprehensible. While Humphreys makes for interesting reading, it also illuminates the exploitative potential of ethnographic research, hence my unease as a researcher in this particular field. He put the desire to collect data above the needs of those he was studying. His deceit made it impossible for them to resist. The power balance between the researcher and the researched rested firmly on his side while his subjects played a bit part in their own story.

With contemporary ethnography, researchers increasingly acknowledge their own presence and explore the impact of the research on those taking part. Addressing the power imbalance between the researcher and researched is a particularly salient point:

> The research is very often focused on relatively powerless groups with the researcher exploiting their powerlessness to carry out the research. ... And even where researcher and researched are social equals, power is still involved because it is the researcher who makes the decisions about what is to be studied, how, for what purposes, etc.
>
> (Hammersley 1990a: 13)

The issues here relate to who has the right to research 'Others'? Historically, as discussed in Chapters 2 and 3, research has been carried out by white, middle-class, heterosexual academics. The new social movements, such as the lesbian and gay movement, feminism, and the disability rights movement have started to challenge whether it is appropriate or legitimate for those with no direct experience or immediate point of identification with those they are researching to research the 'Other' (Fawcett and Hearn 2004). The tension relates to whether such a depth of understanding is needed to produce authentic accounts of the lived experience of the oppressed group. This seems a valid point, but raises other concerns, in that adopting this stance could replicate the oppression the research sets out to challenge. Similarly, it is an essentialist argument to assume that because two or more people share a common experience of marginalization, they are the same. I clearly fell into this category of having direct experience and point of identification, but this did not make the group members and me social equals, nor mean that the power relations between us did not need addressing. I still felt like a fake!

My awkwardness did not come from the sense of 'Was I deceiving the group?' as I was not. Nor did it come from what Fine (1995: 271) described

134

as the 'agony of betrayal', where he notes how ethnographers present an illusion of 'sympathy' towards their participants to aid their research. As he points out, ethnographers cannot 'like' everyone but tend to 'gloss' over this. To some degree, I had experienced this in a previous piece of ethnographic research, where I had been able to use my working-class status to access a socially deprived community (see Sixsmith *et al.* 2003). In that project, I did give an impression of sympathetic understanding towards many of the participants I encountered, but managed to maintain a degree of distance and detachment from those who took part. I certainly did not like everyone who took part in the research, but, rather, respected them.

Yet, at the same time, the nature of ethnography will surely mean that friendships develop between the researcher and at least some of the researched. This was certainly the case for Mahoney (2007), who makes great play of the strength of the friendships that came about in the course of his ethnographic research. With the current research, however, my 'insider' status bestowed upon me a 'genuine' empathy towards members of the group. Moreover, while I did not 'like' every member, it would have been difficult to remain aloof from some of them, with whom I developed close and friendly relations. Yet, in spite of this, the fact remained that I chose to be there for the purpose of research, while they were there for support. What seemed to be causing me the most anxiety was the clash between my multiple roles of researcher, volunteer, trusted confidant and friend.

The curse of reflection

It seemed that one way to overcome my uneasiness within this group was to find ways I could contribute to the group. Gomm (2004) has suggested how participatory research can focus on direct benefits to the group, and only secondarily on the knowledge produced for use by others. I wanted to put the needs of the group if not above, then at least level with the requirement for data. I began to see my role in the group as less about data collection and more about the emancipatory agenda. Adopting this stance meant I was able to 'put something back' rather than just take from the group or 'return the favor' (Fine 1993: 272). Becoming the principal volunteer allowed me to achieve this. But doing so opened up the proverbial 'can of worms', and a plethora of other issues that would need addressing.

A key issue related to the extent my more active role would influence the nature of the group. As a researcher, I was there to observe and collect data. As the main volunteer, I had to ensure the success of the group. It was unclear to what extent it was appropriate, or not, to influence the direction of the group. Fine (1993: 281) suggests that we need not worry excessively about the researcher presence 'as long as the impact is not excessively directive or sub-stantive'. The difficulty is, as he goes on to point out, realistically, 'participant observation often becomes participant intervention' (1993: 287). Clearly, adopting the role of principal volunteer for the group meant I was also influencing the direction of the group's proceedings.

At the group level, I had developed a web page,[1] had promotional material made, chaired the meetings and introduced topics of conversation, applied for grants, liaised with professionals at the Lesbian and Gay Foundation (LGF) among a host of other day-to-day activities. There was clearly a clash between the research influencing the group and the effectiveness of the group. I could not offer any guarantees that my input would be minimal or free from direction. For instance, one recurrent theme discussed within the group related to a desire to meet other gay married men. On one level, this seemed quite a sensible strategy, as then both men would have the necessary understanding of each other's life and commitments and so be able to offer support. However, enmeshed within these accounts was a sexual element, and the assumption that having sex with men in a similar position was in some way safer in terms of HIV transmission.

This highlighted how some in the group had a general lack of knowledge and understanding about gay issues. After all, they had not lived as gay men, why would they? It seemed that they lapsed back into a discourse, thinking that HIV only related to 'gay men'. My research had brought me into contact with many of the issues surrounding safer sex, making it possible to explore how such risks can be properly managed. I therefore felt I had to point out the advantages of practising safer sex, along with the catastrophic consequences of failing to do so. As a friend, how could I not? I would like to think that, in some respects, there was an element of Vygotsky's (1978) socio-cultural theory of the 'Zone of Proximal Development' embedded in the group, in that learning was socially supported by a more experienced party.

In truth, participating in the group made me feel extremely powerful compared to the members, who, for all intents and purposes, were at the start of their 'gay career' (Goldring 2007). Did my lengthier 'gay career' bestow on me wisdom I could impart to others? Perhaps I was behaving like a concerned parent. So as well as addressing my feelings of inauthenticity, I also needed to explore my motives for choosing to get involved with the group. Constantly reflecting on my position and role within the group seemed at times like a curse, instilling doubts about my 'insider' role and my basis for 'being there'. This was no act of altruism, nor was it simply about me getting another qualification. We shared several forms of social relations in that we all identified as males who, through our 'non-heterosexuality' and relationships with women, had experienced psychological distress. My initial research agenda had been influenced by the involvement of the participants in unforeseen ways. I could neither escape my own experience of marginalization as a former gay married man nor ignore my privileged social position as 'apprentice' academic, imbued with practical 'facts' and health tips. What I could do, however, was acknowledge them and keep a close scrutiny on how my presence in the group could empower, disempower or smother.

Gently elevating the quiet voices

Acknowledging the power of my presence as a researcher helped resolve my feeling that the research relationship was in some way exploitative. The bigger picture was not my inability to 'decentre' from the group, but rather, how I could quietly tell the stories of a group of men. Shouting 'injustice' from the rooftops would most likely have members 'running for the hills'. In essence, I was not necessarily attempting to 'give voice', but rather quietly elevate the voices of those men still silenced by heterosexism and fears over discrimination. The emancipatory approach I had adopted meant the research might 'do some good' to group members directly, and to other men in this situation more generally.

Looking at the group itself, you might think it difficult to paint a positive picture of many of these men, who face such tremendous anguish. Yet there have been some great success stories. Attending the GMMG allowed members to escape the silence that engulfed their sexuality. When some men first attend the group they are trembling with fear and anxiety, often failing to hold back their tears as they search for words to describe their lives. Some talk about their attempts at suicide, of tossing coins: heads they leave their wife, tails they kill themselves. However, the changes can be fast and sudden. An early sign was catching a brief smile on someone's face. It had been such a long time since they had found much to smile about and the smiles led to laughter leading to boisterousness, jokes and good old-fashioned male banter. Consequently, the strength of the group did not come from members being offered advice or receiving benefits from the group. As Cheung *et al.* state:

> by entering into social relations with other people faced with similar problems and participating in activities of the group, self-help group members are able to generate social capital in the form of personal empowerment that, in turn, increases the benefits that they could obtain from the group

> (2005: 357)

The applied research setting facilitated the necessary conditions under which members could equip themselves to take advantage of the benefits offered by the group. However, this is just at the group, two hours every other week. What happens outside of the group is important too. Many members have become happy, self-fulfilled individuals. Some start to take and keep control of aspects of their lives, and cut down on the harmful behaviours that once acted as a prop. Some begin to take control of their mental health, finding the strength to cut down and eventually stop taking the anti-depressants, while others acknowledge the need to seek help and perhaps start medical treatments. Some start to renew their contribution to family life. 'Be the best person you can' is the only advice the group offers, be it the best husband, father, son, uncle, friend and so on, rather than let the guilt paralyse and limit them. These are the success stories, and how success is measured. Therefore, at this level, the 'process of the ethnography' has the ability to be empowering; in this instance, by supporting the environment from which gay married men can empower themselves through exploring their sexual orientation. However, I cannot help but think of all those who have not been able to take advantage of what the group has to offer. Where are their voices in this account?

Of course, whether 'giving voice' is enough to evoke social change is questionable (Gorelick 1996). Clearly, knowing about oppression is worthless without the will to challenge it (Fawcett and Hearn 2004; Truman 2000). Nevertheless, how do we begin to challenge injustice without knowing it? It must be easy for those who occupy inherently powerful positions to reject the identity politics of difference (Villenas 2000). However, it is worth thinking about the causes of oppression in this population. It is not brought about by the fluidity of sexual orientation, or the fact that gay men enter into long-term relationships with women. To think that would be to blame the victim and focus on the wound rather than the blade. Rather, it is heterosexism, prejudice and a general lack of understanding that oppress this group. Consequently, to 'give voice' (however feebly) has the potential to be empancipatory and empowering on at least three levels.

First, showing others the daily struggles faced by this group of men starts to raise their profile, or 'give voice'. There is no claim that these accounts are representative of all gay married men. The claim is that an important first step has been taken in quietly elevating the voices of this group who are a disenfranchised population. At this point in time, it seems more important to raise awareness of the unique issues they face. Not only does this let others know of their plight, it also informs others in a similar situation that they are not the only married men in the world to be attracted to other men.

The second way that the current research evokes social change is by including accounts from those on the fringes of the gay community. Gay married men are easily missed out from inclusion in mainstream gay identity. In some respects, it seems that the gay movement has tried to impose a fictional reality to which some cannot subscribe. We need to broaden the definition of what it is to be gay. Doing this challenges the essentialism and hegemony that sustains the narrow gay stereotype of the young, single and sexually promiscuous white male. Confronting this narrow view reveals how current notions of gay identity are not only limited, but also limiting to all those who do not conform to such representations.

The third way social change may be 'provoked' is by reminding us all of the shameful role of the state in sanctioning such discriminatory ideologies. It would be wrong to focus simply on individual acts of homophobia, important though they are. It is also necessary to reflect on the active role the state took when inflicting symbolic and actual violence on gay men. Doing so led to generations going without the social and legal protection afforded the majority population. Gay men have been victim to both institutionalized acts of heterosexism and individual acts of homophobia. Although we currently live in more egalitarian times, gay married men continue to bear the brunt of past acts of discrimination.

Bang!

Writing this chapter has been an emotional rollercoaster that has brought back many painful memories of my own experiences, and experiences where I felt helpless to support adequately some members of the group. I have not received training for this, and I have made many mistakes. Reflecting on some of my methodological decisions, I am now beginning to question my decision to curtail data collection. At the time, when I started to run the group, it seems that my ethical underpinning of 'do no harm' may have overshadowed the potential usefulness that this research could have had for more people facing the same dilemma. I felt uneasy and unable to obtain informed consent from members who were attending the group in search of support. I was concerned that declaring myself a researcher could act as an obstacle to new members receiving support when they most needed it. On reflection, perhaps my past experiences made me too risk-averse. Fortunately, writing this chapter has allowed me to re-evaluate this stance. The Gay Married Men's Group is a rich source of data and, importantly, members' stories deserve to be told. The fact that people have stories to tell and that I have the direct experience to relate and understand them, along with the training, does not necessarily make the relationship exploitative. So why does telling them make me feel so exposed? I wonder what Laud Humphreys felt as he wrote his accounts from the 'Tearooms' of America? Did he realize he would be remembered as the classic case of unethical ethnography? It feels as if I am painting a target on my academic career from which to invite others to judge and shoot: BANG!

Suggested further reading

Bott, E. (1971) *Family and Social Networks: Roles, Norms, and External Relationships in Ordinary Urban Families*, New York: Free Press.

Cornwell, J. (1984). *Hard-earned Lives: Accounts of Health and Illness from East London*, London and New York: Tavistock.

Weeks, J., Heaphy, B. and Donavan, C. (2001) *Same Sex Intimacies: Families of Choice and Other Life Experiments*, New York: Routledge.

Reflective activities

1   An important characteristic of contemporary ethnographic research is the ability to build strong trusting relationships between the researcher and researched. Much of the debate appears to focus on the well-being of those taking part in the research: the participants. However, what about the welfare of the researcher? In this activity, you are asked to:

a Consider whether the strategies that ethnographic research adopts objectify researchers as mere 'research tools'?

b How much of yourself do you feel is appropriate to put into a research process? For instance, just how much personal and private information are you willing to reveal to others? These processes are adopted to aid the building of relationships etc., but this information may be highly sensitive and leave you as a researcher feeling quite exposed.

c What if you favoured some participants over others, would you treat them differently? What about your availability and contactability?

d Is it sensible to have an 'open door' policy or should you take a degree of control over how participants are able to contact you?

2 In this activity, you are asked to reflect on what takes precedence, the research or the participant? Good research governance suggests that a decision must be taken between the need to collect data and the potential harm that this process might do to the participant, versus the good the research can do for society. Many of the members of the Gay Married Men's Group were in distress and in search of support, making it difficult to ask for informed consent. However, being able to collect data and tell others of the seriousness of the situation could be of great benefit to others in a similar situation: where would you draw the line?

Note

1 www.gaymarriedmen.co.uk.

10

OBSERVING WITH A FOCUS

Field notes and data recording

Clive Palmer

The main focus of this chapter is to introduce fieldwork strategies and note-taking, the objective being to lift the act of spectating to that of observing: observing with a focus, in other words – researching. The ethnographic research discussed in this chapter originated from a philosophical enquiry into the artistic evaluation of Men's Artistic Gymnastics. Therefore, a concept of aesthetics in relation to sport and gymnastics in particular, will be examined to help establish a theoretical context from which to follow this ethnographic study. Such an examination also indicates a point of departure for the procedures used during fieldwork activities. Some of the data collection strategies used in the field will be discussed in the context of the aesthetic details and some tentative findings from the research are outlined.

Field notes and note-taking for the novice researcher

Observations in the field are a valuable part of the research process within an ethnographic study. For those with prior experience of the phenomena, or in this case the sport to be studied, there will be for them the strange (new) experience of being the researcher looking in on a familiar setting. Instead of spectating, working or taking part as an enthusiast, the 'researcher' now has a mission to put themselves in a position that may yield useful data about the experience of the group they are studying. Fieldwork may be carried out overtly or covertly, which places different demands upon the researcher, some of which are explained later in context for this chapter. Given this new responsibility to observe in a structured way, it is apparently important to have a plan for organizing field notes of observations that reflects this investigative agenda. Writing field notes can be difficult at times, but what is written at the time or immediately after the event will constitute the data for that part of the study and, consequently, field notes are all the researcher may have to rely upon from an observation phase of research.

It may be important to consider in advance the location, what position to observe from or the specific group to be observed, and note these thoughts beforehand. Such a calculation may lead to a more beneficial use of research time, given that observing in the field can be very time-intensive. Depending on the study, it may be advisable to arrange a schedule of observation with a person in a position of authority within the group or organization. Consider whether or not you want to be open about your study with the people you are observing. Some people may feel uncomfortable or act differently when they know they are being watched. Getting close to the lived experience presents some ethical dilemmas for covert investigations; the interplay between self-preservation, spoiling data, permission or consent are factors which are worth the researcher taking some advice about before they embark upon their fieldwork.[1]

It may be prudent to be discreet and protect your notes. Field notes are documentation of what was witnessed and may include conflicts or utterances that you regarded as important at the time. Try to use significant keywords that aid recall and refer back to keywords to develop thorough notes after you have left the field. Type up a detailed version of your notes for future analysis; develop your notes, fill in the gaps before the memory fades. If relevant, use code-names for the people you observed to protect their identities. Think carefully about telling others of your research; while it may not affect them directly it may affect your research later if people know your mission to observe and research in the field. Also, the sensitive nature of what is written may include what people do not want revealed about themselves or their group, so think carefully about the confidentiality of field notes and how they might be used within your research. Try to complete your field notes immediately after leaving the field; writing them up with greater detail while the experience is fresh in your mind may strengthen your data.

Origin and development of the research: focusing on aesthetic language in gymnastics

My research originated from a philosophical enquiry into the artistic evaluation of Men's Artistic Gymnastics. If the name of the sport was to be taken literally, it might be expected that *artistic criteria* were used to judge the quality of their distinctly artistic products. Indeed, that the judges, coaches and gymnasts at top levels within the sport might be perceived as being educated in and knowledgeable about the artistic criteria they (supposedly) used to define and value their products. A real-life consequence of their artistic education would be their critical judgements made of others' performances at competition, particularly on the international stage. Working from a broad basis of theories about 'Form in art' and 'Expression in art', my initial philosophical investigation sought to identify which artistic theories might be most frequently used by practitioners to interpret their artistic sport. It was quickly discovered that their knowledge of gymnastics was not informed by any artistic theories such as, for example, minimalism or symbolism, or other artistic concepts of form or expression through art (see Gombrich 1995 and Hospers 1969 for a range

142

of possibilities for artistic evaluation of artistic products). Rather, it was found that practitioners' knowledge was informed by concepts of Risk, Originality, Virtuosity, Harmony and Rhythm in performance as it related to gymnastics.

The FIG's (Federation Internationale Gymnastique) explanations to the judges of these aspects used predominantly artistic language and therefore had strong artistic connotations. These words featured in the FIG's *Code of Points* (i.e. rule books) during the 1970s and 1980s, with lengthy explanations to help judges interpret these qualities and award marks: Up to 0.60 as a maximum allocation for 'ROV' ('Risk, Originality, Virtuosity') within the possible 10.00 available in the 1979 *Code* (Lylo 1979:14). However, suspicion of unreliable or unfair awarding of marks for 'ROV' may have eroded the confidence of some judges to have faith in the marks from others for their national gymnasts. One practitioner commented that 'if you wore a Russian leotard you automatically got ROV', which may be indicative of the perceived imparity in interpretation of this aspect of the rules. In the superseding *Codes* the marks for 'ROV' were reduced until these words (essentially descriptors of artistic qualities) and their explanatory notes were removed from the FIG *Codes* in the 1990s in order to reduce ambiguity or wild interpretation and, perhaps, abuse. However, simply deleting the words from the rulebook may not have been sufficient to remove these concepts from the stock of knowledge held by expert practitioners to inform their decisions. Consequently, when routines contained the same or similar level of difficulty and were performed with little or no error, the interpretation of the finer aspects of performance became more critical, so judgements or the awarding of points were hotly debated for active discrimination.

Such a debate would require some specific language. In the 1990s, prac-titioners seemed to be reverting to the kind of aesthetic language that had been officially removed from earlier *Codes*, in the form of 'ROV', to express their opinions about who performed 'the best' gymnastics. Consequently, I was now curious to discover, between the FIG *Codes* of 1997 and 2001, what the aesthetic language of Men's Artistic Gymnastics was. This insight might be afforded by looking within the sport; by listening to gymnastic language; and observing gymnastics behaviour 'close up' at international levels of competition. The data showed that a 'new' range of aesthetic vocabulary seemed to be informing the interpretation of performances, for example, terms such as 'grace', 'elegance', 'beautiful', 'élan', 'lightness of touch', 'quiet', 'powerful', 'commanding', 'heavy', 'sloppy', 'frenetic', 'shaky', 'thumpy', 'weak', 'skilful', 'technical', 'crafty', 'safe', 'tactical', 'measured' and 'standard', were some terms being utilized. Such a finding may present the FIG with a dilemma relating to their use of aesthetic language. How to embrace the 'new' descriptions being used by practitioners to communicate and justify their aesthetic evaluations, which appear to retain the spirit of the traditional 'ROV' descriptions but are seemingly unrestrained by any formal recognition within the FIG *Code*?

A word about aesthetics and aesthetics in sport

Aesthetics is a branch of philosophy concerned with the interpretation and understanding of the appearance of objects in its broadest sense – although originally the attention of seventeenth- and eighteenth-century Continental philosophers, such as Kant and Schiller, was focused principally upon art and beauty. However, a contemporary view of applied and philosophical aesthetics may be that it is understood to be a developing set of ideas about how objects, people or places 'appear' to us: how they may be perceived, reasoned about and made sense of; how they could be measured, communicated, valued and rewarded, or even discarded.[2] In broadening the basic boundaries of the term 'aesthetic', it is not simply a byword for 'artistic' or 'beautiful', which might be further compounded by a common error that these words are alternative adjectives for pleasant phenomena: nice, pretty, lovely, etc. The scope of the 'aesthetic' seemingly includes ugliness and discord both in art and in many of life's experiences, which present equally valid dimensions of the aesthetic, which can be reasoned about. That is, aesthetic reasoning may be explanations of aesthetic value judgements, not merely irrational subjective responses. In this manner, the meaning of aesthetics for the purposes of philosophy may be closer to the Greek sense of the word: *aisthetikos*, 'a sense of perception'.

While all art has an aesthetic not everything aesthetic is art, which may be a key that permits the researcher to explore an aesthetic of sport. That is, sport may be regarded as having an aesthetic dimension but not an artistic one. As Best (1978: 122) points out, 'sport can be the subject of art, but art could not be the subject of sport'. Sport is not presented to its spectators as art and spectators do not use artistic criteria to judge the sport. Most actions within sport are seemingly motivated by the 'contest' and viewers' interests may be focused upon the outcome of competition, which will stem from competitive actions. That is, actions within a sport seem to require related aesthetic criteria for sensible judgements to be made about them and perhaps valued in the context of that sport. For example, within football, 'football knowledge' about attacking, defending or player formation may constitute the aesthetic details for some critical judgements. Conversely, if a football match were presented as art, it may be of very little consequence who actually wins. An own goal could be interpreted as an artistic challenge to the norms of football protocol, which would be an absurdity in sport and perhaps the game would cease to be called football. As Best (1985: 39) states: 'Superb aesthetically, sport can undoubtedly be. Why not judge it by its own standards, including aesthetic standards?'

With sport now categorized as 'aesthetic' there may be subdivisions of a sports aesthetic to help us make sense of individual sports. While all sports have a scoring system of some kind to denote winners and losers, the principal features of assessment for scoring seem to vary between tallies – *how much* – and appearance – *how well* something is performed.

A valuable reference at this point would be to Best's (1978: 99–122) useful distinction between *purposive* and *aesthetic* sports. According to Best (1978), sports are purposive when the manner of, for example, scoring goals in football or registering times and distances in athletics, is incidental to the outcome of competition. To illustrate the distinction, a good high jump is one that clears the bar; the style demonstrated by the jumper is incidental and contributes little to the validity of the attempt. Conversely, a stylish, 'elegant' jump, which knocks the bar off, counts only as a failure, however admirable the physical prowess displayed in doing so. Alternatively, aesthetic sport is when the manner of performance is the principal feature for critical judgements, as in figure skating or gymnastics. The quality of appearance that is judged against set criteria to discriminate between performances for competition outcomes. For example, the performance of a gymnast who visibly struggles through their routine, but completes it without error will be judged as demonstrating poor quality compared to a similar routine performed by another gymnast with apparent ease; the latter would win.

So, if the sport of Men's Artistic Gymnastics was not artistic as its name suggested but 'aesthetic', there seemed to be significant mileage in exploring what the aesthetic standards might be for critical judgements to be made about the quality of gymnastic performance, particularly when medals, money, fame and opportunity were at stake. In very close contests, such as for Olympic medals, the rules seemingly needed some further 'interpretation' to decide between podium positions. In such instances, what aesthetic criteria did these practitioners use? Was it possible that socio-cultural preferences for gymnastic style could be accommodated within the rules and tip the balance at competitions? Would that be fair? Was there such a thing as cultural style in gymnastics performance? How could this be accounted for and communicated? Could informed personal preference for one gymnastic style over another legitimize the awarding of Gold over Silver? It may be that an aesthetic experience for a gymnast, coach or judge could be more than just a casual response to the visual. Making judgements about *how well* something was performed seemingly involved reference to a vast stock of gymnastic knowledge accrued over a lifetime. Consequently, in this research it was the various interpretations, the language and applications of aesthetic criteria by experts in gymnastics, that were of central interest. This was where aesthetics met ethnography; a philosophically based ethnographic investigation of practitioners' socio-cultural understanding to make aesthetic judgements in their sport.

Ethnographic fieldwork: data collection strategies through participant observation

The fieldwork activities undertaken included an extended period of observation 'deep' within the world of gymnastics, followed by a number of unstructured in-depth interviews with practitioners, gymnasts, coaches and judges. The phases of observation lasted for three years, followed by one year of progressive interviewing and data analysis. Both phases of fieldwork were regarded as dimensions of participant observation. A key feature of the whole research process was that new discoveries made from the data signposted fresh areas to investigate. At every turn the data led or directed the research: indeed, the sign of a healthy project may be that it grows, or 'snowballs' with new opportunities to collect data. The main problem facing the researcher was one of how and when to stop the research, not what to do next. Each fresh area of investigation was typically exploring a new theme in aesthetic understanding, or it was a new observation opportunity for existing themes but in a new context. As Hammersley and Atkinson (1995: 1) point out,

> In its most characteristic form it involves the ethnographer partici-pating, overtly or covertly, in people's daily lives for an extended period of time, watching what happens, listening to what is said, asking questions – in fact collecting whatever data are available to throw light on the issues that are the focus of the research.

By examining successive versions of the FIG *Code of Points* (which is revised every four years following the Olympic cycle) and, importantly, listening to practitioners' dialogue, it was discovered that the concepts of 'Rules', 'Skill' and 'Technicality' had significant meaning in the gymnastics world. Also emerging from discussions in relation to these key words were the terms 'Standards', 'Skilfulness' and 'Technique'. The tactic was then to contrast these key words from *their* gymnastics dialogue to develop an understanding of *their* aesthetic inference. A model for theorizing about aesthetic discourse in gymnastics was constructed using these words. Interestingly, these 'new' terms seemed to allow practitioners to have similar kinds of discussion to those exchanged during the reign of previous FIG *Codes*, i.e. under the guise of 'Risk', 'Originality', 'Virtuosity', 'Harmony' and 'Rhythm'. The identification of these 'new' key words created a theoretical context in gymnastics aesthetics, which could be 'fleshed out' progressively with ongoing field observations of gymnastic behaviour and practitioners' interpretations.

A model for theorizing about aesthetic discourse in gymnastics

In my research, I chose to focus on the following three aspects of gymnastics scoring criteria and used these as a means to focus my data recording:

- Rules and Standards
- Skill and Skilfulness
- Technical and Technique

A necessary condition of researching in gymnastics, or any sport for that matter, may be that the researcher is bound to follow the competition calendar and that observational opportunities are dictated by this to a large extent. Also there was the issue of negotiating access with 'gatekeepers' (key players and officials) in order to become privy to some otherwise restricted situations, such as attending judges' courses or getting behind the scenes at competitions. Some of the events where observation took place are listed, followed by some examples of field notes made on these occasions. Observing at these events required the researcher to adopt variously a covert or overt role within participant observation. These roles were dictated by the situation and practical setting, which either facilitated note-taking at the time or restricted it, forcing notes to be written immediately after the event. The research developed systematically and chronologically, following the FIG calendar of events and collecting data from a range of sources.

Data sources: literature, documentation and the gymnastics world

My data sources included the following:

- FIG *Code of Points* (rules and conditions) past and present.
- FIG documentation; letters, updates, clarifications on rules and conditions.
- Samples of national documentation from Governing Bodies, which *interpreted* FIG rules. This may be seen to develop a cultural identity in gymnastics, if only in the majority of cases, by pointing out the faults/ implications of others' preferences.
- Gymnastic press: performance trends and national preferences evidenced on internet websites and contemporary gym publications (national and international).
- International judges' conferences and symposia.
- Attendance at major international competitions and video evidence of these performances, for example:

  2000 European Championships, Kunstturn, Bremen, Germany
  2000 Olympics, Sydney, Australia (video only)
  2001 World Championships, Ghent, Belgium
  2002 Commonwealth Games, Manchester
- Gymnastic literature: historical, cultural and technical information.
- Aesthetics literature: the analysis of aesthetic theory has enabled the researcher to consider a central question about gymnastics, 'If not artistic then how aesthetic?'
- Peer-reviewed journals in sport, aspects of judging, coaching or perform- ance in gymnastics indicated some evidence for international bias/ preference in performance style as might affect scoring.

- Formal in-depth interviews with international practitioners: the data indicated that eliciting experts' comments upon experts would be informative. A contextually bound means of collecting new data was to ask practitioners to give verbal commentaries on a video of selected performances from an international event. These unstructured interviews represented minimal researcher bias but did reveal the true mission of the researcher. The interviews were the final phase of data collection within the research 'window'.

Organizing field notes

The opportunity to record information in field notes was dictated by the social and practical situation, along with the implications for protecting the researcher's role as well as recognizing any limitations upon the data. Consequently, a method of organizing field notes that accommodated these considerations was adapted from Schatzman and Strauss (1973), who argue that data should be recorded in distinct packages of material according to whether they constitute Observational Notes (ON), Theoretical Notes (TN) or Methodological Notes (MN). This proved to be an effective way of structuring and sorting data collected during the extensive observational phase of research. The researcher was able to select and record significant observations and theorize about them as they occurred. This was vital to expanding the detail within the aesthetic model identified above. Burgess (1982) developed a similar structure of organizing field notes, which he termed as 'Substantive' field notes, 'Methodological' field notes and 'Analytic' field notes. However, the conceptual operations within this and other interpretations of organizing field notes (Burgess 1984; Hughes 1994; Kirk and Miller 1986) seemed similar in essence to that of Schatzman and Strauss (1973) which, for user friendliness, was adopted as the model for use in this research. Schatzman and Strauss (1973) explain that:

> **ON Observational Notes** are [descriptive] statements bearing upon events experienced principally through watching and listening. They contain as little interpretation as possible and are as reliable as the researcher can construct them. Each 'ON' represents an event deemed important enough to be included in the fund of recorded experience. An 'ON' is the *who, what, when, where* and *how* of human activity. It tells who said or did what under stated circumstance. If the observer wishes to go beyond the facts in the instance, he writes a theoretical note.
> **TN Theoretical Notes** represent self-conscious controlled attempts to derive meaning from any one or several observation notes. The observer as recorder thinks about what he has experienced and makes whatever private declaration of meaning he feels will bear conceptual

fruit. He interprets, infers, hypothesizes, and conjectures; he develops new concepts, links these to older ones, or relates any observation to any other in this presently private effort to create social science.

MN Methodological Notes A methodological note is a statement that reflects an operational act completed or planned: an instruction to oneself, a reminder and a critique of one's own tactics. It notes timing, sequencing, stationing, stage setting or manoeuvring.

Schatzman and Strauss (1973) clarify that a package of data is an abstract rendering in brief paragraph form, which tells of a single distinct event (ON) then draws an inference (TN) or makes a tactical decision (MN). This is not the only way of organizing field notes, although it did prove to be effective in this instance. For variations on the theme of organizing field notes see also Spradley (1980: 78), Hammersley and Atkinson (1995: 185), Polit and Hungler (1999: 368–9), Richardson (2000: 923–49 cited in Silverman (2004: 251)) and Bailey (2007: 79–93). The following extracts are examples of field notes taken when observer-as-participant and participant-as-observer fieldwork roles were adopted by the researcher.

Example of field notes: observer-as-participant fieldwork role

These field notes were made while spectating at the 2001 World Championships in Ghent, Belgium Team Competition, while adopting an observer-as-participant field role; 'a position of relative detachment' (Hammersley and Atkinson 1995: 104).

ON (Observational Notes): Teams from Mexico, Argentina, Venezuela, Turkey and Korea are competing in this round, 2.00–4.00pm.

I have a good vantage point being close to the competition podium but fairly central in the stadium. I have a good overview to see all the teams as they rotate from one piece of apparatus to the next.

The team from Mexico seem to stand out visually for some reason. Their gymnastics is not very high in difficulty terms but as a team they seem well coordinated, well matched compared to the others.

All the Mexican gymnasts did Vende swings on Floor, all did Magyar hop on Pommels and all did a drop-chute action before their dismount sequence on Parallel Bars.

The Mexican gymnasts have different individual routines but include repetition of certain elements, which are common to all. The other teams competing this afternoon did not do this so apparently.

I have watched gymnasts from over sixty countries, four gymnasts in each team in the last two days – this team had a very strong aesthetic team image.

TN (Theoretical Notes): The Mexican team seems to have a corporate image to their performance, which is impressive compared to the other teams on display.

Initial impressions; looks very tidy, coordinated, together, traces of similarity but all different.

There seems to be an expectation set up in me (spectating) that each gymnast in the Mexican team would perform a visually similar action. Something that identifies them with that team.

Strong aesthetic impact as a team but their difficulty (of elements) is relatively low in world gymnastic terms.

This collective image seems to identify them as a team rather than a group of individuals.

There may be some kind of aesthetic synergy in that the visual affect is greater than the sum of its parts.

The repeating of aesthetic material seems to create/leave a national signature that identifies them as a team.

The expectation of team image set up by watching this Mexican team seems to influence what I am looking for in other teams.

MN (Methodological Notes): I can make these observations from this secluded position in the stand and they seem quite apparent from this vantage point.

I am quite detached, a fly on the wall so to speak.

I wonder if judges down on the podium see this 'corporate image' as clearly as I do? And how do they respond to it?

Is there is an expectation set up by judges for a team aesthetic? I must think of a way to find out if a judge recognizes aesthetic team image. I am unable to question right now as the competition is going on and I can't get access to them from up here in the stands. Nor is this the time or place to interrupt others' duties and viewing of the competition. Any questions will necessarily be reflective.

I may have to reveal my research role in asking such questions or may get ignored; suspicion of being sponsored or just an idealistic gymnastic crank! I will have to think of a social setting and situation for such a conversation to take place; it should be relaxed, unthreatening allowing the practitioner to talk freely, uninterrupted allowing them to reflect, formulate and verbalise their opinion; I'd like to know their opinion on this aesthetic point of team image and aesthetic expectation.

Interestingly, this situation did arise later during that week in Ghent in a hotel lobby bar. In relaxed circumstances, I took the opportunity to introduce myself and my interests (observer-as-participant; my role as researcher revealed) to a judge from a Mediterranean country, with the intention of discussing the concepts of cultural/corporate image. His response was recorded in field notes, which read as follows:

ON: This judge is absolutely adamant that cultural visual image exists in gymnastics; in both men's and women's gymnastics but particularly obvious to them in the women's sport.

The judge stated, *verbatim*, that they 'could tell which culture and usually which country a gymnast comes from in terms of their historical, religious and social gesture patterns without seeing the leotard or flag'.

Then the judge proceeded to demonstrate with arms and hands some examples of subtle gestures noticed from gymnasts from Catholic countries. This [European] judge had clearly thought about cultural influences presented in gymnastics, which they have had to make sense of over the years.

The judge went on to state, as if evident for all to see, i.e. it was obvious for this person that, 'the USA have ignored their strong cultural traditions in contemporary dance and ballet in gymnastic presentation whereas other countries have utilized their cultural identity to the full.'

In the judge's words about the aesthetic style in the USA 'they embrace Hollywood, it's all Fred Astaire and Ginger Rogers, entertaining, but not deeply cultural, it's superficial and glitzy.' She continued that 'they have not tapped their cultural dance heritage' and seemed to be shaking her head, indicating that it's a shame that a great opportunity for them (USA) to develop a significant style in gymnastic performance, is being missed.

The opportunity to gather this data was presented by chance and seized upon in an observer-as-participant field role in the relaxed surroundings of a hotel bar alluded to in the previous MN which was made (envisaged) at the gymnastics stadium. Consequently, I was aware of how valuable this opportunity was and was keen to conduct the exchange appropriately. I was careful not to lead the judge into making the kind of specific comments she did make about religious and social gesture and the Hollywood interpretation of aesthetic in American performance. This judge's comments were offered independently and in response to my own (apparently innocent but actually loaded) enquiry as to whether gymnasts displayed any aesthetic differences in terms of cultural image that did not conflict with the rules directly. This fieldwork tactic was noted in Methodological notes for that fieldwork episode.

Example of field notes: participant-as-observer fieldwork role

The following field notes were made while attending an international judges' assessment course, when I adopted a participant-as-observer field role; a position of relative involvement (Hammersley and Atkinson 1995).

ON: There is a presentation in the main lecture theatre at the centre with about 40 practitioners attending. Some of our national coaches are also judges being assessed for this *Code*.

Speaker reports that under the new *Code*, straddling of legs is to be deducted in certain (most/all) circumstances.

No straddle lifts to handstand, must always be a pike lift.

Refer to *Code* for verification – quote, 'if it's not in the *Code* it's not allowed.'

Different kinds of straddling of legs affect deductions and recognition of Special Requirements.

What kinds of situations for straddle of legs? When is it 'typical' and when is it 'atypical'? Clarification; quote 'it's judgement call, if straddling makes the move easier then deduct.'

This ruling seems to have provoked a great deal of confusion and shaking of heads but the context of this course is an assessment and the candidates want 'pass'. These people seem to accept the rule submissively, perhaps in the hope of passing the exam rather than it being a forum to discuss their beliefs and implications of the rule; this would have been the normal course of events at national judges' symposiums where no international assessment was at stake.

TN: Straddling of legs is a basic aesthetic shape that visually occupies more time and space than the other basic shapes of gymnastics, tuck, straight, pike.

Straddle is a splayed out shape – a larger aspect of body is presented – guides the eyes to furthest points, spreading of 'wings', illusory; ease of action.

Bigger space and time occupied but with some elements biomechanically easier to do than in straight shape e.g. front planche straight compared to front planche with straddle. Biomechanically it reduces the distance of weight supported from the base making some straddled elements easier.

Risk: straddle shape could be phased out completely; elements at risk: flairs, shears, straddle planches, straddle lifts to handstand; affects straddle elements on most apparatus.

Risk that gymnasts will not perform them because they are not worth doing as devalued (by number) and will be deducted despite looking impressive and distinctly gymnastic.

The straddling issue is discussed here as a 'technical' issue but it seems to be more than that. It is a rule issue with associated problems of evaluating the aesthetic of performance which include:

- perception/conception; understanding the aesthetic values of that shape in a gymnastic context

- judgement and appreciation of difficulty as an aesthetically defining factor of the sport; all getting labelled at this event as technical aspects of judging
- What does 'technical' actually mean here for these practitioners in terms of the specific examples and specific gymnasts they make reference to?

Taste selection and sieving out fundamental aesthetic material, devaluing the straddle shape, reducing the number of basic shapes with which the gymnast has to work; motivation for this? Making gymnastics more difficult to perform in order to make it easier for judges to score.

What will be removed next to promote difficulty?

There may be some serious consequences for this reductive action; if a gymnast can't do the most difficult elements in the *Code* is it worth doing anything?

Aesthetic monotony from pursuing difficulty results in reduced range of shapes on display, to make scoring easier.

This seems like naïve motivation from an aesthetic point of view.

Aesthetically seems a bit drastic; gymnastic shape sieved out and lost forever. It reduces the gymnast's ability to show variety within the performance gymnastically, i.e. the range of shapes and elements reduced that the gymnast's body is capable of exhibiting, i.e. occupation of time and space that was the preserve of the gymnast is minimized in this way.

MN: Within this formal situation my participant-as-observer field role seems quite obvious to me in the here and now. In a way it is socially defined by context, i.e. it is an assessment course to which I do not contribute nor am I being assessed. I know I can't ask for clarification or point out aesthetic consequences to the sport or aesthetic consequences of their interpretations for fear of causing an imbalance in the proceedings and therefore the data I am collecting.

My role is to observe, listen and record. I make sure I am sat to the side of the lecture theatre so as not to distract people or draw attention to myself but close enough to the people so as to appear part of the group. If someone asked 'What's he doing up the back there?' my cover would be gone, but more importantly I would have disrupted their formal setting and therefore my data under this strategy for fieldwork.

I think these experts are talking in aesthetic terms about the straddle issue and many other aspects for the new *Code*, such as Rings and the new emphasis on strength moves, but they don't seem to realize the formal aesthetic significance of what they are saying. They are talking aesthetics but not using aesthetic language as they understand it. Their gymnastic language alludes to their 'technical' understanding of appearance but would happily disregard the notion that gymnastic language is aesthetic language in their world; aesthetic language seems to be regarded by them as flimsy, subjective and biased, emotionally driven and unreliable; there is no place for this kind of language in the 'objective' and clinical act of scoring (or is there?)

The degree of self-reflection on my strategy and the aesthetic content being discussed seems much greater in this situation for me as a researcher than in any other to date only because it is a lecture theatre and I am free to think my thoughts and write my notes; no contribution and no demands to interrupt me, I am a fly on the wall.

The method of data collection during this fieldwork episode was clearly defined by the formal context of the meeting and therefore demanded appropriate conduct from the researcher as a visitor to that situation. The field role of participant-as-observer required that the researcher appeared to take part in a similar manner to the judges and coaches around him. To all intents and purposes, I was one of them. Following their lead, I listened attentively and gave an outward appearance of being studious. However, if I had been asked for a judging contribution to the meeting (as opposed to a philosophical aesthetic point) my role may have been exposed. This, while not posing any personal danger, could disrupt the 'natural' proceedings unnecessarily and potentially affect the data that might otherwise be collected from this essentially private meeting of gymnastics experts. It could also affect data from these practitioners from this point forward in the study.

Drawing conclusions

The act of researching in the field and the development of detailed field notes were vital to this investigation and formed the core of information from which all other research activities were grounded and directed. Interviews were carried out towards the end of the research some three years later, when my role as a researcher was known, but also when field data indicated that interviews may have been a relevant thing to do at that point. Each round of field observations was punctuated with periods of analytical writing to develop concepts and theorizing around the aesthetic model identified. In the early stages of the research a detailed exploration of the aesthetic heritage of gymnastics was indicated because a great deal of cultural *reference*, and cultural *preference* seemed to be informed by practitioners' understanding of gymnastic history (Palmer and Sellers 2009). This historical perspective was significant because gymnastic innovation may only be understood in the context of that which has preceded it. Also, that gymnastics history reveals a tradition of constantly changing preferences for different styles of gymnastics over time. Discoveries in the data were indicating that culturally influenced preferences in Men's Artistic Gymnastics may be as prevalent as they ever were in history, although not formally acknowledged in the *Code(s)*. This may have contributed to the fiasco of scoring at the Athens 2004 Olympics (see Da Cunha 2004), where competitive desires and clashes in aesthetic tastes were the most detrimental to the sport in recent times.

A conclusion from this research would be that meaningful language in gymnastics may be hindered by practitioners' understanding that 'technical' details are somehow not aesthetic details. The separation of the two may be a mistake which could be compounded further by an unhelpful distinction between 'objective' and 'subjective' notions of quality in their sport. For example, in revising the *Code*, the FIG have made significant strides towards 'making more objective the judging of gymnastics exercises' (Zschocke 1993: 3). However, the use of numbers alone may not remove 'subjectivity' in the scoring process and the score, once arrived at, may rightly direct our attentions to concepts of beauty, grace, elegance or power, or its opposites, in performance. Perhaps something more than just a number may be required from the FIG to demonstrate sound critical reasoning about the aesthetic qualities of Men's Artistic Gymnastics.

Suggested further reading

Best, D. (1978) *Philosophy and Human Movement*, London: Allen and Unwin.

Harvey, F. J. (1903) *The Fighting Gladiators or the Games and Combats of the Greeks and Romans: A Short History of Physical Culture*, Exeter: The Physical Training Publishing Company.

Kunzle, G. C. (1960) *Olympic Gymnastics, vols 1–4*, London: Barrie and Rockcliffe.

Lowe, B. (1977) *The Beauty of Sport: A Cross-disciplinary Inquiry*, New York: Prentice Hall.

Newton, E. (1950) *The Meaning of Beauty*, London: Longmans Green and Co.

Prestidge, J. (1988) *The History of British Gymnastics*, London: British Amateur Gymnastics Association.

Ryan, J. (1996) *Little Girls in Pretty Boxes: The Making and Breaking of Elite Gymnasts and Figure Skaters*, New York: Grand Central Publishing.

Sparkes, A. C. (2002) *Telling Tales in Sport and Physical Activity: A Qualitative Journey*, Champaign, IL: Human Kinetics Publishers.

Reflective activities

1 Practise observing and making field notes: go to a sports event to observe as a researcher rather than being a spectator. Make field notes from two field roles (i) on aspects of spectator behaviour of those immediately around you, and (ii) aspects of performer behaviour or that of officials. In each case describe how it feels to be a researcher rather than a spectator. Explain what roles in participant observation were most appropriate to the situations. What ideas were spurred on from your notes as to where or what you might observe next?

2   Practice observing. Carry out an observation in a setting which is convenient: community meeting, work, in a sport, or at a restaurant perhaps. Envisage where to sit, who to observe and how you will make notes; at the time or after. Make notes of these factors before you enter the setting. Plan your notes in accordance with the details in this chapter. (i) Carry out the observation. Consider what emerged and consequently what you might observe for next time (your reason for observing will have been grounded in your data which is good). (ii) Write a brief account; creative writing or write a poem about how you felt being the researcher in that situation, the 'outsider' looking in?

Notes

1   See Mauthner *et al.* (2002) for some useful discussions in this area.
2   See Hospers (1969), Best (1978), McFee (1992) and Palmer and Torevell (2008) for various discussions concerning aesthetic criteria.

11

MAKING SENSE OF IT ALL

Analysing ethnographic data

Julie Scott Jones and Sal Watt

The process of analysing ethnographic data has until fairly recently been absent from discussion in either completed ethnographies or textbooks on ethnographies. Much discussion could be found on how to go about doing fieldwork; what to expect during it; and the importance of keeping up-to-date field notes; but the final stage processes of analysis and 'writing up' remained 'hidden'. We can understand this as part of the mystification process of 'being' an ethnographer in the classical sense, particularly in the anthropological tradition; perhaps to shine a light on the process would serve to detract from its magic and meaning. However, as was noted in Chapter 2, post-structuralism's preoccupation with text meant that, from the 1980s onwards, writing and text construction became almost as important as the act of fieldwork itself. Yet how to analyse data remained under-discussed. Quantitative data by its nature is easy to collate, manage and analyse; there are clear strategies to employ irrespective of discipline or subject area. The highly subjective nature of ethnographic data is probably the central reason why its analysis was ignored for so long. Although such data remain subjective, there is still a range of strategies that an ethnographer can follow to make the job of analysis easier. This chapter will explore the stages of ethnographic data analysis, drawing on two contrastive fieldwork examples to illustrate different approaches that you could take towards handling ethnographic data. The case studies also focus on commonalities within ethnographic data analysis.

The myth of ethnographic data analysis

Qualitative data analysis and ethnographic analysis, in particular, is subject to fierce debates about how much the process of analysis can be systematized (Brewer 2000; Hammersley and Atkinson 1995). For many ethnographers any form of system goes against the interpretivist values of ethnography (Hammersley and Atkinson 1995). The data should exist to 'speak for itself' as proponents of grounded theory would maintain (Bryman 2008). However, such debates ignore the reality of the research process: the ethnographer is continually editing and managing, consciously or subconsciously, what they are recording throughout their time in the field. Before entering the field setting, ethnographers will have some basic questions: issues that they want to explore which will ultimately frame what they do in the field setting. In reality, few ethnographers genuinely turn up at a field setting as a 'blank slate' to allow data to emerge *sui generis*; this is a myth akin to constructing ethnographer as magician rather than researcher. From the development of a research interest, we are making decisions, asking questions and imposing basic interpretative frames on our work, even before data collection. That is not to discount the importance ethnographers place on letting data emerge from the field setting (ethnography is an inductive approach at heart), but this is not a neutral process: it is highly subjective and directed by the ethnographer. Thus, offering a system for processing and analysing ethnographic data should not be seen as against 'true' ethnography.

Can technology help?

Quantitative data analysis has utilized computer assisted data analysis software (CADAS) since the late 1960s, for example SPSS is used widely in sociology and psychology. This means that quantitative data can be coded, processed and analysed with great ease and in a cost- and time-efficient way. CADAS software for qualitative research has been a more recent development, partly due to technological limitations and the view that qualitative data cannot be (and should not be) analysed in a mechanical way. The first qualitative CADAS packages emerged in the late 1980s and the two most popular today are *NVivo* and *Ethnograph*. Nevertheless, their use is still not widespread, particularly in relation to ethnographic work. Hammersley and Atkinson provide a strong critique of the limitations of software, in particular *Ethnograph*:

> Whatever merits are to be found in computer applications, however, we must recognize that they only provide adjuncts to the sociological or anthropological imagination. They certainly do not provide 'automatic' solutions to problems of representation and analysis. Understanding and interpretation are the outcome of interactions between ethnographer and the data, which are themselves constructs. There are no mechanistic substitutes for those complex processes of reading and interpretation.
>
> (Hammersley and Atkinson 1995: 203)

In other words, the key skills required for analysis of ethnographic data are reading, reflection and interpretation (Geertz 1984), and for these tasks computers are no substitute for a human ethnographer. For that reason, most ethnographers still do manual data analysis. The two case studies in this chapter will provide an illustration of how to go about doing that.

Data analysis case study 1: Julie Scott Jones's ethnography of 'God's Way'[1] religious community

Field notes and field data

Chapter 10 discussed the importance of field notes and outlined ways to code and categorize such notes. Field notes are at the heart of ethnographic research (Sanjek 1990) and therefore analysis; so it is important that you ensure you keep field notes updated and as detailed as possible, as you go along. The depth and detail of your field notes will depend on your research approach; for example, in my covert fieldwork on 'God's Way' community I had to 'write up' my field notes each night, quickly, in a toilet therefore they lacked the detail overt research would have afforded. I also had to try to remember details from throughout the day: key recollections, events and sayings. However, field notes are not the only forms of data available to the ethnographer: photographs, diagrams, maps, a personal field journal, artefacts, sacred scriptures, official documents and so forth are all potential forms of data. In my research, I took photographs of the community, drew diagrams of the community's layout and constructed a family tree showing the kinship ties of all the members. These forms of data proved invaluable when I came to analysis. I also drew on quotes from their sacred scripture, of which I had a copy while in the community; and I kept community recipes, personal letters between me and my gatekeeper 'Isaac', and my key informant 'Rachel', and gifts made and shared with community members through my year there. The point I am labouring is that ethnographic data does not just have to entail your field notes, so try to collect a range of forms of data. I did not keep a field journal, for obvious practical reasons, but these can be a potential source of insight particularly when it comes to incorporating reflexivity into your completed ethnography.

Getting started with analysis: creating a sense of order

When ethnographers finish fieldwork and 'return' to academic life, usually with the intention of 'writing up' their data into an ethnography, most experience a sense of being overwhelmed by the task ahead. There just seems to be so much data and so little sense of order to it: I have yet to meet an ethnographer who did not spend the first few months 'back' from fieldwork bewildered and unable to see where to start or what is relevant. It took me the best part of a year to order my data and start my writing, and I remember there being little advice around at that time as to how to go about analysis. Things have changed since then, as most ethnography textbooks offer some discussion of analysis (see for example Brewer 2000; Hammersley and Atkinson 1995). Data analysis should be seen as a two-stage process:

- Stage one involves ordering, collating and managing your data in a way that makes analysis possible.
- Stage two involves actual data analysis.

Dealing with it all!

Let us start by looking at stage one of this process. When I returned from my fieldwork, I dumped all my field data unceremoniously in a large 'banker's box' box file, scrawled 'fieldwork' on the top and shoved it under my desk. It sat there for several months as I indulged in displacement and distraction activities: anything but have to deal with all my data. This is a common experience following fieldwork, where the ethnographer needs time to decompress from the often emotionally intense experience of fieldwork. Nevertheless, the sooner you 'deal' with your data and confront the analysis task ahead the better. My continual procrastination meant that the thought of getting started overwhelmed me beyond all logic. After some months, I opened the box file, took a deep breath and emptied out its contents on to the floor.

First impressions: the 'read through'

Once you have opened your filed away data, the first thing you should do is read through and look at everything. Take the time to do this read through and do not worry about being systematic or ordered at this stage. I literally sat on the floor of my room, surrounded by field notes, pictures, photos and so forth and took the time to look at everything. This allowed me to go back into that feeling of the 'field', which I had left months before; I recalled things I thought I had forgotten and I began to see significances. This may sound touchy feely and intuitive but that is part of ethnographic analysis: go with what you feel (Shweder 1991). As I read everything, I jotted down brief notes about things I thought were important, relevant or stood out. By the end of this process, I had reconnected with 'God's Way' community and had begun to 'see' some of the issues that I wanted to discuss in my ethnography. The notes did two key things; first, they were a shorthand means to locate specific issues within specific parts of my data and, second, they would later facilitate the reflexive process by highlighting some of my reactions and feelings.

Once I had read everything, I repeated the process; this sounds convoluted but it allowed me to catch things I missed the first time and made me reflect further on the notes I had initially jotted down. I stuck post-it notes on significant sections with preliminary ideas and highlighted what looked like key extracts. There is no hard-and-fast rule as to how long you should take to read all your field materials; a lot depends on how much material you have. The important thing is not to rush this process. Another consequence of 'reading through' is that it makes you feel more confident about the quality of your data (ethnographers are always worried that their data will not garner sufficient analysis) and of your ability to manage data analysis.

Finding significances: coding/indexing data

I then approached my data in a more systematic way by starting to 'code' or 'index' it. Coding/indexing is a means to make data more manageable by highlighting key words/quotes/issues, etc. My notes from the 'read through' stages served to help me start coding by guiding me to significant pieces of data. Having read through all my field notes I had already noted which sections discussed which key issues so I did not have to reread everything again; instead I could go straight to the relevant sections. For example, one key first impression noted from my 'read through' had been the use of two recurring phrases: '*God sees dust*' and '*We are as significant as dust*'. During fieldwork, I had become so used to the phrases I did not really think that much about them, yet both phrases recurred throughout my field notes. I had noted their use as speech acts during specific activities, as a motif in communal art and in their sacred scripture. During coding, I went through all the pieces of data that featured these phrases and highlighted the context of their use. I then wrote on post-it notes key words such as 'use in chores', 'artwork hung in dining room' and 'quoted to children', which allowed me to code usage. I used post-it notes and a highlighter pen; other people write directly on their data, but this can make data messy. I repeated this process with other seemingly significant themes.

Creating summaries: filing data

Once I had covered my data in post-it notes and highlighter pen, I then needed to draw 'data bundles' that linked together. A good strategy is to write short summaries of 'data bundles'. I did this on old fashioned filing cards but an easier way today would be to use a computer. Table 11.1 shows an example of this.

From my summary card, you can see that not only have I provided a 'snapshot' of this data but also recorded possible further issues to explore. Once filed away, the data summary is always available to give me instant access to that material, and I can use it as an *aide mémoire* to direct me to further analysis at a later date. A really well done data summary would record the exact location (page numbers of field notes/journals) at the end of the summary. I was not that organized.

Table 11.1 Data summary

Use of recurring phrases
Community use series of recurring phrases. 'God sees dust'; 'We are as significant as dust'. Repeated in same way, always initiated by senior adult members. Echoed in repetition by everyone else. Almost chant like quality that goes on for a few minutes. Occurs repeatedly through day. Context specific – during 'chores', during external farm work, in chastising children, in 'rallying the troops', in response to poor treatment from 'outsiders'. Meaning heavy but never said in chapel. Embroidered and hung in dining room. **Both sayings of founder. What is 'dust' . . . explore symbolism. Link to belief system as embodied in everyday living on 'chosen' land. God monitoring 'chosen'. Explore 'chosen' status and relationship to God.**

What does it all mean? Data analysis strategies

Coding and filing are not data analysis, rather they are stages of preparing and managing the data to allow the ethnographer to start actual analysis. In a sense the preparatory stage does frame the data in a raw analytical fashion, but you cannot yet make full sense of it all. The main form of data analysis used by ethnographers is broadly labelled 'thematic analysis' and there are a variety of different versions that can be used. Versions differ depending on discipline, theoretical approach and type of data collected.

Thematic analysis

I used a basic form of thematic analysis, what you might call 'regular' or mainstream thematic analysis. Thematic analysis involves drawing out key themes from the data and then theoretically framing them, in other words making sense of them. I started my analysis by going through all my file card summaries and rereading them. I noted down all the key themes/issues: a number emerged including:

- 'chosen' status
- importance of founder's vision
- recurring phrases
- outside/inside spatial divide,
- end of the world
- belief as the mundane everyday
- gender
- prejudice
- rituals
- animal symbolism
- 'true Americans'

I did not try to edit this list; the key is to generate as many key themes as possible at this early stage of analysis. This means you will be less likely to miss something significant. I then went through all my coded data again to locate sub-themes within the broader headings. I then constructed a data matrix to illustrate each, see Table 11.2.

The data matrix can include quotes, descriptions, impressions and key words; anything that adds to your analysis. Data matrices can get quite large but again they are invaluable for making sense of data; so try to avoid editing them. I did a data matrix for all my key themes and then I started to arrange the themes in a hierarchy of significance; thus I ended up with just five central themes that I wanted to explore which were 'chosen' status; 'end of the world'; 'views of space'; 'embodiment of belief in the everyday'; and 'communal history'. The other themes were either discounted or more typically subsumed

162

Table 11.2 Thematic analysis

Communal history	Role of founder	Expression of 'chosen' status	Impact on communal beliefs/life
Given special book to replace Bible	Chosen by God	Outside/inside divide	Strict diet
	Series of visions		Strict moral/gender
Tested by God		Chosen/fallen	codes
	Recurring use of	divide	
Rewarded by God	stories about the		Constant vigilance
	founder and his	Highly racist/	of self and others
Schism and conflict	key quotes during	homophobic	
	daily life	(all Blacks drug	Censorship of radio/
Will be rewarded		dealers, Clinton	music/TV/newspapers
after apocalypse		White House	
		dominated by	'God sees dust'/
		queers)	'We are as significant
			as dust' phrases
		Anticipating end	
		of world	
		'A chicken ain't	
		a hoss' phrase/	
		animal symbolism	

within main themes, for example, the community's high levels of prejudice fitted under the main themes of both 'chosen' status and 'views of space', while gender was best placed under 'embodiment of belief in the everyday' along with the use of recurring phrases. If well done, the data matrix stage should give you a template for 'writing up' your work: my main themes eventually became the chapters of my completed ethnography.

Do not forget the theory

The final stage of data analysis, and often the one most students omit, is the framing of analysis with theory. All good research starts with literature searches and reviews done well ahead of fieldwork. Alongside data analysis, the ethnographer should be reading related literature, guided by their key themes. Themes are not themselves fully analysed unless linked to wider literature and theory. I found that a lot of the literature that I read before my fieldwork was irrelevant on my return, as my subject focus had changed during my fieldwork, so you should expect to be reading when you return from fieldwork. In addition, ethnographers let data emerge from the field setting, thus themes you might not have anticipated prior to fieldwork will become significant and require reading up on when you return. Ethnography without a theoretical framework is just description – a key criticism of ethnographic work.

Data analysis case study 2: Sal Watt's ethnography of a Civil Service department

My experience of analysing data on the Civil Service research was very similar to Julie's; certainly around reading, re-reading and making notes. I too used post-its by the dozen to highlight sections and similarly used coloured highlighters. However, unlike Julie, I did write messily all over my notes and transcripts, which, in hindsight, was not the best of ideas. Part of my PhD training was to undertake various courses, one of which was a two-day course on the analysis software package *NUDIST*. In terms of its capabilities, I could see its usefulness if you wanted to know the number of times someone said a particular word or phrase, but the whole process left me ambivalent around how warmth or emotion could be conveyed via software 'output'. While without doubt, such packages can be extremely useful, the beauty of ethnography is in its rich and fine detail and, as such, analysis should be reflective, reflexive and necessarily takes time.

Secondary and primary research

Ethnographic data inevitably comes from various directions and employs different methods. Before embarking on my research in the field, I undertook several months of secondary research. It seemed logical to start at the very beginning and investigate the origins and history of the Civil Service. This revealed the rapid expansion of the Service and, thereafter, a protracted history of criticism around its cost and efficiency (Drewry and Butcher 1991; Pyper 1995). It immediately struck me that the Civil Service has never stood still and its survival has always depended on its critical response to change. I progressed my investigations through government websites to New Labour's call for 'Modernizing government' and therein the call for open government and communication. This gave me a solid grounding in understanding 'top-down' messages, from which I could then investigate how this information informed and was disseminated across individual departments through, for example, their aims, objectives and so on. The gathering of this information was sequential and, aside from making notes and highlighting various internet documents, I also started to construct a 'mind map'.

As Julie has already pointed out, dealing with a lot of information can be overwhelming and sometimes linear notes do not always reveal the wider picture or the synergy between field notes and the concepts therein. 'Mind mapping' is a really useful way of bringing data together and allows you to creatively play with themes or ideas. I am sure you will be very familiar with the term 'mind mapping' but, for the sake of clarity, a 'mind map' can be made up of words in bubbles, rectangles or just clusters of words that are then linked together by arrowed lines. My 'mind maps' looked incredibly messy and quite honestly would make no sense to anyone else. However, as a visual thinker, they made perfect sense to me and, when dealing with a lot of themes, concepts or theories, they allowed me to be creative and play with ideas. A word of caution though, as a procrastinatory diversion as I set about 'writing up' my PhD I did try to 'mind map' the whole thing: this was taking things just a bit too far and I would not advocate it as good practice.

When I entered the field, I was given IT access to the department's intranet and so, while I was getting to know people in the 'division' where I was to conduct my research, I continued doing secondary research around the department's change and communication strategies. This background knowledge proved invaluable as I started getting to know my participants and explore their working lives. I had two cohorts of participants; 'key' and 'peripheral' participants, and the research was conducted in two phases. In phase one, I came in and out of the working lives of the 'key' participants over a 14-month period. I gathered data by overt participant observation, shadowing, semi-structured interviews and through conversation. The emergent themes of phase one informed the questions I later posed to the 'peripheral' participants via semi-structured interviews in phase two of the research. The objective here was to ascertain whether the views expressed by phase one participants were typical of the wider community and, as far as possible, reliable.

Field notes

As the research was overt, with the key participants in phase one it was relatively easy to record field notes concerning procedural and departmental observations throughout the day. My participants often would nod to my book as if to say 'you need to write this down', and I think it served as affirmation that I was indeed listening and valuing the things they told me. I kept my field notes simply and chronologically in a diary format. However, when 'writing up' notes I always spaced my notes out so that I had room to write additional notes when I was on my own concerning things I did not want to write in front of the participants. For example, if I had noticed a tension between workers; or if I had noticed a contradiction in what they said that did not tie in with an earlier comment or behaviour; or if an ad hoc 'off the record' conversation or comment was made.

The same but different

Analysing the data was, by and large, through thematic analysis similar to that described earlier in the chapter. The only difference being that in psychology the process I had been taught was perhaps more laborious, in that the idea is to generate as many themes as possible; to number each theme; and then to go through a process of collapsing themes that overlap with each other. This process is repeated several times until the data is reduced to a manageable number of themes that can be explored further via a data matrix and then subsequently 'written up'. However, as Julie has pointed out, there are

165

numerous ways of describing and undertaking thematic analysis and the difference is often negligible if not semantic.

However, in the interests of clarity, below is an example of a short quote that I sometimes use in class and from which students then generate themes. The subjective nature of qualitative analysis means that interpretation of a quote will throw up differences and the themes you might come up with might well illustrate this. But have a look below at the initial themes students typically generate. Note that, in the second column of the collapsing down process, a new theme name has emerged and below are the numbers of those themes that have been collapsed down as similar or overlapping. This process continues until the key overarching theme or themes emerge. In some methods books you will see this collapsing down process referred to in terms of 'first, second and third ordering'. Have a look at the process and see what you think? What initial themes would you have generated? Remember these are likely to be different.

Table 11.3 Numerical thematic analysis

14 themes ‡	5 themes ‡	2 themes ‡	Overarching theme/ conclusion
1. Job (career?)			
2. Passionate			
3. Sarcasm?			
4. Emphasis	Self 1, 2, 5, 6, 14, 10		
5. Enjoyment			
6. Satisfaction	Descriptors 2, 3, 4, 5, 6, 13	Work identity 1, 2, 3, 4, 5, 6, 7, 8,11, 12, 13, 14	Job satisfaction *This worker's identity is closely aligned with working as part of a*
7. Solidarity			
8. Small	Satisfaction 5, 6, 11, 12, 13	Team member 7, 8, 9, 10, 11, 12, 13, 14	*team and this results in job satisfaction.*
9. Few people			
10. Only – doubt?	Colleagues 8, 9, 10, 11, 12, 12, 14		
11. Mutual liking			
12. Plural voice	Group Cohesion 7, 10, 13, 14		
13. Group satisfaction			
14. Spokesperson			

This is a very simple example and your interpretation might well be very different. However, it serves to illustrate the process. You will see that some of the themes students identify question whether the individual was being sincere, or possibly sarcastic, and this is where I think a thematic analysis in isolation can fall down. My constant advice to students is always to read the transcripts while listening to the audio version. In isolation, written words do not convey the full essence of how something is said. The tone and pitch is really important and informative, and I think you can also even 'hear' non-verbal behaviour. Listening to the way words are spoken alongside the transcript can throw you and, importantly, your memory back into the interview situation. This allows you to recall the minutiae that might not have seemed important at the time but might well be highly significant later when seen in conjunction with the whole interaction.

Practical considerations and analytic deviations

When I analysed my PhD research I think at the time the psychologist in me liked the idea of what seemed like a bit of qualitative 'number crunching' and the numerical system outlined above seemed ideal. However, despite my best intentions, when applied to my data, the numeric system proved unwieldy and far too time-consuming alongside the number and duration of the interviews I had, especially when there was also a wealth of field notes and secondary data to analyse. Instead, I found myself undertaking what Julie describes as a more 'regular' thematic analysis, which is less prescriptive or numeric in approach.

Earlier, Julie commented on the fact that only relatively recently have texts begun to appear giving advice on how to analyse ethnographic data. This was certainly my experience. The diversity of ethnographic location, experience and data perhaps renders this dearth of information somewhat understandable. However, that data analysis is to some extent individual to the research and the researcher is not helpful to budding ethnographers. I found myself betwixt and between methods, training in psychology and sociology, and the way I approached my analysis was far from ideal. On the one hand, I felt the need to somehow qualitatively 'number crunch', and initially focused on the above system that would ensure I did not miss some vital minutiae that would affect my interpretation of meaning. On the other hand, I was anxious to ensure I fully engaged with the meaning of my participants' worldviews through their words and the way they conveyed them. I worried about whether discourse analysis or perhaps a Foucauldian discourse analysis (Foucault 1972, 1976) was the way forward to ensure hermeneutical understanding. In truth, I think I floundered around taking a 'pick 'n' mix' approach, harnessing methods of analysis that ensured each aspect of my research was explored to its full extent holistically and phenomenologically. When my PhD was completed, I commenced a full-time teaching position in psychology and, while refreshing my knowledge on psychological methods, I hit upon what is a relatively new approach in psychology, which I instantly identified with and which lends itself to analysing ethnographic interview data.

Interpretative Phenomenological Analysis

The Interpretative Phenomenological Analysis (IPA) approach developed by Professor Jonathan Smith takes an inductive and ideographic approach. Its concern is around capturing a detailed understanding of an individual's personal lived experience, and how the individual makes sense of experience, both socially and personally (Smith 2008). Smith *et al.* (2009: 1) make the point that the focus is phenomenologically on 'exploring experience in its own terms' and the important distinction is that it does not attempt to 'fix experience in predefined or overly abstract categories'. An important element of this approach and its subsequent analysis is to recognize the role of the researcher. Interpretivism necessarily relies on hermeneutical understanding and IPA drives home the point that research is 'a dynamic process' which must include the researcher (Smith 2008: 53). The idea here is that a double hermeneutic is at work, which recognizes that the researcher's own perceptions are important. Students can sometimes struggle with this concept but Smith (2008: 53) succinctly sums up this two-stage process as follows: 'the participants are trying to make sense of their world' while 'the researcher is trying to make sense of the participants trying to make sense of their world'. Too often students ask the specific questions they want answers to, which are then subjectively interpreted to fit neatly with the researcher's predefined perceptions and assumptions. IPA takes a phenomenological approach through a double hermeneutic that is both questioning and, importantly, empathetic, and seeks to achieve an 'insider' view that accurately reflects and respects how individuals make sense of and attribute meaning to their personal and social worlds.

Smith *et al.* (2009) make the point that IPA is ideographic and that IPA studies tend to be relatively small. In addition to individual analyses, a small sample that is homogeneous then allows for a further examination that looks at differences and similarities. This is a strategy that I adopted with my ethnographic sample, my six key participants with whom, as I have previously outlined, I spent considerable time, allowed me to do an individual analysis of their worldviews that were to varying extents personal, social and, of course, work orientated. For example, while the focus of my research was how change was communicated to them and how they experienced it, I also necessarily got to know them very well around their work history, their career pathways and their social and familial influences and experiences. From the 'pick 'n' mix' analyses I undertook, and my subsequent interpretation of their worldviews, I then drew conclusions that allowed for comparisons to be made around how the civil servants made sense of their working environment and, in particular, organizational change.

The development of IPA in the mid 1990s as Smith *et al.* (2009) make clear, draws on theoretical frameworks from other disciplines. In doing so it produces an approach within psychology that draws on phenomenology, which values the experiential, thus giving psychology an exciting and cohesive framework to progress qualitative research and analysis. In Chapter 4, I discuss the disciplinary dominance in psychology that has traditionally privileged the scientific model and assert that ethnography could be utilized far more in psychology. I would suggest that an IPA analysis is highly useful, if not complementary to ethnographic projects, and, in particular, interview data. So let us have a look at the analysis process of IPA.[2]

IPA analysis: stages one and two

As with the thematic analyses already outlined, transcripts should be read and reread so that you become highly familiar with its content and flow. It is always a good idea to leave wide margins on the transcript so that there is sufficient room for note-taking. In IPA, the left-hand margin is used to make note of anything significant that catches your attention. It could be what is actually said, the way it is said, the language used, a quote or a non-verbal. Smith (2008: 67) describes this as being close to 'a free textual analysis', and as such there are no rules around what should or should not be notated. The next stage is to go back through the transcript and, in the right-hand column, to transform the original notes into emergent themes that encapsulate the essence of the notes; and potentially move the original note to a 'slightly higher level of abstraction', which may include 'psychological terminology' (Smith, 2008: 68). Smith (2008) suggests that the skill in doing this is to make links at the second stage that are at a higher level of abstraction and form theoretical connections. Although Smith (2008) talks of psychological terminology, I would suggest that this analysis can equally accommodate terminology from other social science disciplines. All transcript data holds potential to be of interest, however, as with any transcript, some sections will be richer than others and so some parts of the transcript will be annotated more than others. The important thing when progressing these two stages is to ensure a balance between the richness of what has been said, the themes that are generated and that theoretical connections are established. Let us have a go with our original quote, see Table 11.4.

Again, this is a very simple example and without analysing the entire transcript, the above emergent themes are highly speculative but hopefully it serves to illustrate the transition from stage one to two of an interpretative phenomenological analysis. To illustrate further the importance of not taking things at face value, whether it is by a regular or numeric thematic analysis or by IPA, I should at this point tell you that the participant who said this to me genuinely did love his job and the words he spoke concerning his colleagues were for the most part an accurate reflection. The participant spoke these words

Table 11.4 Example of IPA

Stage 1 – initial notes	*Quote*	*Stage 2 – emergent themes*
Job or career? Language – highly descriptive – love, wonderful	*I love my job, it's* *wonderful, it is. . . . I*	Over-emphasis
Added emphasis – 'really really'	*really, really enjoy it and*	
Speaks for 'everybody'?	*everybody on the* *section does which I*	Group identity – conformist
Hesitation – 'I think is . . .' I becomes 'we' . . .	*think is . . . we are only a*	
Size . . . Important?	*small section, but* *everybody there really*	Role/identity conflict
Everybody enjoys	*enjoys what they do.*	Lack of self-confidence

with real enthusiasm and this was evident in his body language or non-verbals, and the tone and pitch with which he spoke them. Throughout the considerable time I spent with him, his words and behaviour rang true; he did indeed love his job. Again, the point of making this clear to you is to illustrate that, phenomenologically, we always need to take a quote or indeed a transcript as just part of the whole and, as you can see through the above example, it would be easy to misinterpret the participant's words and the meaning he attributes to his world.

Themes and clustering

Once you have worked through stages one and two on the transcript, the next step is to bring order to the themes generated. You do this by constructing an 'initial list of themes', chronologically, in the order that they appeared, in the right-hand column of the transcript (Smith, 2008). Once these are compiled the next step requires a closer analysis that theoretically 'clusters' and orders the themes. Some themes will immediately be apparent as superordinate themes – that is, as overarching themes under which other themes naturally cluster. 'Clustering' can take some time and should not be rushed. Interpretation can be highly subjective and, to avoid any misrepresentation, conclusions drawn must be checked through continued referral to the transcript. As Smith (2008: 72) states: 'this form of analysis is iterative and involves a close interaction between reader and text'.

Once the list of 'clusters' has been compiled, the next stage is to bring order and coherence to the superordinate themes. You do this by producing a table that lists the superordinate themes. Under each superordinate theme the themes that were 'clustered' need to be listed, and alongside where to find them in the transcript, for example, page 2 line 15 can be represented as 2.15 'I love my job'. Accurate cross-referencing like this can prove invaluable at later stages, when you might want to recheck something, and especially during the 'writing up' process. It is highly likely that some themes will be discounted during the process because they do not fit comfortably under any of the superordinate themes, or are simply not rich enough in meaning to take forward.

IPA: the final stage

How themes are taken forward into the 'writing up' stage very much depends on the sample. If the sample of participants is small, then each case can be 'written up' on an individual basis and overall conclusions can be drawn between the cases. Alternatively, if the sample and amount of data warrant it, it might be more manageable if the themes across a number of cases are drawn together in a final 'master' table of themes (Smith 2008). The scope of the study in question might well determine how many themes can be explored in the 'write up' and so a master table allows us to see which of the superordinate themes are most prevalent or important. For example, in a dissertation, assuming the data is rich and has been analysed thoroughly, I suggest to students that four (or at a push six) key or superordinate themes are probably enough to unpack in detail in the final 'write up'. A master table or matrix can be invaluable in ordering and determining which themes should be 'written up' and the order in which they should appear.

Variations on a theme

IPA and 'regular' thematic analysis are variations on a theme; ethnographers draw on some form of themes-based approach to their data analysis. This form of analysis is inductive in nature and is predicated on the view that one lets data 'talk' for itself, with themes emerging from the data with as little initial framing as possible. Ethnographic data analysis takes time and effort; it is painstaking and it can feel overwhelming at first, but once analysis starts you will find that you have more themes and issues than you will need for your 'write-up'. All good data analysis relies on good data in the first place, which in turn relies on well designed and well planned fieldwork. If you have taken the time to plan and think through your fieldwork, then the chances are that you will have collected valuable data and, in turn, will be able to generate interesting and insightful themes and findings.

Looking ahead to writing

The next chapter deals more specifically with 'writing up' ethnographies. However, if you have taken the time (and it is time-consuming) to thoroughly go through your data, then 'writing up' will be much easier than you might expect. One final thing to say about analysis would be to remember to make reflexive notes about your views, feelings, reactions and so forth; as has been noted in several of the chapters of this book, the act of reflexivity is a key aspect of doing an ethnography. Field journals are useful repositories of reflexive material, but, even if you did not keep a journal, try to write reflexive material throughout your field notes. Do not leave reflexive writing until 'writing up', as you might become distanced from the field experience by that stage. Use the data preparation stage to make reflexive notes and summaries. Again, as with thematic analysis, do not try to edit reflexive notes; note as much as you can and see if you can attach reflections to wider data themes.

Suggested further reading

Brewer, J. D. (2000) *Ethnography*, Milton Keynes: Open University Press.

Bryman, A. and Burgess, R. G. (eds) (1994) *Analyzing Qualitative Data*, London: Routledge.

Fetterman, D. M. (1998) *Ethnography*, London: Sage.

Hammersley, M. and Atkinson, P. (1995) *Ethnography, Principles in Practice*, London: Routledge.

Smith, J. (1996) 'Beyond the divide between cognition and discourse: Using interpretative phenomenological analysis in health psychology', *Psychology and Health* 11: 261–71.

Smith, J. A., Flowers, P. and Larkin, M. (2009) *Interpretative Phenomenological Analysis: Theory, Method and Research*, London: Sage.

Reflective activities

1   In Chapters 2, 8 and 10, various participant observation activities are suggested. Select one and conduct a short piece of participant observation research. Try to collect as much data as you can. What types of data could you collect that would help create a picture of your field setting?

2   Using the data collected in the above exercise, follow the steps outlined in this chapter to conduct either a thematic analysis or an IPA analysis of your data. What themes emerge?

3   Reflecting on your research, think about what you might incorporate in a reflexive account of your research.

4   Looking at your themes and data, try to construct a plan for a 'write up' of your fieldwork into a brief ethnography.

Notes

1   A pseudonym.
2   For a more in-depth illustration of the IPA process, see Smith (2008) and Smith *et al.* (2009).

12

THE FINAL STAGE?

Writing up ethnographic research

Duncan Light

By this stage, it should be clear to you that ethnography is a distinctive and challenging way of 'doing' research. Ethnography aims to understand something – a community, event or way of life – from the inside, with a particular focus on 'everyday, lived experiences' (Cook 2005: 167). It uses overtly qualitative methods, such as in-depth interviews, focus groups, fieldwork diaries and behavioural observation, in order to get close to the people being studied and to understand them better on their own terms. Ethnography shuns the view (widespread in much social science research) that the researcher is a detached and impartial 'scientist' who seeks the 'truth': instead, ethnography openly acknowledges the subjectivity of the researcher (Crang and Cook 2007).

Bearing all this in mind, it is not surprising that the writing stage of ethnography is also a distinctive process. For ethnographers, 'writing up' is not simply a mechanical and relatively insignificant 'final stage' of the research process. Instead, writing is a central part of 'doing' ethnography. As Hammersley and Atkinson (2007: 191) have pointed out, ethnography 'is produced as much by how we write as by the processes of data collection and analysis'. Writing ethnographic research is a complex and demanding task. The aim is to convey the feel of what has been studied, representing reality in a concise but complete way (Fetterman 1998). Its aim is to evoke, as much as analyse, the setting, people or event that has been studied (Shurmer-Smith and Hannan 1994). Regardless of how much care has been taken over data collection, or the quality of the data that has been generated, a piece of ethnographic research can be clumsy, incomplete or unconvincing if it is not written effectively. Thus, writing ethnography requires particular writing skills, although the good news is that anybody who is committed to ethnographic research can develop these skills.

In this chapter, I will introduce some of the most important aspects of 'writing up' ethnographic research. I start by examining the role of writing within the overall research process, with particular reference to 'when' to start writing ethnographic research. I then outline some general guidelines for organizing and structuring your writing, and some key principles for ethnographic writing, particularly the use of 'thick' description, direct quotations and first-person writing. Finally, I consider the importance of being reflexive in your writing and of writing with particular audiences in mind.

How does writing fit into ethnographic research?

Students in the social sciences are conventionally taught a particular model of research (Crang and Cook 2007; Flick 2009). This treats research as a linear process, where various stages follow each other in a consistent and logical order. This model usually goes something like this: first select a research field; then undertake a review of relevant literature; refine and focus the aims of your specific project; collect data using whatever method is appropriate to the research aims; analyse that data using appropriate techniques; interpret and discuss the results; and, finally, 'write up' your research findings. This model has its origins in an approach to research derived from a philosophy known as positivism (Mansvelt and Berg 2005). Broadly speaking, positivism (and the 'post-positivist' variants, which have followed it) is an approach that stresses knowledge of the world derived from observation and/or experiment. It is an approach that underpins much research in the natural sciences, but which also enjoyed some popularity in the social sciences up until the 1960s. Although it has subsequently fallen out of favour, a broadly positivist model of research (in particular, the use of the 'scientific method') is still widespread in the social sciences (Graham 2005).

You can see that this conventional model of research treats 'writing up' as the last stage of the research process. Indeed, note how this book, like many others about qualitative research in general, and ethnography in particular, places the 'writing' chapter at the end! Writing is frequently regarded as something that happens *after* the 'proper' research has been undertaken and completed. It is simply a matter of reporting what has taken place (Holliday 2007). Moreover, 'writing up' is often treated as something straightforward, less significant and less problematic than the other parts of the research process (Mansvelt and Berg 2005).

However, ethnographers do not treat 'writing up' in this way. In particular, writing is not a mechanical process that can be routinely undertaken at the end of the 'real' research (Hammersley and Atkinson 2007). Instead, in ethnographic research, writing is something that starts much earlier and is embedded throughout the process of data collection, analysis and interpretation. For example, as you collect data and then go on to analyse it, all sorts of thoughts, ideas and interpretations will be occurring to you (Mansvelt and Berg 2005). These may be about which ideas or themes recur most often in your data, or those topics that generate the greatest range of responses, or ways of interpreting a particular research finding, or simply phrases or expressions that will sound good in the final product. All these ideas that you generate as you go along can then feed into the way that you finally write your ethnography.

As a result, research and writing are mutually constitutive, so that 'writing helps shape the research as much as it reflects it' (Mansvelt and Berg 2005: 225).

It is therefore good practice to keep a record of the additional ideas, observations, connections and interpretations that you generate during the collection and analysis of your field data. These notes might take the form of annotations or commentaries added to your original research field notes. Alternatively, you could keep a separate notebook that is, in effect, a commentary on your original field notes. These notes and ideas will feed into what becomes the final written product. In this way, reading, writing and doing research are deliberately entangled (Crang and Cook 2007), so that writing becomes an 'unfolding story' in which an argument progressively develops as the research progresses (Holliday 2007). The outcome is a more complex, nuanced and detailed 'write up' of your research than might be achieved by the conventional approach of leaving the 'writing up' until after all the data has been collected and analysed.

Finding a structure for your writing

Doing ethnography can generate huge quantities of data: including your original field notes, your subsequent comments and annotations, and the ideas that emerge as you analyse and interpret the data and link it back to existing theory and the wider academic literature. At some stage, you will have to make sense of this mass of data and present it in a written form for others to read. At the start you might feel, understandably, overwhelmed by the task. How are you going to organize and structure all of this data and then present it in a way that makes sense to someone reading your work?

There are some general principles to keep in mind. In particular it is important to recognize that 'ethnographic writing is a process of compression ... The goal is to represent reality concisely but completely and not to reproduce every detail and word' (Fetterman 1998: 123). In other words, you are aiming to capture the complexity of your data but at the same time, you have to recognize that some things will have to be left out. You cannot present all of your data and if you did so your written account would probably be unreadable. Hence, writing will involve a process of simplifying and synthesizing your data, to some extent, in order to distil the most significant findings for your reader.

Another point always to bear in mind is that there is no universal formula or method for 'writing up' an ethnography. Beware of thinking that there is a single, 'correct', 'true' way to 'write up' ethnographic research that you should be following. On the contrary, there is no 'right' or 'wrong' way to 'write up' an ethnography (Hammersley and Atkinson 2007). Two ethnographers working on the same project might independently 'write up' their work in completely different ways. Neither would necessarily be 'right' or 'wrong', although one account might be more insightful or convincing than the other. You should be aiming for a nuanced and coherent account that fully captures the complexity of the event or people that you studied. In order to achieve this you will have to make choices about what you will include in your written account and how you will frame and structure this account (see Mansvelt and Berg 2005). These choices may initially appear daunting. However, one of the advantages of beginning your writing during the period of data collection and interpretation is that the ideas you generate as you go along will frequently feed into the choices you need to make about writing and presenting your final product.

There are many ways of structuring and organizing your written report. A logical structure may suggest itself to you during the collection and analysis of your data. Failing that, there are a number of conventions for 'writing up' ethnographic research that you may decide to follow. One way is to organize your 'write up' around groups of ideas: categories, themes and concepts that are generated by, and recur during, your data analysis (Woods 2006). 'Categories' are basic ideas, perspectives or events that are identified by your analysis. Indeed, a common technique for analysing qualitative data involves the identification of discrete categories within your data and then allocating codes to these categories (see for example Crang 2005). 'Themes' are broader unifying links that run through or underpin your data, while 'concepts' are more abstract and theoretical notions. As you analyse your data you will notice that particular categories, themes or ideas reoccur. You can then organize your 'write up' around these analytic categories or themes, grouping together all material relating to a particular category/theme. This offers a clear and readable way of structuring your writing. You may decide to put all material about a particular theme into a separate chapter of the 'write up', or alternatively to subdivide a single chapter into sections, each of which has its own sub-heading and deals with a particular subject or idea. An alternative way of structuring your writing is chronologically (Hammersley and Atkinson 2007). As such, your written account would be an analytical narrative that charts the development of something over time. This can be a useful approach if you have undertaken a longitudinal study.

Key principles for ethnographic writing

Although individuals will have their own styles, there are a number of characteristics that distinguish ethnographic writing from other forms of writing in the social sciences. In particular, Fetterman (1998) argues that writing ethnography is underpinned by two stylistic conventions: 'thick description' and the use of extensive references to (or quotations from) the original field data.

'Thick description' is a technique originally developed by the anthropologist Clifford Geertz (1975). It is perhaps most easily understood by contrasting it with 'thin' description, which is simply an account (description) of something that has happened, such as a report of observed behaviour or something that was said during an interview. However, 'thick description' seeks to put something into a wider context, in order to explore and understand all the various meanings behind it (Holliday 2007). Indeed, it aims for as broad a contextualization as possible. The aim is to 'take the reader to the centre of an experience, event or action, providing an in-depth study of the context and the reasons, intentions, understandings, and motivations that surround that experience of occurrence' (Mansvelt and Berg 2005: 260). Hence, a simple presentation of research findings does not constitute 'thick description'. Instead, 'thick description' is a form of dense and elaborate (and ideally exhaustive) commentary on those findings that aims to give the reader a greater depth of understanding by fully contextualizing what the researcher has observed or experienced.

Let me illustrate this with an example from my own research (see Light 2009). A few years ago I accompanied a group of about twenty Dracula enthusiasts on a Halloween tour in Transylvania, Romania, that ended at 'Hotel Castle Dracula', high in the Carpathian Mountains. In interviews, a majority of people told me that they were disappointed with the hotel and that it did not look as they had expected. To stop there would constitute 'thin description'. However, 'thick description' would attempt to put this finding into a much wider context. We need to look at why these tourists were disappointed. Many of them were fans of Dracula/vampire films and Castle Dracula is an established trope of such films. The castle has been frequently portrayed as a dilapidated, sinister, haunted place on a mountain peak, inhabited by Count Dracula and all manner of other supernatural creatures. The tourists were expecting to find something that accorded with their expectations from (western) cinema. Moreover, at Halloween (a time when the boundaries between the material and the spiritual worlds are believed to temporarily break down) many of these tourists were expecting some sort of strange, otherworldly and supernatural experience on Halloween night (and a number of them regularly sought such experiences on Halloween). Indeed, several people were expecting to encounter Count Dracula in some form on Halloween night. They were not expecting 'Hotel Castle Dracula' to be a modern building with only a superficial resemblance to a castle. But then they were unaware that the building was constructed during Romania's Communist period (where any sort of engagement with Dracula and the supernatural was forbidden) and was designed by an architect who had never read *Dracula* or seen any western Dracula films. Hence, they found themselves in a not very frightening building in a not very sinister part of Transylvania. Indeed, many in the group said that they had encountered more 'realistic' representations of Castle Dracula in their home country. They were also unaware that the western Halloween is almost unknown in Romania and that very few Romanians are aware of the significance of Castle Dracula for western Dracula enthusiasts.

You can easily appreciate that it is a laborious and time-consuming task to write a 'thick description' well. Moreover you need to be thoroughly familiar with the cultural context which underlies whatever you are studying and sometimes developing this knowledge can itself take time. You also need to be aware that writing 'thick description' can use a lot of words. Undergraduate or postgraduate dissertations frequently impose word limits and these might constrain what you can say. To write ethnography effectively you may need to develop skills in being concise. Ultimately, however, your word limits might be such that you have to leave out a lot of material, in which case your 'thick description' cannot be as 'thick' as you might intend!

A second characteristic of ethnographic writing is the extensive reference to your original field data when writing a 'thick description'. This will usually take the form of verbatim quotations from interviews/focus groups, or detailed descriptions of behaviour that you have observed. The aim is to 'give voice' to your research participants (see Coffey 1999) and to let them express themselves in their own words (or their own behaviour). In this way you acknowledge that your participants are people and not simply objects of study (Wolcott 2009). This is one of the tenets of ethnography and enables you to capture the feel of the situation you were studying. However, when you make use of verbatim quotations resist the temptation to correct or improve on what people say. For example, listen to how often people say 'erm' or 'sort of' or 'you know' or 'like' in their everyday speech. You might feel that to include such verbal 'tics' will make your respondents appear ridiculous or that such expressions are not appropriate in a piece of academic research. However, an important part of giving 'voice' to your respondents is to allow them to speak in their own way (Coffey 1999). To attempt to improve or clarify what people have said is to deny them their own voice and also to impose your views about what is normal and acceptable speech on to the research data. In short, be faithful to your original field data, whether interviews or observations, and leave it in its original form so as to evoke fully the situation or event that you were studying.

When using verbatim quotations in your writing you should do so in a way that attempts to demonstrate the full range of views or responses in your field data. This is sometimes called 'polyvocality', meaning 'many voices' (Coffey 1999). For example, if you have interviewed people, you will rarely find that there is full agreement on a topic. Instead, there will usually be a broad spectrum of views. Similarly, if you have been observing behaviour you are unlikely to find that people all behave in the same way. Ethnography aims to engage with and represent the complexity of the everyday world. In particular, it recognizes that there are multiple versions of 'reality' (see Coffey 1999). Consequently, in your writing you should try to capture the depth and diversity of (and in) your field data.

One way of doing this might look something like this:

When asked about . . . [subject] . . . the most common response was . . . [brief summary]. For example, one person said . . . [verbatim

quote 1] . . . Similarly, another person said . . . [verbatim quote 2].
On the other hand, some people took the opposite view. For example
. . . [verbatim quote 3]. There were also a number of respondents
who expressed no strong view on the subject. For example . . .
[verbatim quote 4].

Note that if your quotes are lengthy (say, more than 15 words) you may choose
to set them apart from the main body of the text as illustrated above, with
indented margins both sides and a blank line above and below.

Although the extensive use of quotations or observations is central to
ethnographic writing, it goes without saying that you should never write
anything that can reveal the identity of the people being researched. Thus, the
identity of the people who have been quoted should always be concealed (unless
they are representing a particular organization and are speaking 'on the
record'). You can preserve the anonymity of your participants simply by
having a brief descriptive comment after a verbatim quotation (for example,
female, aged 29, manager). Alternatively, you can devise pseudonyms (invented
names) for your respondents.

Of course, writing an ethnography is about more than just assembling
quotations or observations in a logical order, so that they capture the complexity
of your data. Simply presenting field data does not constitute ethnography.
While the voices of your participants are important, of equal importance
is your interpretation of your research data. Hence, you need to embed
your quotations (or observations) within a 'thick description' by adding a
commentary, contextualization and analysis of those quotations and their
broader significance. In addition, your written account should not isolate itself
from existing literature and theories on the subject you are studying. Overall,
then, you need to produce a written account that weaves together your field
data (verbatim quotations or observations) and your interpretation and
discussion of the data (the 'thick description'), which also links to the work
of other researchers and the wider academic literature. The aim is for a text
that is dense and 'busy' (Hammersley and Atkinson 2007).

Below is an illustration, from my own research, of how writing an ethnography involves weaving together data, interpretation, contextualization and the
wider literature. This particular study was concerned with tourists who had
travelled to Transylvania for Halloween and, in particular, the importance to
them of Halloween night. You will see that the passage begins with a paragraph
that establishes the academic and theoretical context for what follows (the
importance of escapism, fun and self-definition for the tourist experience). I
then go on to explore my interview data in this context (another, equally valid,
way to go about this is to present research data first and then link back to a
theoretical context). You can see that this passage makes use of field data
in the form of direct quotes, anecdotes and observations. This example is, of
course, not definitive and there are many different ways of 'writing up' an

179

ethnography: indeed, another researcher might have written up the same data in a completely different way.

An example of how to write up ethnographic research

Contemporary analysis of tourism as a cultural phenomenon (e.g. Urry 2002; Franklin 2003) focuses on the meaning and significance of holidays for the individuals who 'perform' tourism. Tourism is framed both by notions of escape and 'letting go' and a belief in the restorative properties of a holiday. The holiday itself is a period of time characterized by freedom from normal routines, obligations and disciplinary gazes (Edensor 2000: 325; Hennig 2002: 179–80). As such, a holiday presents an opportunity for self-actualization or 'self-making' (Urry 2002: 84): it is an occasion for making and affirming senses of personal identity. Tourism is an occasion when we can be (if only for a limited time) our true or 'authentic' selves (Wang 1999: 363). Consequently, Hennig (2002: 185) argues tourism takes place as much in the realm of the imagination as in the physical world and being on holiday is often a chance to engage in fantasy and escapism.

Many of the tourists evoked their visit to Transylvania in just such ludic terms. A visit to 'Dracula's Castle' was an opportunity to engage in a little fantasy and play. Being in Transylvania for Halloween offered excitement and adventure, particularly the *frisson* of an imagined encounter with the ineffable and the mysterious (cf. Inglis and Holmes 2003). Thus several people mentioned their excitement about *sleeping* in Dracula's Castle in the Borgo Pass. Others declared their hope of encountering Dracula in some form or other during their stay there. One visitor mentioned the thrill of being slightly afraid while staying in the Borgo Pass:

> I don't believe in the supernatural, but I can enjoy it and I can get a thrill out of pretending it exists . . . it's escapism, it's a chance to, you know, suspend the rules . . . let's pretend there are vampires and . . . I'm also looking forward to being scared.

> Three of the group mentioned that they hoped to hear wolves howling in the surrounding mountains. And one woman told me how she was intending to quietly creep back to her room at midnight and leave a glass of chilled wine on the windowsill for Count Dracula. For these tourists, Halloween was a time – and Transylvania a place – for giving full rein to the imagination.

> For almost all the visitors the most eagerly anticipated part of the tour was the costumed Halloween Ball at Hotel Castle Dracula. One English visitor stated: 'It's not often you can relax and do something quite mad without any inhibitions or restrictions.' Another described the Ball as an opportunity to 'dress up and leave reality

behind for an evening'. Similarly, an American stated: 'Halloween's my favourite holiday in the world ... I love dressing up. I love costume, I love acting out.' Many of the group invested considerable time and expense in their costumes: several came as Count (or Countess) Dracula, others as vampires, devils, witches, wolves and assorted monsters. Again we see the ludic dimensions of Halloween. The evening was an opportunity to leave behind normal routines, boundaries and inhibitions, and to dress up and fully engage with, and celebrate, the Transylvania place myth with little regard for the views of other people.

(extract from Light 2009: 193–5)

'Writing up' across the social sciences

Finally, it is important to recognize that ethnography is different from other 'standard' approaches to 'writing up' data in the social sciences. To reiterate the point I made earlier, many students are still taught a model where the written account is separated into clear sections: presentation of data; analysis of data; interpretation of data; discussion of findings. This is an effective (if rather blunt) way of 'writing-up' a piece of research so that it has a clear and logical structure. However, it goes without saying that this approach simply does not work with ethnographic writing. It is not realistic to separate out presentation, interpretation and discussion of data in this way. Instead, as already mentioned, writing an ethnography involves producing a narrative where presentation, interpretation, discussion and contextualization are seamlessly interwoven. This is a challenging task, and in many ways it is more difficult than the rather mechanical 'present data, analyse data, interpret data, discuss findings' approach.

The voice of the author

A lot of research in the social sciences is written in a 'standard' and rather bland academic style. It is characterized by a neutral, detached and pseudo-scientific tone that gives away nothing about the author. In turn, this is another legacy of the positivist/scientific turn in the social sciences, which emphasized a particular model of the researcher: an objective, detached 'scientist', who simply sought the truth and who maintained a professional distance from whatever he or she was researching. The 'scientist' was expected to 'write up' his or her research in an impersonal and objective tone, since it was believed that this was appropriate and somehow gave the research greater credibility. Indeed, any indication of the presence of the author/researcher was somehow regarded as 'contamination' of the rigour of the research (Holliday 2007). Hence, research papers in the social sciences are littered with expressions such as 'An experiment was designed . . .', 'interviews were undertaken . . .', 'from this it is apparent that . . .' and 'the author considers that . . .'. Nobody speaks in this curious and stilted way (characterized by excessive use of the passive voice) but many social scientists still write like this. Indeed, some academic journals only accept papers written in this way. And, of course, many students are strongly encouraged to adopt this 'correct' style of academic writing in their assignments.

Needless to say, this way of writing is inappropriate for ethnography. Indeed, ethnographic researchers do not pretend to be detached and impartial in the way that they 'do' ethnography. Instead, there is a recognition that the 'positionality' of the researcher; their social and ideological background, biography, prior experiences, attitudes, values and so on, will all influence what they choose to research and how they go about it (Crang and Cook 2007; Hay 2005). This approach also influences the way that ethnographers 'write up' their work. In particular, as Coffey (1999: 126) argues, there 'is general agreement that "silent" authorship – writing the text without a visible presence – works against the contemporary spirit of ethnography'. As such, rather than trying to exclude the voice of the researcher/author, ethnographers actively try to write the author *in* to their research (Coffey 1999; Mansvelt and Berg 2005).

In practical terms, this means writing in the first person (using 'I', 'We' and so on). As Holliday (2007: 136) argues, using the first person in this way is a 'major device for separating the researcher's agenda from the other voices in the text, thus increasing transparency and accountability'. This could mean using expressions such as: 'In this study I will explore . . .', 'I interpret this as meaning . . .', 'a number of people told me that . . .' and so on. This enables you to express your positionality and subjectivity, and demonstrate how *you* as an individual are involved in the process of collecting and interpreting data. On the other hand, try to avoid the 'naïve' use of the first person ('I went to my field site and there I did 20 interviews . . .' in which you simply describe what you have thought or done. Furthermore, be careful not to make your voice the dominant one (Fetterman 1998). Too much reference to *you* risks drowning out the voices of your participants, but it is their voices and experiences that are the most important part of an ethnographic study. Therefore limit references to *you* to those that are necessary for a coherent narrative. For more discussion on writing in this way see Coffey (1999) and Crang and Cook (2007).

Finally, a cautionary note: there are still many people working in universities who are unsympathetic to first-person writing (and some have little time for ethnography either). If your ethnography is undertaken as part of a dissertation or thesis that will be submitted for assessment you may want to keep in mind the person who will be marking it. In particular, if you know that the marker is not sympathetic to first-person writing you may unfortunately feel it more prudent to adopt a more conventional and detached writing style, even if it goes against your instincts to do so.

Representation, responsibility and reflexivity

Writing ethnography raises fundamental and problematic issues of power and knowledge. Ethnographers are engaged in writing about 'Other' people and their lives; they are telling their stories for them (James *et al.* 1997). In effect they are creating knowledge about the people they have researched. Writing an ethnography, then, is a process of representation on the part of the writer/researcher. The writer will make choices and decisions (sometimes unacknowledged) about what to say (and how) about the people being studied. Indeed, if word limits are an issue these choices can be as fundamental as what to include and what to leave out. Thus, the way in which the 'researched' are portrayed will be informed and mediated by the complex positionality of the writer: his or her background, personal biography, prior experiences, attitudes, values, agenda, cultural baggage and so on. Consequently, writing ethnography is not a neutral or value-free process but instead involves an active shaping of the worlds and peoples that are being represented (Crang and Cook 2007). As one ethnographer has noted: 'there is little question that, through our fieldwork . . . we are engaged in the construction of the lives of others' (Coffey 1999: 130). And we need to keep in mind that the representation of 'the researched' by the ethnographer may not necessarily be the way that they would choose to represent themselves.

Writing ethnography, then, entails certain responsibilities on the part of the writer (Crang and Cook 2007; Hammersley and Atkinson 2007). In particular, ethnographic researchers need to develop 'reflexivity'. Put simply, reflexivity (or being 'reflexive') is about engaging in self-critical and self-conscious introspection and scrutiny (Hay 2005). It is about deliberately asking yourself how *you*, as a human being, researcher and writer, might have shaped the very thing that you are studying (Hammersley and Atkinson 2007). It also includes reflecting on the self–Other relationship, between you and your research participants that was at the core of your research. Being reflexive includes acknowledging that you are not some authoritative figure who is master of all that you survey (Crang and Cook 2007). Instead it means recognizing the limitations of your research and of you as a researcher. Reflexivity is a crucial skill to develop at all stages of ethnographic research, but it is especially important when you are 'writing-up' your research.

Considering your audience

An obvious point about writing ethnography is to write with your audience, whoever will be reading it, in mind. Ethnographies can be written for many different audiences; undergraduate markers, doctoral examiners, peer-reviewed journals, policy makers and so on. Each audience will be different in terms of their background knowledge, assumptions and expectations (Hammersley and Atkinson 2007). Therefore, what you write needs to be appropriate, accessible and understandable to your readers, as Fetterman argues: 'the ethnographer's ability to write to different audiences will determine the effectiveness of the work' (1998: 112). From this it follows that the same material could be 'written up' in different ways for different audiences (Woods 2006).

I can give another example from my own research in Romania. For some years I have been researching 'Dracula tourism' in Transylvania. This is an activity generated in Western Europe and America in which Dracula enthusiasts visit Transylvania (part of modern Romania) in search of the literary and supernatural roots of Bram Stoker's famous novel *Dracula*. Most educated Romanians are well aware that in the West their country has become synonymous with vampires and the supernatural, and many of them are rather weary of being stereotyped in this way. Some Romanians are also resentful about the (groundless) confusion between the Count Dracula of fiction and a fifteenth-century prince called Vlad Țepeș, known sometimes as 'Dracula' during his lifetime. This prince is regarded as something of a national hero for his efforts to restore order to his country in turbulent times: Romanians are not happy that he is sometimes equated with a blood-drinking vampire. On top of this, there is a degree of bewilderment that some international tourists overlook Transylvania's abundant other attractions in their single-minded quest for an entirely fictional Dracula.

This context has significant implications for the way I 'write up', or talk about, my research to Romanian and non-Romanian audiences. If I am addressing an audience outside Romania (whether verbally or in writing) I approach the subject from a 'western' perspective. I take it as read that my audience is aware of the international popularity of Dracula and vampires, and I then go on to consider why Dracula presents Romania with a dilemma. The root of this dilemma is that Bram Stoker's famous novel is little known in Romania. Instead, for Romanians the term 'Dracula' evokes a national hero: thus, Romanians often feel the need to 'defend' the reputation of one of their leaders against associations with vampirism. This in turn explains why Romanians are so reluctant to embrace the fictional Count Dracula and their unwillingness to cater for Dracula enthusiasts wanting to find vampires in Romania. However, when I am addressing a Romanian audience I need to take a different approach. When I talk of 'Dracula', my audience will immediately think of Vlad Țepeș and will know little about the fictional Count Dracula. Therefore I need to spend some time discussing Stoker's novel, including its Transylvanian setting, its global popularity and its importance in western popular culture. Moreover, in order to gain the respect and attention of my audience I feel it important to situate myself outside western stereotypes about Romania. Thus, I make it clear that I know there are no vampires in Romania; that I am well aware that Vlad Țepeș was not a vampire; and that I understand why many Romanians hold Vlad Țepeș in high regard. I can then go on to explore the nature of Romania's dilemma with Dracula and help my audience to understand why their country is equated with vampires in the western popular imagination. In other words, I can present a broadly similar argument in completely different ways for different audiences.

Of course, for most students the question of audiences is unproblematic. If you are an undergraduate then your audience is the lecturer who will be marking your dissertation. If you are a postgraduate, your audience will probably be the expert who will be examining your thesis. In such cases, the audience you should be writing for is clear. Remember that you will be writing for an experienced academic who will probably be an ethnographer himself or herself. Your marker will be looking for evidence that you have undertaken ethnographic field research, situated your research findings in a wider academic context, and that you have been able to 'write up' your findings by interweaving 'thick' contextualization and interpretation with extracts from your original field data. If you are an undergraduate student, it is important to remember that your marker will only be expecting undergraduate-level work.

One last point about audiences: you need to keep in mind that the people who were the subject of your ethnography may be among your audience. You should not assume that your research participants will never see the results of your research (Hammersley and Atkinson 2007). Indeed, in some circumstances your participants may insist on seeing a copy of your work, particularly if you have undertaken your research in a place of work. In such circumstances you will need to write with several audiences in mind; the marker of your dissertation, but also the organization or institution that sponsored or permitted your research. To safeguard your participants you may have to (reluctantly) censor yourself and leave out details that you do not want the organization to know about.

And so the story ends . . .

Ethnography is a complex and challenging way of doing research. Similarly, 'writing up' ethnographic research is an equally challenging task; as Fetterman (1998) notes, writing ethnography is hard work! There are certain 'golden rules' with ethnographic writing. First, the process of writing should not be left until the very end. Instead, writing should begin with data collection and should evolve through the entire research process. Second, your writing should aim for as deep a discussion, interpretation and contextualization as possible. Such 'thick description' helps you evoke your data in the deepest and most nuanced way. Third, your writing should make extensive reference to your original data, whether through the use of verbatim quotations or descriptions of observed behaviour.

Perhaps the easiest way to get to grips with ethnographic writing is to read what other ethnographers have written (Hammersley and Atkinson 2007). Of course reading around the subject is an essential part of being a student, but it is especially important with ethnography. By looking at what other researchers have written you will see the ways in which they have approached the task and tackled the problem of presenting and structuring their data. The more you read the work of other writers, the more you will appreciate and understand what 'works'. Indeed, you could do worse than model your writing style on that of other ethnographers whose work you admire.

Finally, keep in mind that writing ethnography can be a long process of trial and error. You may start writing only to find that your structure does not work, or that the 'feel' of your data is not coming through, or that your argument or contextualization is not convincing. In such cases, you may need to start all over again. Indeed, writing and re-writing is a quite normal part of ethnographic research (Crang and Cook 2007). However, this can be a useful experience. Through redrafting your work, you will be able to produce a final version, which succeeds in being 'true' to the data. Writing ethnography can be demanding, but when you produce a final version which 'works', which captures and evokes the situation, event or people that you were studying, you will know that it was worth the effort.

Suggested further reading

Clifford, J. and Marcus, G. E. (eds) (1986) *Writing Culture: The Poetics and Politics of Ethnography*, Berkeley: University of California Press.

Crang, M. and Cook, I. (2007) *Doing Ethnographies*, London: Sage.

Hammersley, M. and Atkinson, P. (2007) *Ethnography: Principles into Practice*, 3rd edn, London: Routledge.

Holliday, A. (2007) *Doing and Writing Qualitative Research*, 2nd edn, London: Sage.

James, A., Hockey, J. and Dawson, A. (eds) (1997) *After Writing Culture: Epistemology and Praxis in Contemporary Anthropology*, London: Routledge.

Wolcott, H. F. (2009) *Writing Up Qualitative Research*, 3rd edn, London: Sage.

Some examples of well-written ethnographies in geography

Edensor, T. (1998) *Tourists at the Taj: Performance and Meaning at a Symbolic Site*, London: Routledge.

Ghodsee, K. (2005) *The Red Riviera: Gender, Tourism and Postsocialism on the Black Sea*, Durham, NC: Duke University Press.

Verdery, K. (2003) *The Vanishing Hectare: Property and Value in Postsocialist Transylvania*, Ithaca, NY: Cornell University Press.

Reflective activities

1 How does ethnography differ from other conventional approaches to research regarding the timing of the writing stage?

2 How does writing an ethnography differ from writing a conventional academic essay?

3 How might you write yourself 'in' to an ethnography? Why is it important to do so?

4 How might you go about being reflexive in 'writing up' an ethnography? How might your written account benefit as a result?

13

LEAVING THE FIELD

A reflexive journey

Sal Watt

When we started talking about this book, we did so based on our experiences as field researchers and teachers of research methods in the social sciences. It was born over many cups of coffee and protracted discussions. We expressed our frustration at the representation of ethnography across the social sciences, in textbooks and among our students, who sometimes think it is simply a question of a 'bit of an observation'. This is hardly surprising because textbooks often describe ethnography in cold or clinical formulaic terms. For example, ethnography is the study of culture, the researcher enters the field, gets to know people, does some interviews, conducts participant observation, writes field notes, analyses the field notes, 'writes up' – and there might be a mention of reflecting on the process or, better still, something on reflexivity.

The aim of this book was to bring alive the process of ethnography: to introduce methodological considerations but to do so alongside our experience of conducting ethnographic research. As you will have seen through the chapters, the researchers have been candid in their reflections about the mistakes they have made and how, in hindsight, they could have done things differently. It is this process of reflection and reflexivity that often becomes lost, gets overlooked or simply is not sufficiently explained in textbooks, or indeed the classroom. In this chapter, we will consider the process and importance of reflection and reflexivity alongside our own experiences, and the often emotional process of 'leaving the field'. So first let us consider what we mean by reflection and reflexivity.

Looking inward: reflection and reflexivity?

We first need to make the distinction between reflection and reflexivity. Put very simply, throughout our lives we continually reflect on both past and present everyday life experiences, for example, what we have just done, seen or experienced. It is a process that involves all the senses: sight, hearing, touch, taste and smell. We draw on memories and often, relatedly, our emotions. However, to be reflexive is to look deeper when drawing on these reflections and to ask questions such as: what was my part in this? How might I have influenced something or some behaviour? If you think about this in terms of an argument, you may have had with your best friend: to be *reflective* is to think back and possibly describe to someone who said what in the argument; to be *reflexive* is to stand back, reflect on the argument and reflexively ask questions around your involvement, for example, what was my part in the argument? Did I say something that may have caused offence? Did I fuel the argument by some comment I made? Reflexivity is first about reflection but then relies on us being introspective, that is, looking inward and taking responsibility for our own thoughts, feelings and actions, and asking ourselves probing questions around our own motivation or involvement. This process is known as reflexive practice and it is something your teachers and lecturers do all the time. We come out of class, reflect on how the class went; what worked; what did not; how could things be done differently next time and, importantly, question how we might have influenced things. In undertaking any form of research, reflexive practice is just the same; and it is crucial that qualitative researchers and, in particular, ethnographers engage in this process.

Throughout this text, we have emphasized that qualitative research, and hence ethnography, is very different from positivistic or scientific means of conducting research. We do not reduce experience to quantifiable data that can be statistically tested, replicated and generalized to a wider population. However, therein lies a problem, because in a world that has come to value a tradition of scientific and rational enquiry, our qualitative findings can be called into question around their reliability and validity. This is problematic because such an expectation is at odds with the ethos of qualitative research; research that values people's subjective experience. As qualitative researchers, although we value subjective life experiences, we strive to conduct our research, and gather and interpret our data, objectively. However, because of the subjective nature of our data, in many respects we have to work all the harder when 'accounting' for our findings and in demonstrating our own objectivity in the research process.

Behar (2003) makes the point that ethnographies need to be taken on trust and at face value with the hope that the ethnographer was both a sensitive and good listener. If our accounts are to be taken on trust then we need to assure the reader and the scientific community more generally, that our research is as authentic and as objective as it possibly can be. In order to achieve this then we must be highly engaged in reflexive practice.

So how do we demonstrate our reflexive practice? In the first instance, as ethnographers we spend extensive time in the 'field', reflect on what we have seen, heard and generally experienced, this then emerges into 'thick' description. However, as previously outlined, the process does not end there because we need to reflexively pose some very pertinent questions. We need to question our own preconceptions before and during the research period; how the researched group presented themselves; the extent to which this may have been influenced by the researcher's presence; how that might then have influenced the data; and, importantly, how it might have impacted on the interpretation process. This list is not exhaustive but it gives you an idea of the many important questions researchers ask in trying to ensure they take full responsibility for their part in the research process and, of course, in striving to maintain their objectivity (see Willig 2008).

The role of a qualitative researcher and, in particular, the journey an ethnographer embarks on can be difficult. To allay criticism around objectivity we need to be open and honest about our engagement with the researched group, our experiences, preconceptions, interpretations and, in short, account for our own potential subjectivity. If our ethnographic accounts are to be taken on trust then we need to demonstrate our full engagement with the reflexive process. We can do this by locating our own subjective and personal stand-points, for example, moral, religious, political, socio-economic and so on, in the final 'write up'. If we do this, then the reader is fully informed of our standpoint and from this can make an informed decision as to whether they trust our account and whether they want to read our research further.

We can see through the chapters of this text that the contributors have been highly reflexive regarding their thoughts, feelings and some of the issues they have faced. Nevertheless, the process of reflexivity is ongoing and it does not simply end when the research ends; our research experiences, thoughts and feelings stay with us and become part of us. We thought one of the best ways to illustrate the ongoing process of reflexivity was to ask some of the contributors to write a small vignette around their experience of 'leaving the field' and to share these with you.

Leaving the field

The following vignettes illustrate the reflexive process in action. You will notice there is an overlap between the thoughts, feelings and concerns that the respective researchers raise. Let us start with Wendy Laverick's thoughts on 'leaving the field'.

Wendy Laverick

Doing justice to it all . . .

Ethnographic researchers are, it is widely acknowledged, notoriously affiliated towards the subjects of their studies. In part it has been argued by theorists such as Brewer (1990), Liebling (1999, 2001), Liebling and Stanko (2001), Burman *et al.* (2001), that such an affiliation provides insight into social processes and groups, allowing the researcher to enter the secret world of the subject. However, my own experience led to a great deal of ambivalence. Ultimately, despite informing the research participants from the outset regarding the selfish objectives of my research task, namely to obtain a PhD qualification, I have since felt a degree of shame, alongside a sense of achievement, at doing just that. Ultimately, it was perhaps inevitable, given the nature of the topic, that the research data would document a degree of the sadness and despair of those involved. However, the extent and depth of such feelings could not possibly be imagined or anticipated prior to the commencement of the interviews themselves. Returning to my own life, post-research, was disturbing. It is perhaps unsurprising that, upon receipt of my doctorate, it took a few years to revisit the narrative accounts, and that I submerged myself in new challenges resulting from a new teaching career and family commitments, in addition to various 'safe' projects. The lingering feelings of frustration, disloyalty, even betrayal, at my detachment and the lack of impact of my research are not, however, far away; they drive my personal need to disseminate the research findings to a wider audience, in order to do 'justice' to their honesty and the contribution they may be able to make.

We can see from Wendy's words that achieving her PhD was perhaps 'bitter sweet'; her sense of achievement seems over shadowed by a degree of shame she felt around the instrumentality of the process. We can see that Wendy's research in the prison service found her unprepared for the depth of feelings she experienced, and that what followed was a difficult period of readjustment that saw her rise to new challenges as a diversionary activity. She talks about feelings of frustration and disloyalty, and the need to do justice to her research findings. Leaving the field for most of us is a very difficult period of readjustment and we all experience this in different ways and to varying degrees. Julie Scott Jones's 'leaving the field' vignette concerning her covert research illustrates just how difficult a transition this can sometimes be.

Julie Scott Jones

Dreams, guilt and writer's block

When I left 'God's Way' community, I was glad to leave and relieved no longer to have the pressure of 'playing a role'. I spent a couple of months in the USA before returning to the UK to 'write up' my doctoral thesis. It was only when I returned to the UK to start writing that the enormity of what I had done and been through hit me. I was unable to write anything about my research for a year: I could not face it. Every time I started to write or think about writing, I felt guilty. I had a recurring dream every night for a year where I was living on the community, unable to leave, feeling trapped and anxious.

Looking back, I was clearly processing the emotional fall-out of my research, but what strikes me now are two things. First, no one talked about fieldwork stress when I was a postgraduate ethnographer and, even today, there are few books on it; yet the emotional consequences of long-term fieldwork may be considerable. Second, I think I was naïve not to expect such an emotional reaction to what I had gone through, and I wonder to this day, why I did not seek some form of counselling. Again, we rarely discuss the aftermath of fieldwork as about anything other than data analysis and 'writing up'; where is our duty of care to support the fieldworker's transition back to 'real life'? I also remember the stress of 'writing up' my data: stress caused by the heavy responsibility to do justice by 'God's Way', to give them 'voice', to make their lives seem understandable, to challenge the stereotypes that people might have of them. Again, this stress of duty of care to participants in the writing stage is not widely discussed and we need to be more open about it.

You do not ever leave the field because it becomes part of who you are; the experience is part of you and informs who you are both personally and academically. The field is your construction, to an extent, and therefore you take it with you: it is not an overstatement to say that 'God's Way' changed my life. 'God's Way' has been part of my life for more than a decade after I left it; I cannot let them go but often wish I could. I went to 'God's Way' and I lived their way of life for almost a year; today they continue and they await the end of the world as they always have done.

As Julie's 'leaving the field' story indicates, her experience was all the more difficult because of its covert nature. Covert research in itself is very difficult, particularly over a sustained period of time; time which inevitably places immense psychological stress on the researcher. In Julie's case, she assumed a different identity and performed a role, which was at odds with her usual identity, social location and social activity. We can see in Julie's account that this dual identity evoked much stress both in and out of the field, resulting in what she earlier described (see Chapter 8) as personality dissonance. Julie makes the point that she cannot let go of 'God's Way', it has changed her and has become part of her. This is not uncommon and we will return to this point later in this chapter. Like Wendy, Julie also could not face her data when she returned from the USA. Avoidance of data is again common as the next story indicates.

Sal Watt

In and out

Leaving the Civil Service perhaps predictably evoked a sense of *déjà vu*. As a former Civil Servant, I prevaricated and finally took a huge decision to take voluntary redundancy. Right up to the point of leaving, I was very unsure I had made the right decision. In truth, going back and researching how change was contemporarily communicated in the Service was partly driven by a personal sense of unfinished business. Going back turned out to be a cathartic journey that brought with it mixed emotions. My research was not conducted in any of the sections in which I had previously worked, and did not involve former colleagues, but when I returned my face was familiar to many and I was generously welcomed back.

My time there threw up many questions and allowed me to reflect on whether I had done the right thing in choosing to leave six years earlier. I pondered how far my career might have progressed had I chosen to stay and I lamented the people that had come and gone with whom I had worked. I felt accepted and part of the community I researched and so leaving again was painful. I worry over the extent I would and should remain in contact with those who had so generously given of their time, thoughts and feelings. To this point, I have been very reticent in sharing this research more widely within the academic community. For several years, I could not bear to revisit my PhD and it gathered dust on its shelf. I recognize now that this was to some extent caught up in the 'leaving the field process'. Writing this book has brought clarity to this and allowed me to think through my publishing reticence. Did I do the right thing in initially leaving the Civil Service? Yes I did. Now it is time to let go and finally do justice to the data that I was privileged to gather and, of course, to those individuals who shared their working lives with me.

Unlike Julie, I knew the environment I was entering and so the transition was far less stressful. However, like Wendy, I also angst over my motivation for undertaking my PhD research and question the foundation of 'unfinished business' on which it was partly built. In common with Wendy and Julie, I too had difficulty facing my data, both at the 'writing up' stage and later through my reticence to publish. Re-entering a familiar setting also brings with it its own set of problems, as does sharing a background with participants. So, in common with my experiences, let us now look at John E. Goldring's 'leaving the field' story, because his association with his research group brought with it unique challenges.

John E. Goldring

Say hello, wave goodbye

At some point in the future, I suspect, I will stop working with the Gay Married Men's Group but that time has not come yet. The

192

continuing changing legal and social climate towards gay men means there is still much to be learnt and reported. In some respects, writing this chapter has reinvigorated my interest in this research, and I now have the confidence to juggle both ethnographic data collection and the participatory activities of the group. Far from leaving the field, I feel I am now better placed to conduct more ethnographic research; possibly even expand the field. Perhaps my initial anxiety over formally collecting data was in some respects my methodological departure. Yet surely there is more to ethnography than the art of collecting data.

First and foremost, it is a relational approach to research that requires some emotional attachment. It seems somewhat aloof and inauthentic to assume that the friendships developed over the years with past and present members could easily be ended. You could read this as a word of caution. Leaving the field is not as straightforward as it may appear. Reflect on my dual roles of researcher and group facilitator: am I cornered into a position of being unable to leave the group? Currently, I am once again the only volunteer. The nature of the group means it is difficult to maintain an active pool of other workers, partly because of the group's success in supporting people to find the necessary strength to take control of their lives. Once they do, they often do not have time even to attend the group, let alone volunteer for it. I do sometimes feel trapped but, as a social capitalist, the rewards still outweigh this concern.

Although John's initial research is complete, he has not left the field and, as he explains, he does not feel he is able to do so at the present time. John concedes there is a tension in researching a group that you are familiar with, but his knowledge and involvement has, without question, been immensely advantageous in understanding the needs of the Gay Married Men's Group. Further, it has allowed him to progress the support offered to group members. Although John sometimes feels trapped, his work with this group is nevertheless rewarding. This is an important point, because so far we seem to have talked a great deal about our anxieties, but our work also brings with it many rewards and, as Duncan Light now explains, can be highly enjoyable and indeed, sometimes even fun!

Duncan Light

Halloween in Transylvania

My most recent experience in the 'field' involved spending a week travelling with a group of tourists who had come to Romania to spend Halloween in Transylvania. For me, it was an interesting experience of wearing different hats and playing different roles. On the one hand, I was an academic researcher. At the start of the week, wearing this hat, I fulfilled my ethical obligations by explaining to these tourists who I was and what I was doing. On the other hand, I was also a tourist in Transylvania on a Halloween tour. Perhaps for this reason the group quickly accepted me as one of them. Hence, I was very much a participant rather than a detached, impartial 'scientist' (and this, after all, is what ethnography is all about). Over the week, I spent a lot of time talking and socializing with the group and a number of them took a keen interest in my research. Although they recognized that I did not share their interest in the supernatural, most of them were more than happy to take part in an interview with me and I really enjoyed talking to them.

Therefore, at the end of the holiday, which for me was my departure from the 'field', I had mixed emotions. On the one hand, I was glad that the exhausting process of interviewing was all over. I was also glad that a week of quite serious partying had ended. I had found it hard work wearing two hats over the course of the week and now I needed some sleep! However, there was also a tinge of sadness: I had really enjoyed meeting these people and I was sorry to say goodbye to them. They did not feel like research participants; they were more like friends. In fact, we did all keep in touch by 'round robin' emails for a couple of weeks after the tour ended. Then, once we had all said goodbye, my academic identity took over again. I was bogged down by questions such as 'when am I going to find time to transcribe all these interviews' and 'how am I going to make sense of all this data?'. But then, when I finally got round to analysing my data and writing something for publication, it was like reliving the fun of that week in Transylvania all over again. It just goes to show that while ethnographic research is hard work it can also be highly enjoyable!

Duncan's ethnography in this instance was not of a long duration but the time spent with his group of tourists was intense and it is clear to see that firm friendships were forged and to some extent maintained. It again demonstrates the dual roles and identities that ethnographers adopt. In this instance, Duncan's identity as an academic and fellow tourist in Romania allowed him to socialize and enjoy the company of the tourists seeking a unique Halloween experience in Transylvania. Although Duncan describes the experience as tiring, hard work and one which evoked a 'tinge of sadness'; it illustrates that ethnography is not necessarily an angst-ridden process but instead can be 'highly enjoyable!' However, returning to a sensitive topic, the final vignette and word comes from Helen Jones's story.

Helen Jones

Farewell for now . . .

Entering sensitive topic areas such as sexual violence takes a lot of negotiation and planning, and so too does leaving the research field. When I first began researching violence in women's lives, I did not think I would still be here twenty years later. Of course, my first research participants have long since moved on. Those women who first spoke to me, sharing their most intimate experiences, gave me more than I ever gave them. At the time, I did not even realize that researchers have obligations and responsibilities to the people involved in their research. Observing the ebb and flow of work at a rape crisis centre, noticing the way the work affected volunteers and paid workers, and speaking with women who had accessed the service for support, made me realize that this was more than 'being nosey with a purpose': these were real people who deserved ethical consideration. I did not want to say goodbye, I wanted to stay in touch; but I also knew it was important not to exploit the situation or try to change the research relationship into an inappropriate form of friendship. Happily, dissemination has always offered a return to the field. The negotiation of what to write and how to write has offered a 'right of return' and often led to further pieces of research. For me, as a researcher committed to her research area, this means that leaving is never a final 'goodbye' but simply a 'farewell'.

In Helen's story, we can see that her research is sustained and ongoing in what is a highly sensitive area. Her commitment, obligation and responsibility to the women that she has researched is realized through dissemination. Helen's concern that participant researcher boundaries should not be breached for exploitative purposes gives a clear indication of her commitment to representing her cohorts responsibly, while dissemination affords her new opportunities, where she can return to her chosen research area and field of expertise. For Helen it is a question of 'farewell' rather than goodbye, which is perhaps an optimistic note on which to draw some conclusions.

A shared understanding

As you can see from these vignettes and from the chapters in this book, there is much overlap and shared understanding between ethnographers. It is underpinned by a shared understanding based on ethnography's ethos of core values. We share reflexive concern over how we conduct our research, we share commitment to our participants and respect as to how we treat them and the groups we research, how we represent them and ultimately how to give them 'voice'. The process can be challenging, frustrating and stressful but, on the other hand, it is also highly rewarding, creative and can be enjoyable. The ethnographic and reflexive process without doubt influences who we are and how we see the world. Ethnographers often have, to paraphrase Fetterman (1983) 'guilty knowledge, dirty hands' and, I would add, 'heavy hearts'; as the vignettes in this chapter illustrate. Ethnography is challenging, problematic and not a methodological approach for the faint-hearted. However, if done well, ethnography has the power and potential to give us an appreciation of how others live their lives, and an understanding, however fleeting, of our own and others' social worlds. Ethnography, as the chapters in this book demonstrate, can change the lives of ethnographers and field subjects alike. It can reveal 'hidden' social worlds and 'make a difference'. I end this book by urging the reader, as Robert E. Park exhorted his students, to 'go and get the seat of your pants dirty in real research' (Park 1915).

Suggested further reading

Alvesson, M. and Skoldberg, K. (2009) *Reflexive Methodology: New Vistas for Qualitative Research*, 2nd edn, London: Sage.

Hammersley, M. and Atkinson, P. (2007) *Ethnography: Principles in Practice*, 3rd edn, London: Routledge.

Willig, C. (2008) *Introducing Qualitative Research in Psychology*, 2nd edn, London: Sage.

Reflective activities

1   Over the next week, keep a reflective diary that details your everyday activities and social interactions. Try to recall the conversations you had and write them down using 'thick' description.

2   Leave your reflective diary for another week and then revisit your entries the following week. Ask yourself were the entries accurate regarding your social interactions? Were they reflective or reflexive?

3   If reflective, then consider the reflexive process described at the beginning of this chapter and ask yourself some of the questions posed there around, for example: 'How you might have influenced an interaction or in hindsight do you think you interpreted and described the situation accurately?'

BIBLIOGRAPHY

Ackroyd, S., Harper, R., Hughes, J., Shapiro, D. and Soothill, K. (1992) *New Technology and Practical Police Work: The Social Context of Technical Innovation*, London: McGraw-Hill Education.

Adler, P. A. and Adler, P. (1994) 'Observational techniques', in N. K. Denzin and Y. S. Lincoln (eds) *Handbook of Qualitative Research*, London: Sage.

Alessi, E. J. (2008) 'Staying put in the closet: examining clinical practice and countertransference issues in work with gay men married to heterosexual women', *Clinical Social Work Journal* 36: 195–201.

Alvesson, M. and Skoldberg, K. (2009) *Reflexive Methodology: New Vistas for Qualitative Research*, 2nd edn, London: Sage.

Anderson, N. (1923) *The Hobo: The Sociology of the Homeless Man*, Chicago: University of Chicago Press.

Angrosino, M. (2007) *Doing Ethnographic and Observation Research*, London: Sage.

Angrosino, M.V. and Mays de Perez, K. A. (2000) 'Rethinking observation: from method to context', in N. K. Denzin and Y. S. Lincoln (eds) *Handbook of Qualitative Research*, 2nd edn, London: Sage.

Arendt, H. (1973) *The Origins of Totalitarianism*, London: Harcourt.

Arens, W. (1979) *The Man-Eating Myth: Anthropology and Anthropophagy*, New York: Oxford University Press.

Ashworth, P. (2008) 'Conceptual foundations of qualitative psychology', in J. A. Smith (ed.) *Qualitative Psychology: A Practical Guide to Research Methods*, 2nd edn, London: Sage.

Bailey, C. A. (2007) *A Guide to Qualitative Research*, 2nd edn, London: Sage.

Ball, L. and Ormerod, T. (2000) 'Putting ethnography to work: the case for a cognitive ethnography of design', *International Journal of Human-Computer Studies* 53: 147–68.

Bandura, A. (1965) 'Influence of model's reinforcement contingencies on the acquisition of imitative responses', *Journal of Personality and Social Psychology* 1: 589–95.

Bandura, A. (1973) *Aggression: A Social Learning Analysis*, London: Prentice Hall.

Banks, M. (2001) *Visual Methods in Social Research*, London: Sage.

Barker, E. (1984) *The Making of a Moonie: Choice or Brainwashing?* Oxford: Basil Blackwell.

Bartlett, A., Smith, G. and King, M. (2009) 'The response of mental health professionals to clients seeking help to change or redirect same-sex sexual orientation', *BMC Psychiatry* 9(11): 1–8.

Barton, B. (2007) 'Managing the toll of stripping: boundary setting among exotic dancers', *Journal of Contemporary Ethnography* 36(5): 571–96.

Beck, K. A. (2005) 'Ethnographic decision tree modelling: a research method for counseling psychology', *Journal of Counseling Psychology* 52(2): 243–9.

Becker, H. S. (1963) *Outsiders: Studies in Sociology of Deviance*, New York: Simon and Schuster.

Becker, H. S. (1967) 'Whose side are we on?', *Social Problems* 14(3): 239–47.

Becker, H. S. (1971) *Sociological Work: Method and Substance*, London: Allen Lane.

Becker, H. S. (1999) 'The Chicago School, so-called', *Qualitative Sociology* 22(1): 3–12.

Becker, H. S., Geer, B., Hughes, E. C. and Strauss, A. L. (1961) *Boys in White: Student Culture in Medical School*, Chicago: University of Chicago Press.

Behar, R. (2003) 'Ethnography and the book that was lost', *Ethnography* 4(1): 15–39.

Belknap, J. (2001) *The Invisible Woman: Gender, Crime and Justice*, Belmont, CA: Wadsworth.

Best, D. (1978) *Philosophy and Human Movement*, London: Allen and Unwin.

Best, D. (1985) 'Sport is not art', *Journal of the Philosophy of Sport* 12: 25–40.

Blass, T. (2004) *The Man Who Shocked the World: The Life and Legacy of Stanley Milgram*, New York: Basic Books.

Blumer, H. (1956) 'Sociological analysis and the "variable"', *American Sociological Review* 21(6): 683–90.

Blumer, H. [1921] (1969) *Symbolic Interactionism: Perspective and Method*, London: Prentice Hall.

Booth, C. (1902) *Labour and Life of the People of London*, London: Macmillan.

Bosworth, M., Campbell, D., Demby, B., Ferranti, S. and Santos, M. (2005) 'Doing prison research: Views from inside', *Qualitative Inquiry* 11: 249–64.

Bott, E. (1971) *Family and Social Networks: Roles, Norms, and External Relationships in Ordinary Urban Families*, New York: Free Press.

Breakwell, G. M., Hammond, S., Fife-Schaw, C. and Smith, J. A. (eds) (2006) *Research Methods in Psychology*, 3rd edn, London: Sage.

Brewer, J. D. (1990) 'Sensitivity as a problem in field research: a study of routine policing in Northern Ireland', *American Behavioural Scientist* 33(5): 578–93.

Brewer, J. D. (2000) *Ethnography*, Milton Keynes: Open University Press.

British Sociological Association (2002) 'Statement of ethical practice for the British Sociological Association, URL (accessed October 2009): http://www.britsoc.co.uk/equality/.

British Society of Criminology (2006) 'Code of ethics for researchers in the field of criminology'. URL (accessed May 2008): http://www.britsoccrim.org/ethical.htm.

Brownmiller, S. (1976) *Against Our Will: Men, Women and Rape*, Harmondsworth: Penguin.

Bryman, A. (2008) *Social Research Methods*, 3rd edn, Oxford: Open University.

Bryman, A. and Burgess, R. G. (eds) (1994) *Analyzing Qualitative Data*, London: Routledge.

Bulmer, M. (1984) *The Chicago School of Sociology: Institutionalization, Diversity, and the Rise of Sociological Research*, Chicago: University of Chicago Press.

Burgess, R. G. (1982) 'Keeping fieldnotes', in R. G. Burgess (ed.) *Field Research: A Sourcebook and Field Manual*, London: Unwin Hyman.

Burgess, R. G. (1984) *In the Field*, London: Allen and Unwin.

Burke, T. (2007) 'Providing ethics a space on the page: social work and ethnography as a case in point', *Qualitative Social Work* 6: 177.

Burman, M., Batchelor, S. and Brown, J. (2001) 'Researching girls and violence: facing the dilemmas of fieldwork', *British Journal of Criminology* 41: 443–59.

Burr, V. (1995) *An Introduction to Social Constructionism*, London: Routledge.

Calvey, D. (2008) 'The art and politics of covert research: doing "situated ethics" in the field', *Sociology* 42(5): 905–18.

Campbell, R. (2001) *Emotionally Involved: The Impact of Researching Rape*, London: Routledge.

Carlen, P. (1983) *Women's Imprisonment: A Study in Social Control*, London: Routledge and Kegan Paul.

Cavadino, M. and Dignan, J. (2007) *The Penal System: An Introduction*, London: Sage.

Chambers, E. (2000) 'Applied Ethnography', in N. K. Denzin and Y. S. Lincoln (eds) *Handbook of Qualitative Research*, 2nd edn, Thousand Oaks, CA: Sage.

Cheung, Y. W., Bong-Ho, M. and Tak-Sing, C. (2005) 'Personal empowerment and life satisfaction among self-help group members in Hong Kong', *Small Group Research* 36(3): 354–77.

Cheverst, K., Cobb, S., Hemmings, T., Kember, S., Mitchell, K., Phillips, P. *et al.* (2001) 'Design with care', *Journal of New Technology in the Human Services* 14(1/2): 39–47.

Christensen, P. and James, A. (eds) (2000) *Research with Children: Perspectives and Practices*, London: Falmer Press.

Clemmer, D. (1940) *The Prison Community*, New York: Holt, Rinehart and Winston (2nd edn 1958).

Clifford, J. and Marcus, G. E. (eds) (1986) *Writing Culture: The Poetics and Politics of Ethnography*, Berkeley: University of California Press.

Code, L. (1995) 'How do we know? Questions of method in feminist practice', in S. Burt and L. Code (eds) *Changing Methods: Feminist Transforming Practice*, Ontario: Broadview Press.

Coffey, A. (1999) *The Ethnographic Self: Fieldwork and the Representation of Identity*, London: Sage.

Comaroff, J. L. and Comaroff, J. (1992) *Ethnography and the Historical Imagination*, Oxford: Westview Press.

Condry, R. (2009) *Families Shamed*, Cullompton: Willan.

Cook, I. (2005) 'Participant observation', in R. Flowerdew and D. Martin (eds) *Methods in Human Geography*, 2nd edn, Harlow: Pearson.

Cornwell, J. (1984) *Hard-earned Lives: Accounts of Health and Illness from East London*, London and New York: Tavistock.

Corston, J. (2007) *The Corston Report: A Review of Women with Particular Vulnerabilities in the Criminal Justice System*, London: Home Office, URL (accessed November 2009): http://www.homeoffice.gov.uk/documents/corston-report.

Craig, E. (2000) *Concise Routledge Encyclopedia of Philosophy*, London: Routledge.

Crang, M. (2005) 'Analysing qualitative materials', in R. Flowerdew and D. Martin (eds) *Methods in Human Geography*, 2nd edn, Harlow: Pearson.

Crang, M. and Cook, I. (2007) *Doing Ethnographies*, London: Sage.

Da Cunha, M. (2004) 'Olympic gold all around gymnast Paul Hamm: only human', *Capitalism Magazine*, URL (accessed 11 February 2009): http://www.capmag.com/article.asp?ID=3876.

Dallos, R. (2006) 'Observational methods', in G. M. Breakwell, S. Hammond, C. Fife-Schaw and J. A. Smith (eds) (2006) *Research Methods in Psychology*, 3rd edn, London: Sage.

deMarrais, K. B (ed.) (1998) *Inside Stories: Qualitative Research Reflections*, Mahwah, NJ: Lawrence Erlbaum.

Denscombe, M. (2002) *Ground Rules for Good Research: A 10-point Guide for Social Researchers*, Buckingham: Open University Press.

De Waal, A. (2005) *Famine that Kills: Darfur, Sudan*, Oxford: Oxford University Press.

Dilthey, W. (1988) *Introduction to the Human Sciences: An Attempt to Lay a Foundation for the Study of Society and History*, London: Harvester Wheatsheaf.

Ditton, J. (1977) *Part-time Crime: An Ethnography of Fiddling and Pilferage*, London: Macmillan.

Dobash, R. E., Dobash, R. P. and Cavanagh, K. (2003) 'Researching homicide: method-ological issues in the exploration of lethal violence', in R. M. Lee and E. A. Stanko (eds) *Researching Violence: Essays on Methodology and Measurement*, London: Routledge.

Drewry, G. and Butcher, T. (1991): *The Civil Service Today*, 2nd edn, Oxford: Blackwell.

Durkheim, E. (1915) *The Elementary Forms of the Religious Life*, London: Allen and Unwin.

Edensor, T. (1998) *Tourists at the Taj: Performance and Meaning at a Symbolic Site*, London: Routledge.

Edensor, T. (2000) 'Staging tourism: tourists as performers', *Annals of Tourism Research* 27: 322–44.

Edles, L. D. (2002) *Cultural Sociology in Practice*, London: Wiley Blackwell.

ESRC (Economic and Social Research Council) (2005) *Research Ethics Framework*, URL (consulted November 2009): http://www.esrc.ac.uk/ESRCInfoCentre/Images/ESRC_Re_ Ethics_Frame_tcm6-11291.pdf.

Evans-Pritchard, E. E. (1940) *The Nuer: A Description of the Modes of Livelihood and Political Institutions of a Nilotic People*, Oxford: Clarendon Press.

Ewald, W. and Lightfoot, A. (2001) *I Wanna Take Me a Picture: Teaching Photography and Writing to Children*, Boston, MA: Beacon Press.

Faraday, A. and Plummer, K. (1979) 'Doing life histories', *Sociological Review* 27(4): 773–97.

Fawcett, B. and Hearn, J. (2004) 'Researching others: Epistemology, experience, standpoints and participation', *International Journal of Social Research Methodology: Theory and Practice* 73: 201–18.

Fawcett Society (2007) *Women and Justice: Third Annual Report of the Commission on Women and the Criminal Justice System*, London: Fawcett Society, URL (consulted November 2009): http://www.fawcettsociety.org.uk/documents/Women%20and%20the% 20criminal%20justice%20system%20-%20The%20facts%204.10.07.pdf.

Fechner, G. T. (1860) *Elements of Psychophysics*, New York: Holt, Rinehart and Winston.

Ferrell, J. (2007) 'For a ruthless cultural criticism of everything existing', *Crime, Media, Culture* 3(1): 91–100.

Festinger, L., Riecken, H. W. and Schachter, S. (1956) *When Prophecy Fails*, New York: Harper Row.

Fetterman, D. M. (1983) 'Guilty knowledge, dirty hands, and other ethical dilemmas: the hazards of contract research', *Human Organization* 42(3): 214–24.

Fetterman, D. M. (1998) *Ethnography*, 2nd edn, London: Sage.

Fielding, N. (1982) 'Observational research on the National Front', in M. Bulmer (ed.) *Social Research Ethics: An Examination of the Merits of Covert Participant Observation*, London: Macmillan.

Fine, G. A. (1993) 'Ten lies of ethnography – moral dilemmas of field research', *Journal of Contemporary Ethnography* 22(3): 267–94.

Fine, G. A. (1995) *A Second Chicago School? The Development of a Postwar American Sociology*, Chicago: University of Chicago Press.

Fine, M. (1994) 'Dis-Stance and Other Stances: Negotiations of Power Inside Feminist Research', in A. Gitlin (ed.) *Power and Method*, New York: Routledge.

Firestone, S. (1970) *The Dialectic of Sex: The Case for Feminist Revolution*, New York: Bantam Books.

Firth, R. W. (1936) *We, the Tikopia: A Sociological Study of Kinship in Primitive Polynesia*, London: Allen and Unwin.

Flick, U. (2009) *An Introduction to Qualitative Research*, 4th edn, London: Sage.

Floud, J., Halsey A. and Martin, F. (1956) *Social Class and Educational Opportunity*, London: Heinemann.

Foley, D. E. and Valenzuela, A. (2008) 'Critical ethnography', in N. K. Denzin and Y. S. Lincoln (eds) *The Landscape of Qualitative Research*, London: Sage.

Foucault, M. (1972) *The Archaeology of Knowledge*, London: Routledge.

Foucault, M. (1976) *The Order of Things: An Archaeology of the Human Sciences*, London: Tavistock.

Fountain, J. (1993) 'Dealing with data', in T. May and D. Hobbs (eds) *Interpreting the Field: Accounts of Ethnography*, Oxford: Clarendon Press.

Franklin, A. (2003) *Tourism: An Introduction*, London: Sage.

Frazer, J. (1890) *The Golden Bough: A Study in Comparative Religion*, London: Macmillan.

Freeman, D. (1984) *Margaret Mead and Samoa: The Making and Unmaking of an Anthropological Myth*, Harmondsworth: Penguin.

Freud, S. (1949) *An Outline of Psycho-analysis*, London: Hogarth.

Gamarnikow, E. and Green, A. (1999) 'Developing social capital: Dilemmas, possibilities and limitations in education', in A. Hayton (ed.) *Tackling Disaffection and Social Exclusion*, London: Kogan Page.

Garfinkel, H. (1967) *Studies in Ethnomethodology*, London: Polity.

Garland, D. (2002) 'Of crimes and criminals: The development of criminology in Britain', in M. Maguire, R. Morgan and R. Reiner (eds) *The Oxford Handbook of Criminology*, 3rd edn, Oxford: Oxford University Press.

Geertz, C. (1975) *The Interpretation of Cultures*, London: Hutchinson.

Geertz, C. (1984) '"From the native's point of view": on the nature of anthropological understanding', in R. Shweder and R. A. Levine (eds) *Culture Theory: Essays on Mind, Self and Emotion*, Cambridge: Cambridge University Press.

Gelsthorpe, L. (1997) 'Feminism and criminology', in M. Maguire, R. Morgan and R. Reiner (eds) *The Oxford Handbook of Criminology*, Oxford: Clarendon.

Gergen, K. J. (2009) *An Invitation to Social Construction*, 2nd edn, London: Sage.

Ghodsee, K. (2005) *The Red Riviera: Gender, Tourism and Postsocialism on the Black Sea*, Durham, NC: Duke University Press.

Gillespie, R. (1991) *Manufacturing Knowledge: A History of the Hawthorne Experiments*, Cambridge: Cambridge University Press.

Gilligan, C. (1990) *In a Different Voice: Psychological Theory and Women's Development*, Cambridge, MA: Harvard University Press.

Goffman, E. (1956) 'Embarrassment and social organization', *American Journal of Sociology* 62(3): 264–71.

Goffman, E. (1959) *The Presentation of Self in Everyday Life*, London: Penguin.

Goffman, E. (1961) *Asylums: Essays on the Social Situation of Mental Patients and Other Inmates*, London: Penguin.

Goffman, E. (1963a) *Stigma: Notes on the Management of Spoiled Identity*, London: Penguin.

Goffman, E. (1963b) *Behavior in Public Places: Notes on Social Organization of Gatherings*, New York: Free Press.

Gold, R. L. (1958) 'Roles in sociological fieldwork', *Social Forces* 36: 217–23.

Goldring, J. E. (2007) 'There's more to health than HIV: Social capital and health in the gay community', PhD thesis, Institute for Public Health Policy Research, University of Salford.

Goldthorpe, J. and Jackson, M. (2007) 'Intergenerational class mobility in contemporary Britain: Political concerns and empirical findings', *British Journal of Sociology* 58(4): 525–46.

Gombrich, E. H. (1995) *The Story of Art*, 16th edn, New York: Phaidon.

Gomm, R. (2004) *Social Research Methodology: A Critical Introduction*, Basingstoke: Palgrave Macmillan.

Goodley, D. (ed.) (1999) *Critical Textwork: An Introduction to Varieties of Discourse and Analysis*, Buckingham: Open University Press.

Goodwin, C. (1994) 'Professional vision', *American Anthropologist* 96: 606–33.

Gorelick, S. (1996) 'Contradictions of feminist methodology', in H. Gottfried, *Feminism and Social Change: Bridging Theory and Practice*, Chicago: University of Illinois Press.

Graham, E. (2005) 'Philosophies underlying human geography research', in R. Flowerdew and D. Martin (eds) *Methods in Human Geography*, 2nd edn, Harlow: Pearson.

Gray, A. (2003) *Research Practice for Cultural Studies*, London: Sage.

Green, S. and Hogan, D. (eds) (2007) *Researching Children's Experience: Approaches and Methods*, London: Sage.

Greenhouse, C. J. (2003) 'Solidarity and objectivity: re-reading Durkheim', in P. C. Parnell and S. C. Kane (eds) *Crime's Power: Anthropologists and the Ethnography of Crime*, New York: Palgrave Macmillan.

Griffin, C. (1985) *Typical Girls? Young Women from School to the Job Market*, London: Routledge.

Griffin, C. (1986) 'Qualitative methods and female experience: young women from school to the job market', in S. Wilkinson (ed.) *Feminist Social Psychology: Developing Theory and Practice*, London: Sage.

Griffin, C. and Bengry-Howell, A. (2008) 'Ethnography', in C. Willig and W. Stainton-Rogers (eds) *The Sage Handbook of Qualitative Research in Psychology*, London: Sage.

Gross, R. (1995) *Themes, Issues and Debates in Psychology*, London: Hodder and Stoughton.

Guillemim, M. and Gillam, L. (2004) 'Ethics, reflexivity and "ethically important moments" in Qualitative Research', *Qualitative Inquiry* 10(2): 261–80.

Hall, S. (1997) *Representation: Cultural Representations and Signifying Practices*, London: Sage.

Halsey, A. H., Heath, A. and Ridge, J. (1980) *Origins and Destinations*, Oxford: Open University Press.

Hamilton, M. (2001) *The Sociology of Religion*, London: Routledge.

Hammersley, M. (1990a) *Reading Ethnographic Research: A Critical Guide*, New York: Longman.

Hammersley, M. (1990b) 'What's wrong with ethnography? The myth of theoretical description', *Sociology* 24: 597–615.

Hammersley, M. and Atkinson, P. (1995) *Ethnography, Principles in Practice*, London: Routledge.

Hammersley, M. and Atkinson, P. (2006) *Ethnography Principles in Practice*, 2nd edn, London: Routledge.

Hammersley, M. and Atkinson, P. (2007) *Ethnography: Principles in Practice*, 3rd edn, London: Routledge.

Hansson, C., Dittrich, Y. and Randall, D. (2006) 'How to include users in the development of off-the-shelf software: A case for complementing participatory design with agile development', *Proceedings of Hawaii International Conference on System Sciences (HICSS)*.

Haraway, D. (1991) *Simians, Cyborgs and Women: The Reinvention of Nature*, London: Free Association Press.

Harding, S. (1987) *Feminism and Methodology*, Buckingham: Open University Press.

Harding, S. (1991) *Whose Science? Whose Knowledge? Thinking from Women's Lives*, New York: Cornell University Press.

Harper, R. (1998) *Inside the IMF: An Ethnography of Documents, Technology and Organizational Action*, London: Academic Press.

Harper, R., Randall, D. and Rouncefield, M. (2000) *Organisational Change and Retail Finance: An Ethnographic Perspective*, London: Routledge.

Harper, R., Randall, D., Smyth, N., Evans, C., Heledd, L. and Moore, R. (2008) 'The past is a foreign country: They do things differently there', *Proceedings of DIS 08*, Capetown, South Africa.

Hartswood, M. and Procter, R. (2000) 'Managing errors in a computer-aided clinical decision-making task', in C. Johnson (ed.) Special Issue on 'Human Error and Clinical Systems', *Journal of Topics in Health Information Management* 20(4): 38–54.

Hartswood, M., Procter, R., Rouncefield, M., Slack, R., Soutter, J. and Voss, A. (2003) '"Repairing" the machine: A case study of evaluating computer-aided detection tools in breast screening', pp. 375–94 in K. Kuutti, E. H. Karsten, G. Fitzpatrick, P. Dourish and K. Schmidt (eds) in *Proceedings of the Eighth Conference on Computer Supported Cooperative Work*, Helsinki, Finland, Dordrecht, Kluwer.

Harvey, F. J. (1903) *The Fighting Gladiators or the Games and Combats of the Greeks and Romans: A Short History of Physical Culture*, Exeter: Physical Training Publishing Company.

Haw, K. (2008) '"Voice" and video: seen, heard and listened to?', in P. Thomson (ed.) *Doing Visual Research with Children and Young People*, Abingdon: Routledge.

Hay, I. (ed.) (2005) *Qualitative Methods in Human Geography*, 2nd edn, Oxford: Oxford University Press.

Headland, T. N., Pike, K. and Harris, M. (1990) *Emics and Etics: The Insider/Outsider Debate*, London: Sage.

Hegel, G. W. (1967 [1821]) *The Philosophy of Right*, Oxford: Oxford University Press.

Hemmings, T., Clarke, K., Francis, D., Marr, L. and Randall, D. (2001) 'Situated knowledge and virtual education', in I. Hutchby and J. Moran-Ellis (eds) *Children, Technology and Culture: The Impacts of Technologies in Children's Everyday Lives*, London: Routledge.

Hennig, C. (2002) 'Tourism: Enacting modern myths', in G. Dann (ed.) *The Tourist as a Metaphor of the Social World*, Wallingford: CABI.

Henning-Stout, M. (1999) 'Learning consultation: An ethnographic analysis', *Journal of School Psychology* 37(1): 73–98.

Hill Collins, P. (2000) *Black Feminist Thought: Knowledge, Consciousness, and the Politics of Empowerment*, New York: Routledge.

Hindle, P. (1994) 'Gay communities and gay space in the city', in S. Whittle (ed.) *The Margins of the City: Gay Men's Urban Lives*, Aldershot: Arena.

Hindle, P. (2001) 'The influence of the Gay Village on migration to central Manchester', *North West Geography* 1(1): 54–60.

Holdaway, S. (1983) *Inside the British Police: A Force at Work*, Oxford: Blackwell.

Holliday, A. (2007) *Doing and Writing Qualitative Research*, 2nd edn, London: Sage.

hooks, b. (2003) 'Choosing the margin as a space of radical openness', in S. Harding (ed.) *The Feminist Standpoint Theory Reader: Intellectual and Political Controversies*, New York: Routledge.

Hopkins, L. (2008) 'Disabled students in higher education: writing stories and hearing voices', Unpublished Doctoral Dissertation, The Open University Press.

Hospers, J. (ed.) (1969) *Introductory Readings in Aesthetics*, New York: Free Press.

Hughes, C. (1994) 'From field notes to dissertation, analysing the stepfamily', in A. Bryman and R. G. Burgess (eds) *Analysing qualitative data*, London: Routledge.

Hughes, J. A., Randall, D. and Shapiro, D. (1993) 'Designing with ethnography: Making work visible', *Interacting with Computers* 15(2): 239–53.

Humphreys, L. (1970) *Tearoom Trade: Impersonal Sex in Public Places*, London: Duckworth.

Husserl, E. (1931) *Ideas: A General Introduction to Pure Phenomenology*, London: Allen and Unwin.

Hutton, F. (2006) *Risky Pleasures? Club Cultures and Feminine Identities*, Aldershot: Ashgate.

Inglis, D. and Holmes, M. (2003) 'Highlands and other haunts: ghosts in Scottish tourism', *Annals of Tourism Research* 30: 50–63.

Israel, M. (2004) 'Strictly confidential? Integrity and the disclosure of criminological and socio–legal research', *British Journal of Criminology* 44(5): 715–40.

Israel, M. and Hay, I. (2006) *Research Ethics for Social Scientists*, London: Sage.

Jackson, A. (ed.) (1987) *Anthropology at Home*, London: Tavistock.

James, A., Hockey, J. and Dawson, A. (eds) (1997) *After Writing Culture: Epistemology and Praxis in Contemporary Anthropology*, London: Routledge.

James, W. (1890) *Principles of Psychology*, New York: Holt.

James, W. (1902) *The Varieties of Religious Experience*, New York: Longmans, Green.

Jones, H. and Cook, K. (2008) *Rape Crisis: Responding to Sexual Violence*, Lyme Regis: Russell House.

Kant, I. (1881 [1771]) *Critique of Pure Reason*, London: Macmillan.

Katz, J. and Csordas, T. J. (2003) 'Phenomenological ethnography in sociology and anthropology', *Ethnography* 4(3): 275–88.

Kilkelly, U., Kilpatrick, R., Lundy, L., Moore, L., Scraton, P., Davey, C. *et al.* (2004) 'Children's rights in Northern Ireland and the UN Convention on the Rights of the Child', Belfast, Northern Ireland Commissioner for Children and Young People (downloadable from: http://www.niccy.org/).

Kincheloe, J. L. and McLaren, P. (2008) 'Rethinking critical theory and qualitative research', in N. K. Denzin and Y. S. Lincoln (eds) (2008) *The Landscape of Qualitative Research*, London: Sage.

Kirk, J. and Miller, M. (1986) *Reliability and Validity in Qualitative Research*, London: Sage.

Kirkwood, C. (1993) *Leaving Abusive Partners*, London: Sage.

Kunzle, G. C. (1960) *Olympic Gymnastics*, vols 1–4, London: Barrie and Rockcliffe.

Kuper, A. (1988) *The Invention of Primitive Society: Transformations of an Illusion*, London: Routledge.

Kuper, A. (1996) *Anthropology and Anthropologists: The Modern British School*, London: Routledge.

Laverick, W. (2007) 'Violence, risk and identity: "doing gender" or negotiation of structural barriers to non-violent alternatives?', in J. Scott Jones and J. Raisborough (eds) *Risks, Identities and the Everyday*, London: Ashgate.

Lazarsfeld, P. (1932) 'An unemployed village', *Character and Personality* 1: 147–51.

Lee, J. and Watson, R. (1993) 'Social interaction in urban public space', Final Report Plan Urban Project, Manchester University.

Lee, S. Y. (2008) 'Who do you think you are? Chinese school children's cultural identity in the context of Northern Ireland', unpublished conference paper.

Lees, S. (1996) *Carnal Knowledge: Rape on Trial*, London: Penguin.

Lees, S. (1997) *Ruling Passions: Sexual Violence, Reputation and the Law*, Buckingham: Open University Press.

Leitch, R. (2008) 'Creatively researching children's narratives through images and drawings', in P. Thomson (ed.) *Doing Visual Research with Children and Young People*, Abingdon: Routledge.

Lévi-Strauss, C. (1968) *Structural Anthropology*, London: Allen Lane.

Liebling, A. (1999) 'Doing research in prison: Breaking the silence?', *Theoretical Criminology* 3(2): 147–73.

Liebling, A. (2001) 'Whose side are we on? Theory, practice and allegiances in prison research', *British Journal of Criminology* 41: 472–84.

Liebling, A. and Stanko, B. (2001) 'Allegiance and ambivalence: some dilemmas in researching disorder and violence', *British Journal of Criminology* 41: 421–30.

Light, D. (2009) 'Halloween in Transylvania', in M. Foley and H. O'Donnell (eds) *Trick or Treat? Halloween in a Globalising World*, Newcastle upon Tyne: Cambridge Scholars.

Lowe, B. (1977) *The Beauty of Sport, A Cross-disciplinary Inquiry*, New York: Prentice Hall.

Lugosi, P. (2006) 'Between overt and covert research: concealment and disclosure in an ethnographic study of commercial hospitality', *Qualitative Inquiry* 12(3): 541–61.

Lylo, A. (1979) *F.I.G. Code of Points, Artistic Gymnastics for Men*, International Gymnastics Federation.

Lyng, S. (ed.) (2005) *Edgework: The Sociology of Risk*, London: Routledge.

Lyotard, J. (1984) *The Postmodern Condition: A Report on Knowledge*, Minneapolis: University of Minnesota Press.

McFee, G. (1992) *Understanding Dance*, London: Taylor and Francis.

Mahoney, D. (2007). 'Constructing reflexive fieldwork relationships: narrating my collaborative storytelling methodology', *Qualitative Inquiry* 13(4): 573–94.

Malinowski, B. (1922) *Argonauts of the Western Pacific: An Account of Native Enterprise and Adventure in the Archipelagoes of Melanesian New Guinea*, London: Routledge.

Malinowski, B. (1929) *The Sexual Life of Savages in North-Western Melanesia: An Ethnographic Account of Courtship, Marriage, and Family Life Among the Natives of the Trobriand Islands, British New Guinea*, London: Routledge and Kegan Paul.

Malinowski, B. (1935) *Coral Gardens and their Magic: A Study of the Methods of Tilling the Soil and of Agricultural Rites in the Trobriand Islands*, London: Allen and Unwin.

Malinowski, B. (1967) *A Diary in the Strict Sense of the Term*, London: Routledge and Kegan Paul.

Mansvelt, J. and Berg, L. D. (2005) 'Writing qualitative geographies: constructing geographical knowledges', in I. Hay (ed.) *Qualitative Methods in Human Geography*, 2nd edn, Oxford: Oxford University Press.

Marvasti, A. B. (2004) *Qualitative Research in Sociology*, London: Sage.

Maton, K. I. and Salem, D. A. (1995) 'Organizational characteristics of empowering community settings: a multiple case study approach', *American Journal of Community Psychology* 23(5): 631–57.

Mauthner, M., Birch, M., Jessop, J. and Miller, T. (eds) (2002) *Ethics in Qualitative Research*, London: Sage.

205

May, T. (2003) *Social Research: Issues, Methods and Process*, 3rd edn, Buckingham: Open University Press.

Mead, G. H. (1934) *Mind, Self, and Society*, Chicago: University of Chicago Press.

Mead, M. (1943) *Coming of Age in Samoa: A Psychological Study of Primitive Youth for Western Civilization*, London: Penguin.

Milgram, S. (1974) *Obedience to Authority: An Experimental View*, New York: Harper and Row.

Millett, K. (1972) *Sexual Politics*, London: Abacus/Sphere.

Mills, D. (2003) 'Quantifying the discipline: some anthropology statistics from the UK', *Anthropology Today* 19(3): 19–22.

Moore, H. (1988) *Feminism and Anthropology*, Cambridge: Polity.

Morgan, R. (ed.) (1970) *Sisterhood is Powerful: An Anthology of Writings from the Woman's Liberation Movement*, New York: Vintage Books.

Neuman, W. L. (2006) *Social Research Methods*, 5th edn, Boston, MA: Pearson/Allyn and Bacon.

Newton, E. (1950) *The Meaning of Beauty*, London: Longmans Green and Co.

Normark, M. and Randall, D. (2005) 'Local expertise at an emergency call centre', *Proceedings of ECSCW 05*, 18–22 Sept, Paris, France: Springer.

Oakley, A. (1974) *Housewife*, Harmondsworth: Penguin.

Okely, J. (1975) 'The self and scientism', *Journal of the Anthropological Society of Oxford* 7(3): 171–88.

Okely, J. (1996) *Own or Other Culture*, London: Routledge.

Okely, J. and Callaway, H. (eds) (1992) *Anthropology and Autobiography*, London: Routledge.

Olesen, V. L. (2008) 'Early millennial feminist qualitative research: Challenges and contours', in N. K. Denzin and Y. S. Lincoln (eds) *The Landscape of Qualitative Research*, London: Sage.

O'Reilly, K. (2009) *Key Concepts in Ethnography*, London: Sage.

Palmer, C. and Sellers, V. (2009) 'Aesthetic heritage of Men's Artistic Gymnastics for Olympic competition', *Journal of Olympic History* 17(1): 23–38.

Palmer, C. and Torevell, D. (eds) (2008) *The Turn to Aesthetics: An Interdisciplinary Exchange of Ideas in Applied and Philosophical Aesthetics*, Liverpool: Liverpool Hope University Press.

Park, R. E. (1915) 'The city: Suggestions for the investigation of behavior in the city environment', *American Journal of Sociology* 20: 579–83.

Park, R. E. and Burgess, E. W. [1921] (1969) *Introduction to the Science of Sociology Including the Original Index to Basic Sociological Concepts*, 3rd edn, Chicago: University of Chicago Press.

Park, R. E., Burgess, E. W. and McKenzie, R. (1925) *The City*, Chicago: University of Chicago Press.

Paulson, S. and Willig, C. (2008) 'Why do both ethnography and narrative interviews?', *Proceedings Qualitative Methods in Psychology Section*, Inaugural Conference, Leeds.

Pavlov, I. P. (1927) *Conditioned Reflexes*, London: Oxford University Press.

Perkins, D. D. and Zimmerman, M. A. (1995) 'Empowerment theory, research, and application', *American Journal of Community Psychology* 23(5): 569–79.

Piaget, J. (1932) *The Moral Judgement of the Child*, London: Routledge and Kegan Paul.

Piaget, J. (1950) *The Psychology of Intelligence*, London: Routledge and Kegan Paul.

Pink, S. (2007) *Doing Visual Ethnography*, 2nd edn, London, Sage.

Plummer, K. (1997) *The Chicago School: Critical Assessments*, London: Routledge.

Polit, D. F. and Hungler, B. P. (1999) *Nursing Research, Principles and Practice*, 6th edn, Philadelphia, PA: Lippincott Williams and Wilkins.

Posada, G., Carbonell, O. A., Alzate, G. and Plata, S. J. (2004) 'Through Colombian lenses: Ethnographic and conventional analyses of maternal care and their associations with secure base behavior', *Developmental Psychology* 40(4): 508–18.

Prestidge, J. (1988) *The History of British Gymnastics*, London: British Amateur Gymnastics Association.

Prosser, J. (ed.) (1998) *Image-based Research: A Sourcebook for Qualitative Researchers*, London: Falmer.

Punch, M. (1994) 'Politics and ethics in qualitative research', in N. K. Denzin and Y. S. Lincoln (eds) *Handbook of Qualitative Research*, Thousand Oaks, CA: Sage.

Pyper, R. (1995) *The British Civil Service*, London: Prentice Hall, Harvester Wheatsheaf.

Radcliffe-Brown, A. R. (1952) 'Historical note on British social anthropology', *American Anthropologist* 5: 276.

Randall, D. (2003) 'Living inside a smart home: A case study', in R. Harper (ed.) *Inside the Smart Home: Interdisciplinary Perspectives on the Design and Shaping of Domestic Computing*, London: Springer Verlag.

Randall, D. and Hughes, J. A. (1995) 'CSCW, sociology, and working with customers', in P. Thomas (ed.) *The Social and Interactional Dimensions of Human–Computer Interfaces*, Cambridge: Cambridge University Press.

Rappaport, J. (1981) 'In praise of paradox: A social policy of empowerment over prevention', *American Journal of Community Psychology* 9: 1–5.

Ribbons, J. and Edwards, R. (eds) (1998) *Feminist Dilemmas in Qualitative Research: Public Knowledge and Private Lives*, London: Sage.

Richardson, L. (2000) 'Writing a method of inquiry', in N. K. Denzin and Y. S. Lincoln (eds) *Handbook of Qualitative Research*, 2nd edn, Thousand Oaks, CA: Sage.

Rissel, C. (1994) 'Empowerment: The holy grail of health promotion?', *Health Promotion International* 9(1): 39–47.

Ritchie, J. and Lewis, J. (2003) *Qualitative Research Practice: A Guide for Social Science Students and Researchers*, London: Sage.

Ritzer, G. (2000) *Sociological Theory*, 5th edn, London: McGraw-Hill.

Rose, G. (2007) *Visual Methodologies: An Introduction to the Interpretation of Visual Material*, 2nd edn, London: Sage.

Rosenhan, D. L. (1973) 'On being sane in insane places', *Sciences* 179: 350–58.

Ryan, J. (1996) *Little Girls in Pretty Boxes: The Making and Breaking of Elite Gymnasts and Figure Skaters*, New York: Grand Central Publishing.

Sanjek, R. (ed.) (1990) *Fieldnotes: The Making of Anthropology*, London: Cornell University Press.

Schatzman, L. and Strauss, A. L. (1973) *Field Research: Strategies for a Natural Sociology*, Englewood Cliffs, NJ: Prentice Hall.

Scheper-Hughes, N. (2004) 'Parts unknown: undercover ethnography of the organs-trafficking underworld', *Ethnography* 5(1): 29–73.

Schlosser, J. (2008) 'Issues in interviewing inmates: Navigating the methodological landmines of prison research', *Qualitative Inquiry* 14(8): 1500–25.

Schutz, A. (1970) *The Phenomenology of the Social World*, Evanston, IL: Northwestern University Press.

Scott, J. (2002) 'The nature of social research and social knowledge', in I. Marsh (ed.) *Theory and Practice in Sociology*, Harlow: Pearson Education.

Scott, J. F. (1996) 'Unfinished sympathy: Embodiment of faith in an American fundamentalist Christian intentional community', unpublished PhD thesis, University of Edinburgh.

Scott, J. F. (1997) 'The truth is out there: The renewal of the Western religious consciousness', *Scottish Journal of Religious Studies* 18(2): 115–28.

Scott, J. F. (2001) 'You and me against the world: Christian fundamentalists and white poverty in the USA', in P. Kennedy and C. Danks (eds) *Globalization and National Identities: Crisis or Opportunity?* Basingstoke: Palgrave.

Sharpe, K. (1998) *Red Light, Blue Light: Prostitutes, Punters and the Police*, London: Ashgate.

Shavit, Y. and Blossfeld, H. P. (eds) (1993) *Persistent Inequality: Changing Educational Attainment in Thirteen Countries*, Boulder, CO: Westview Press.

Shaw, C. R. (1930) *The Jack-Roller: A Delinquent Boy's Own Story*, Chicago: University of Chicago Press.

Shurmer-Smith, P. and Hannan, K. (1994) *Worlds of Desire, Realms of Power: A Cultural Geography*, London: Arnold.

Shweder, R. A. (1991) *Thinking through Cultures: Expeditions in Cultural Psychology*, London: Harvard University Press.

Shweder, R. A. and Levine, R. A. (eds) (1984) *Culture Theory: Essays on Mind, Self and Emotion*, Cambridge: Cambridge University Press.

Silverman, D. (ed.) (1997) *Qualitative Research: Theory, Method and Practice*, London: Sage.

Silverman, D. (2001) *Interpreting Qualitative Research*, London: Sage.

Silverman, D. (2004) *Doing Qualitative Research*, 2nd edn, London: Sage.

Sixsmith, J., Boneham, M. and Goldring, J. E. (2003) 'Accessing the community: gaining insider perspectives from the outside', *Qualitative Health Research* 13(4): 578–89.

Skinner, B. F. (1938) *The Behaviour of Organisms*, New York: Appleton-Century-Crofts.

Skinner, B. F. (1957) *Verbal Behaviour*, New York: Appleton-Century-Crofts.

Smith, J. A. (1996) 'Beyond the divide between cognition and discourse: Using interpretative phenomenological analysis in health psychology', *Psychology and Health* 11: 261–71.

Smith, J. A. (2008) *Qualitative Psychology: A Practical Guide to Research Methods*, 2nd edn, London: Sage.

Smith, J. A. and Osborn, M. (2008) Interpretative phenomenological analysis', in J. A. Smith (ed.) *Qualitative Psychology: A Practical Guide to Research Methods*, 2nd edn, London: Sage.

Smith, J. A., Flowers, P. and Larkin, M. (2009) *Interpretative Phenomenological Analysis: Theory, Method and Research*, London: Sage.

Smith, M. (1998) *Social Science in Question*, London: Sage.

Social Research Association (SRA) (2003) *Ethical Guidelines*, URL (accessed 19 March 2009): http://www.the-sra.org.uk/documents/pdfs/ethics03.pdf.

Sparkes, A. C. (2002) *Telling Tales in Sport and Physical Activity: A Qualitative Journey*, Champaign, IL: Human Kinetics Publishers.

Sparks, J. and Glennerster, H. (2002) 'Preventing social exclusion: Education's contribution', in J. Hills, J. Le Grand and D. Piachaud (eds) *Understanding Social Exclusion*, Oxford: Oxford University Press.

Spradley, J. P. (1980) *Participant Observation*, New York: Holt, Rinehart and Winston.

Stacey, J. (1988) 'Can there be a feminist ethnography?', *Women's Studies International Forum* 12(6): 579–92.

Stocking, G. W. (1983) *Observers Observed: Essays on Ethnographic Fieldwork*, London: University of Wisconsin Press.

Stocking, G. W. (1991) *Colonial Situations: Essays on the Contextualization of Ethnographic Knowledge*, London: University of Wisconsin Press.

Sykes, G. (1958) *The Society of Captives*, Princeton, NJ: Princeton University Press.

Taylor, M. (1994) 'Ethnography', in P. Banister, E. Burman, I. Parker, M. Taylor and C. Tindall, *Qualitative Methods in Psychology: A Research Guide*, Maidenhead: Open University Press.

Thomas, J. (1993) *Doing Critical Ethnography*, Newbury Park, CA: Sage.

Thomas, W. I. (1937) *Primitive Behavior: An Introduction to the Social Sciences*, New York: McGraw-Hill.

Thompson, W. E. and Harred, J. L. (1992) 'Topless dancers: managing stigma in a deviant occupation', *Deviant Behavior, An Interdisciplinary Journal* 13: 291–311.

Thomson, P. (ed.) (2008) *Doing Visual Research with Children and Young People*, Abingdon: Routledge.

Thrasher, F. M. (1927) *The Gang: A Study of 1,313 Gangs in Chicago*, Chicago: University of Chicago Press.

Tomlinson, S. (2001) *Education in a Post-Welfare Society*, Buckingham: Open University Press.

Truman, C. (2000) 'New social movements and social research', in C. Truman, D. Mertens and B. Humphries (eds) *Research and inequality*, London: UCL Press.

Urry, J. (2002) *The Tourist Gaze*, 2nd edn, London: Sage.

Verdery, K. (2003) *The Vanishing Hectare: Property and Value in Postsocialist Transylvania*, Ithaca, NY: Cornell University Press.

Villenas, S. (2000) 'This ethnography called my back: writings of the exotic gaze, "othering" Latina, and recuperating Xicanisma', in E. St. Pierre and W. Pillow (eds) *Working the Ruins: Poststructural Feminist Theory and Methods in Education*, New York: Routledge.

Visweswaran, K. (1997) 'Histories of feminist ethnography', *Annual Review of Anthropology*, 26: 591–621.

Vygotsky, L. S. (1978) *Mind in Society: The Development of Higher Psychological Processes*, Cambridge, MA: Harvard University Press.

Wacquant, L. (2002) 'The curious eclipse of prison ethnography in the age of mass incarceration', *Ethnography* 3: 371–97.

Wacquant, L. (2003) 'Ethnograpfeast: A progress report on the practice and promise of ethnography', *Ethnography* 4(1): 5–14.

Walker, M. U. (2007) *Moral Understandings: A Feminist Study in Ethics*, Studies in Feminist Philosophy, New York: Oxford University Press.

Walker, R., Schratz, B. and Egg, P. (2008) 'Seeing beyond violence: visual research applied to policy and practice', in P. Thomson (ed.) *Doing Visual Research with Children and Young People*, Abingdon: Routledge.

Wallis, R. (1976) *The Road to Total Freedom: A Sociological Analysis of Scientology*, London: Heinemann Educational.

Wang, N. (1999) 'Rethinking authenticity in tourism experience', *Annals of Tourism Research* 26: 349–70.

Watson, J. B. (1913) 'Psychology as the behaviourist views it', *Psychological Review* 20: 158: 77.

Watson, J. B. and Rayner, R. (1920) 'Conditioned emotional reactions', *Journal of Experimental Psychology* 3: 1–14.

Watt, S. (2005) 'There and Back Again: A Sociological Case Study of HRM as a Force for Cultural Change in a Division of a Civil Service Department', unpublished PhD, University of Liverpool.

Watt, S. (2007) 'Get with the programme: human resource management a risky strategy?', in J. Scott Jones and J. Raisborough (eds) *Risk Identities and the Everyday*, Aldershot: Ashgate.

Watt, S. (2008) 'The uses and abuses of ethnography', *Proceedings Qualitative Methods in Psychology Section*, Inaugural Conference, Leeds.

Weber, M. (1949) *The Methodology of the Social Sciences*, New York: Free Press.

Weeks, J., Heaphy, B. and Donavan, C. (2001) *Same Sex Intimacies: Families of Choice and Other Life Experiments*, New York: Routledge.

Weiner, A. B. (1976) *Women of Value, Men of Renown: New Perspectives in Trobriand Exchange*, London: University of Texas Press.

Weinreich, P. and Saunderson, W. (eds) (2003) *Analysing Identity: Cross-cultural, Societal and Clinical Contexts*, London: Routledge/Taylor and Francis.

Westmarland, N. (2001) 'The quantitative/qualitative debate and feminist research: A subjective view of objectivity', *Forum: Qualitative Social Research* 2(1):13, URL (accessed 19 March 2009): http://www.qualitative-research.net/index.php/fqs/article/view/974/2125.

Whyte, W. F. [1943] (1955) *Street Corner Society: The Social Structure of an Italian Slum*, Chicago: University of Chicago Press.

Wilkinson, S. and Kitzinger, C. (1995) *Feminism and Discourse: Psychological Perspectives*, London: Sage.

Wilkinson, S. and Kitzinger, C. (1996) *Representing the Other: A Feminism and Psychology Reader*, London: Sage.

Willig, C. (2008) *Introducing Qualitative Research in Psychology*, 2nd edn, London: Sage.

Willig, C. and Stainton-Rogers, W. (2008) *The Sage Handbook of Qualitative Research in Psychology*, London: Sage.

Willis, P. E. (1977) *Learning to Labour: How Working Class Kids get Working Class Jobs*, New York: Columbia University Press.

Willis, P. (2000) *The Ethnographic Imagination*, Cambridge: Polity.

Wirth, L. (1928) *The Ghetto*, Chicago: University of Chicago Press.

Wolcott, H. F. (2009) *Writing Up Qualitative Research*, 3rd edn, London: Sage.

Wood, J. and Duck, S. (eds) (1995) *Understudied Relationships: Off the Beaten Track*, London: Sage.

Woods, P. (2006) *Successful Writing for Qualitative Researchers*, 2nd edn, London: Routledge.

Yates, J. (1989) *Control through Communication: The Rise of System in American Management*, Baltimore, MD: Johns Hopkins University Press.

Young, M. (1979) *The Ethnography of Malinowski: The Trobriand Islands, 1915–18*, London: Routledge and Kegan Paul.

Zimbardo, P. (1973) 'On the ethics of intervention in human psychological research with special reference to the "Stanford Prison Experiment"', *Cognition* 2: 243–55.

Zimbardo, P. (2007) *The Lucifer Effect: Understanding How Good People Turn Evil*, London: Random House.

Zimbardo, P., Malah, C. and Haney, C. (2000) *Reflections on the Stanford Prison Experiment: Genesis, Transformations, Consequences*, URL (accessed 19 March 2009): http://www.prisonexp.org/pdf/blass.pdf

Zisman, M. D. (1977) *Representation, Specification and Automation of Office Procedures*, Report from the Department of Decision Science, The Wharton School, University of Pennsylvania.

Zschocke, K. H. (1993) *F.I.G. Code of Points, Artistic Gymnastics for Men*, International Gymnastics Federation.

INDEX